SPECIAL NEEDS EDUCATION

Special Needs Education
Children with Exceptionalities

Kim Fong Poon-McBrayer

and

Ming-gon John Lian

The Chinese University Press

Special Needs Education: Children with Exceptionalities
By Kim Fong Poon-McBrayer and Ming-gon John Lian

© **The Chinese University of Hong Kong,** 2002

ISBN 962–996–052–4

THE CHINESE UNIVERSITY PRESS
The Chinese University of Hong Kong
SHA TIN, N.T., HONG KONG
Fax: +852 2603 6692
     +852 2603 7355
E-mail: cup@cuhk.edu.hk
Web-site: www.chineseupress.com

Printed in Hong Kong

Contents

Chapter 3 Giftedness and Talent

Chapter 4 Mental Retardation

Chapter 5 Learning Disabilities

Chapter 6 Emotional and Behavior Disorders

Preface

For their specific professional programs to be effective and successful, school teachers and other related service providers such as educational administrators, educational psychologists, physical and occupational therapists, speech and language pathologists, social workers, music and recreational therapists, and school nurses need to have basic knowledge of the increasing students with special needs. There have been a number of textbooks relating to exceptional children and youth, as well as introduction to special needs education. Most of these textbooks, however, are published in other countries (e.g., the United States and the United Kingdom) and tend to lack information for the preservice and inservice field practitioners in Hong Kong as well as the surrounding Southeast Asian areas.

The main purpose of this book, *Special Needs Education: Children with Exceptionalities*, is to provide teachers and other school, social welfare and rehabilitation personnel with fundamental information in order to enhance their knowledge base and professional competence in their daily career. We tried to write into this textbook systematic, practical, and concise contents which are expected to be conveniently applied to various educational and non-school settings.

There are twelve chapters in this book. The first chapter includes general introduction of exceptionality and special needs education. Chapter two focuses on special needs education in Hong Kong. Chapter three addresses issues regarding gifted and talented learners. Chapters four through seven form a special unit relating to high incidence disabilities: mental retardation, learning disabilities, emotional and behavior disorders, and communication disorders. Chapters eight through ten form another unit about low incidence disabilities, i.e., visual impairments, hearing impairments, and physical and health disabilities. The last two chapters provide additional information regarding parents and families of special needs children, and use of technology in special needs education.

Each chapter in the book begins with a list of topic-related questions as well as key terms and phrases for advanced thinking, which is designed to guide readers for them to have a clear overview and to be able to look for key issues and related information. Each chapter is concluded with a summary for an overall review, a number of recommended activities for further learning and enrichment, available local and international resources, and the references for the corresponding chapter. At the end of the book, a glossary, an author index, and a subject index are provided.

We owe a great debt of gratitude to many people who helped bring this textbook to its successful completion. Many thanks must be given to members of our families, who provided us with continuous support and allowed us to spend a huge amount of time to work on this book. Great appreciation also goes to our respectful colleagues and friends for their encouragement and editorial comments which have improved the quality of this book. Above all, we thank all the children and adults with exceptionalities we have worked with and the Creator from whom we have learned so much!

Kim Fong Poon-McBrayer

Ming-gon John Lian

1

Exceptionality and Special Needs Education

ADVANCED THINKING

Answer the following questions as you read this chapter:

1. What factors led to the development of special needs education?
2. What are the key principles that drive special needs education today?
3. Why do some students receive special needs education?
4. Who is eligible for special needs education?
5. What are the advantages and disadvantages of classifying students for special needs education?
6. What are some of the differences between general and special needs education?

KEY TERMS AND PHRASES

classification	prevalence
exceptionality	right to education
history	special education
labeling	special educational needs
legislation	special needs education
parents and families	

INTRODUCTION

The study of children with *exceptionality* is the study of differences and diversity. A child with exceptionality may have difficulties or special talents in seeing, hearing, speaking, thinking, moving, or socializing. The study of children with exceptionality is also the study of similarities. A child with exceptionality is not different from the average child in every way. There are probably more similarities in characteristics, needs, and ways of learning than differences between exceptional and nonexceptional children. For educational purposes, children with exceptionality are defined as those who require special needs education and related services if they are to realize their full potential. We must remember, however, they are very diverse in characteristics and educational needs.

SCOPE OF SPECIAL NEEDS EDUCATION

In the early days, education was a right of the privileged all around the world. Today, most children in developed countries have the right to attend school. These nations have implemented compulsory education to varying degrees. The governments are required to provide education and the parents to send their children to schools. Girls and boys, rich and poor, and children of all abilities and backgrounds arrive at schools each morning. Such student diversity demands skilled teachers and other professionals — a challenge for all.

In many nations, children with disabilities are now part of the public education system and have a right to a free, appropriate, public education. Children with special gifts and talents have historically been included in discussions of special needs education while programs for gifted children may not be as universal as programs for children with disabilities. At present, children with special needs include those with mental retardation, communication disorders, learning disabilities, behavioral disorders, visual impairments, hearing impairments, physical disabilities and health impairments, gifted and creative abilities, or a combination of multiple disabilities and/or special talents.

Special Needs Education Defined

The term "special education" is traditionally associated with children with disabilities, impairments, or difficulties. Yet the scope of *special needs education* has expanded to include children with special gifts or talents or even children from a different culture speaking a different language. Many existing books and publications on special education in countries such as the United States, the United Kingdom, Canada, and Australia include those two groups of children. The broadened scope of the field has also accepted the interchangeability of the terms such as "special needs education" and "special education."

The federal regulation of the United States defines "special education" as individualized education specially designed "at no cost to the parent to meet the unique needs of a child with a disability, including instruction conducted in the classroom, in the home, in hospitals and institutions, and in other settings; and instruction in physical education" (34 Code of Federal 17 [a], [1]). To be eligible for special needs education services, "a child with special needs" or, often times, the "exceptional child" is defined as "any individual whose physical, mental, or behavioral performance deviates substantially from the norm, either higher or lower." (Hardman, Drew, & Egan, 1996, p. 5)

In Hong Kong, "special needs education" is defined within the context of children who may qualify to receive special services. The official definition of "children with special needs" is:

> Children are considered to have special educational needs if they cannot derive full benefit from the curriculum provided for children of their age cohort and/ or who cannot be catered for adequately in the ordinary educational setting. Children with one or more of the following characteristics can be considered as children with special educational needs: visual impairment, hearing impairment, physical handicap, mental handicap, maladjustment and learning difficulties. (Board of Education, 1996, p. 16)

There is a major difference between the regulations adopted by the United States and Hong Kong education system. The U.S. system guarantees a free, appropriate, public education from birth up to age 21, which includes necessary equipment to participate in school activities and transportation to take students back and forth between home and school without delay, while Hong Kong education system does not. Children with special needs are guaranteed a free, compulsory education from kindergarten up to age 15 but various services are more or less provided on the basis of availability rather than legal mandates. For example, children who qualify for special services such as speech therapy often times have to wait for a vacancy to receive services and the government bears no legal responsibilities if services are not available in a timely manner. The government and the schools bear minimal legal responsibilities in making such provisions.

LABELING AND CLASSIFICATION

Students with special needs are individuals who require special education services in order to achieve their fullest potential. A seemingly natural way to determine who qualifies for special education services is to organize children with various learning needs into categories of classification. Children whose needs or abilities fit certain categories are given labels for identification and reference. The difference between labeling and classification is that labels are given and attached to individuals and can include such stigmatizing terms as "lunatics" and "idiots," while classification refers to "a structured system that identifies and organizes characteristics to establish order" (Smith & Luckasson, 1995, p. 5).

When laws were introduced to guarantee a right to an education, the classification system and labels become the gatekeepers to ensure only those who carry the labels are eligible for special education services under a classification system. Such a relationship between laws and school obligations is very well reflected and practiced in developed countries such as the United States. Even though there is not yet a special education law per se, the Hong Kong government funds schools and programs for children with special needs based on whether they are proven to have needs in the designated categories of special needs.

Labeling identifies individuals or groups according to a category assigned to them. The effect of labeling an individual because his/her special needs has received widespread attention in special education. The terms we use to describe persons with special needs, e.g., "crippled," "feebleminded," or "handicapped," can influence the way people think about these individuals and their abilities and/or potential of achievement. Opponents of using labels insist that labeling a person with a category of disabilities may negatively affect the perception of this individual's ability. On the other hand, proponents of labeling argue that labeling would help the professionals to identify the particular needs of an individual and to design appropriate instructional intervention for him/her.

There are indeed a few advantages of *classification* for special needs education. First, a classification system allows us to name disabilities, to differentiate one from another, and to communicate about a specific disability meaningfully and efficiently. Second, a classification system is crucial for research. Researchers may focus and specialize in particular categories of special needs and seek an in-depth understanding of issues related to those categories. Third, the system makes it easier to relate a certain treatment to a certain diagnosis. The major disadvantage of a classification system is to place too much emphasis on the group under a specific category and insufficient emphasis on matching services to individual needs.

The classification used in this book is categorical, organizing special needs into the categories. Each category has its own sub-categorization. For instance, the category of mental retardation is subcategorized into three intensities of supports: mild, moderate, and severe and profound. Nevertheless, we must keep in mind that a person cannot be precisely categorized. A student may have the special education needs of more than one disability such as those who have multiple disabilities.

History of Special Needs Education

Special education grew from an initial awareness that some children require a type of education different from the typical education in order to achieve their potential. The roots of this awareness can be traced to Europe in the 1700s when certain pioneers began to make isolated attempts to educate children with disabilities.

One pioneer was Jean-Marc-Gaspard Itard, a French physician considered to be the father of special needs education. Itard's most important work was his effort to help the so-called wild boy of Aveyron, who was found in the woods of France in 1799 and was later named Victor. He was likely to have mental retardation and environmental deprivation. Itard taught Victor all the things that typical children learn from their families and in school. Victor learned to speak a few words, to walk upright, to eat with dishes and utensils, and to interact with other people via carefully designed techniques. Itard recorded details of techniques used and relevant philosophy along with Victor's progress. Many of those techniques are still used today.

Another key pioneer in the field of special education is Edouard Seguin, a student of Itard. He published the first special education treatise, *The Moral Treatment, Hygiene, and Education of Idiots and Other Backward Children*, in 1846. After moving to the United States, he assisted in founding the Association of Medical Officers of American Institutions for Idiots and Feebleminded Persons in 1876. This organization became the American Association on Mental Deficiency (AAMD) and later the American Association on Mental Retardation (AAMR), the oldest and largest professional association in the field of mental retardation.

Seguin also influenced Maria Montessori, the first female physician in Italy. Montessori worked with children who had mental retardation before she worked with young children. She believed and demonstrated that concrete experience and an environment rich in manipulative materials would facilitate young children's learning. Montessori is well known as the founder of the Montessori preschool movement today.

Residential institutions were established in the United States for teaching children with most disabilities by early 1800s. Special education classes in regular schools began to appear in large cities in late 19th century, for example, the classroom for children with physical disabilities in a Chicago public school in 1900 (Lian, 1999). Nevertheless, only 12 percent of all children and youth with disabilities received special education instruction by the time of 1948 (Ballard, Ramirez, & Weintraub, 1982). Many of other disabled children were probably able to function to some degree in their home communities while the rest were forced to enter segregated institutions.

Once the efforts of educating children with disabilities were planted in the United States, this nation began to lead other countries in the development of special education services in many aspects. As early as 1905, the first training opportunity for special education teachers was offered by the New Jersey Training School for Feebleminded Boys and Girls during the summer time (Kanner, 1964). The gradual recognition of special education as a profession that required an expertise stimulated the development of the field.

Professional organizations and advocacy groups began to be established and became powerful forces behind many changes that have rooted and strengthened the provision of special education services. In 1922, Elizabeth Farrell founded the International Council for the Education of Exceptional Children (Aiello, 1976) to allow members of a summer special education class at the Teachers' College of Columbia University to meet annually in order to exchange ideas about special education. This organization later became the Council for Exceptional Children, or CEC. Today, CEC remains the largest special education professional organization in the United States.

Many volunteer and parent organizations were formed in the mid-twentieth century. The National Association for Retarded Citizens (NARC), or the ARC (formerly the Association for Retarded Children of the United States) was founded in 1950; The United Cerebral Palsy Associations, Inc. in 1949; the National Society for Autistic Children in 1961; the Learning Disability Association of America in 1963; and the Epilepsy Foundation of America in 1968.

Human rights movements have aided significantly the development of providing special education services to children with disabilities worldwide in the 20th century. The concept of normalization brought the movement of deinstitutionalization (Wolfensberger, 1972), which later nurtured the concepts and movements of the *least restrictive environment* and *inclusion* for children with disabilities.

The development of special needs education has been highly associated with laws and worldwide agreements since the 1950s. The United States led the world in legalizing education rights of children and adults with disabilities. The most significant civil rights law for children with disabilities is the Individuals with Disabilities Education Act (IDEA) of 1990 [initiated and signed into law under the original title of the Education for All Handicapped Children Act in 1975] and, for adults the Americans with Disabilities Act (ADA) of 1990. European, Australasian, and Asian nations later also had similar provisions with varying degrees of legal obligations as stated in the Individuals with Disabilities Education Act and the Americans with Disabilities Act.

In Spain, delegates to a world conference on special education in 1994 urged governments and non-governmental organizations to promote integration in all countries (United Nations Educational, Scientific and Cultural Organization and Ministry of Education and Science, Spain, 1994). Though considered a third world nation with a comparatively late economic development, China has also participated in the movement of integration and compulsory education for all, with or without disabilities, in the last decade. Debates over to what extent children with disabilities should participate in regular education with their nondisabled peers have been zealous in the last two to three decades and continue in many parts of the world.

Whether children with special needs are educated in segregated or inclusive settings, they are attending schools today. Different nations provide different types of services based on their financial resources. The provision of special education will continue to draw attention from policy makers. Parents, educators, and advocacy groups will continue to solicit legal mandates to guarantee provisions.

HISTORY OF SPECIAL NEEDS EDUCATION IN HONG KONG

The history of special needs education reflects a chronological development of care-giving activities of philanthropic institutions and individuals to slowly involve more organized governmental effort with increasing legal mandates. The development of special needs education in Hong Kong follows a similar path. According to Yung (1997), the establishment of a home for the blind by the Canossian sisters in 1863 brought the first form of special education services. Several decades later, in 1935, three missionaries established the Hong Kong School for the Deaf. The governmental involvement was minimal and insignificant during this period.

After the Second World War, the Hong Kong government directed the majority of community resources to reconstruct the society and to expand the primary education system for the children of refugees from China. Taking care of the socially deprived group such as the homeless and the orphans became the main task of special education, a form of welfare for children, during this period of time. Most of the institutions serving children with disabilities were in the form of recreational centers and/or training centers under the responsibility of the Social Welfare Department.

In 1960, the Education Department set up a Special School Section. Training for special education teachers began in 1961. Even though the Hong Kong government began to contribute more to the provision of special education services with the vast economic expansion, donations from charitable organizations to initiate various types of services remained the key financial source. As early as 1963, the concept of having a normal education for children with disabilities was stated in the first report of the Education Commission (Marsh & Sampson, 1963). The philosophy to integrate children with disabilities was reiterated in the 1968 Annual Report of the Education Department (Education Department, 1968). Meanwhile, the Education Department attempted for the first time to include a special class for children with partial hearing within ordinary schools. In 1969, five schools for socially-deprived children were transferred from the Social Welfare Department to the Education Department. These schools were later renamed as schools for maladjusted children in the 1970s.

Similar to the United States, the 1970s represented a period of significant expansion and development for special needs education in Hong Kong. The 6-year compulsory education implemented in 1971 helped the government realize the need to provide services for children with special needs, and to have a comprehensive system to identify these children because they have to remain in the education system. Screening services for early identification of children with special needs began in the early 1970s. Additional places for children with disabilities in special or ordinary schools were provided. In 1973 and 1974, two assessment centers were established under the Special Education Section on Hong Kong Island and in Kowloon. Later on, the 1977 White Paper (i.e., the 1977 Rehabilitation Program Plan) provided more rigorous policy recommendations. The Education Department was required to assume a more active role in various types of special education service provisions.

In 1978, compulsory education regulations again influenced the provision of services for children with special needs. The implementation of the 9-year, free and compulsory education further pushed the Education Department to include children with special needs in their planning. Remedial teaching and student guidance service for primary schools were introduced at this time to deal with learning, behavioral, and emotional difficulties partly brought by compulsory education with which some children, who would not otherwise have been in school, were forced to stay and strive for success.

Two important instruments for identifying children with special needs were developed in the early 1980s. The Hong Kong Wechsler Intelligence Scale for Children (Hong Kong Government, 1981) and the Raven's Progressive Matrices Tests (Education Department, 1986) were standardized at about the same time. The 1980s was mainly a period of development and consolidation of the support services for children with special needs in Hong Kong. The 1990s reflected the government's realization of the need to strengthen the professional development of teachers and to ensure delivery of quality services to the students, while the beginning of the new century includes new trends, such as integration of children with special education needs in mainstream schools (Hong Kong Education Department, 2001) and use of technology (Lian, 2001).

SPECIAL NEEDS PREVALENCE

According to Hong Kong Council of Social Welfare (1995), the total number of persons with disabilities was estimated as 264,000 in 1994, among whom approximately 20% to 25% were at school age. Distribution of disabilities in these persons included mental handicap (44.9%), physical handicap (29.0%), mental illness (8.8%), hearing impairment (5.0%), speech impairment (3.6%), maladjustment (2.5%), and autism (0,5%). It is predicted that, by the year of 2004, the total number will be increased to 310,000 (Hong Kong Council of Social Welfare, 1995).

FAMILIES OF CHILDREN WITH SPECIAL NEEDS

When serving children with special needs, professionals must view them as members of their society, community, and families. Parents and professionals must develop a partnership as parents are the primary caretakers and advocates of their children. Professionals must be sensitive to the entire family's needs, not just the child with disabilities. Professionals need to have a basic understanding of the effects of having a child with disabilities in the family and to have respect for parents who may not be trained special educators. Such understanding and respect will facilitate effective partnership between home and school. Further discussion relating to parents and families of children with special needs will be included in Chapter 11.

SUMMARY

1. Exceptional children and their nondisabled peers share a lot of similarities as well as individual differences.
2. Special needs education is to provide opportunities for children with exceptionality to achieve their full potential.
3. The right to education should not be a privilege for some. Students with special needs in the 21st century are entitled to a free, appropriate, public education provided in the least restrictive environment.
4. Children with special needs may include those who have mental retardation, communication disorders, learning disabilities, behavior disorders, visual impairments, hearing impairments, physical disabilities and health impairments, gifted and creative abilities, and a combination of multiple disabilities and/or special talents.
5. In Hong Kong, special needs education is defined within the context of children who meet the eligibility criteria to receive special services in school. We need to compare with special needs education in leading countries and adopt what is suitable for the Hong Kong education system.
6. Labeling and classification of children with special needs tend to have both advantages and disadvantages. It is recommended that administration and policy makers, school personnel, and the general public have positive attitudes, use appropriate and productive terminology and language, and avoid harmful stigmas and negative influences in the effort to fulfill special needs students' individualized educational goals.
7. The history of special needs education includes pioneers in the early

years, formation of parent or advocacy groups and professional organizations, human rights movement, legislation and other legal actions, and governmental involvement.

8. The development of special needs education in Hong Kong follows the similar path of progressive efforts of charity programs, social welfare services, compulsory education and, later, increased governmental leadership.

9. Estimation of special needs prevalence is necessary for consumer-based planning in resource allocation, personnel preparation, and development of appropriate programs and services.

10. Parents and other family members of a child with special needs play an important role in effective educational programs and related services. They should be well-accepted in school and the community and treated as equal partners in all efforts for nurturing a quality life for their children.

ACTIVITIES

1. Write definitions of special education services in small groups or individually in your own words. Share the definitions, comparing and contrasting them.

2. In Hong Kong, a 14-year-old boy was first diagnosed with mild mental retardation at preschool age. He was later reclassified as having learning disabilities in Primary 2. When he was in Primary 5, he was again reclassified as having autism. Discuss factors that may have contributed to such changes of classification and diagnosis and ways to avoid this type of confusion.

3. Compile a directory of services and supports for individuals with special education and their families. The directory should include the name of the provider agency, address, telephone number, target population, and a brief description of the supports provided.

4. After having a quick review on the brief history of the development of special education worldwide, discuss how the provision of special education may be like in the 21st century.

5. Read the Education Reform blueprint and the Chief Executive's policy address on ways to improve education in Hong Kong. Discuss in small groups how they may change the provision of special education services.

RESOURCES

Resources in Hong Kong

The Boys' and Girls' Club Association of Hong Kong
3 Lockhart Road, Wanchai, Hong Kong
Web address: http://www.bgcahk.org/

Cactus Special Education Internet Resource
Web address: http://cactus-sped.uhome.net/

Caritas Chan Chun Ha Day Activity Centre
2/F, 227–252 On Tao House, Cheung On Estate
Tsing Yi, New Territories

Caritas Chan Chun Ha Hostel
2/F, 227–252 On Tao House, Cheung On Estate
Tsing Yi, New Territories

Caritas Clinical Psychological Service
Caritas Hosue, 2–8 Caine Road, Hong Kong

Caritas Comprehensive Intervention Programme for Autistic Children
Room 607, 42 St. Francis Street, Wanchai, Hong Kong

Caritas Dr. & Mrs. Olinto De Sousa Family Service (Shatin)
Unit 102–107, G/F, Block A, Herring Gull House, Sha Kok Estate
Shatin, New Territories

Caritas Hong Kong
Web address: http://www.caritas.org.hk/

Caritas Family Service — Chai Wan
Unit 112, G/F, Lei Tsui house, Wan Tsui Estate
Chaiwan, Hong Kong

Caritas Family Aide Service — Chai Wan
Unit 112,G/F Lei Tsui House, Wan Tsui Estate
Chai Wan, Hong Kong

Caritas Family Service — Aberdeen
1/F, 20 Tin Wan Street, Aberdeen, Hong Kong

Caritas Family Service — Caine Road
1/F, Caritas House, 2 Caine Road, Hong Kong

Caritas Family Service — Fanling
Unit 217–220, Cheung Lai House, Cheung Wah Estate
Fanling, New Territories

Caritas Family Service — Kowloon
Caritas Social Centre — Kowloon
2/F, 134 Boundary Street, Kowloon

Caritas Family Service — Ngau Tau Kok
G/F, 1 On Tak Road, Ngau Tau Kok, Kowloon

Caritas Family Service — Tsuen Wan
No. 9, Shing Mun Road
Tsuen Wan, New Territories

Caritas Family Service — Tuen Mun (North)
Unit 32, G/F, Hing Shing House, Tai Hing Estate
Tuen Mun, New Territories

Caritas Family Service — Tuen Mun (South)
Unit 11–16, G/F, High Block, Wu Boon Hosue
Wu King Estate, Tuen Mun, New Territories

Caritas Family Service — Tung Tau
12, G/F, Wing Tung House, Tung Tau Estate, Kowloon

Caritas Family Service — Yuen Long
4/F, Tin Shui Community Centre, Tin Shui Estate
Tin Shui Wai, Yuen Long, New Territories

Caritas Lok Fung Day Activity Centre
G/F, Wah Lai House, 8 Wah Kwai Estate, Hong Kong

Caritas Lok Hang Workshop
5/F, Caritas Social Centre — Yaumatei, 4 Cliff Road
Yaumatei, Kowloon

Caritas Lok Heep Club — Hong Kong Centre
130 Hennessy Road, 12/F, Southern Center
Wanchai, Hong Kong

Caritas Lok Heep Club — Kowloon Centre
G/F, Yiu Tong House, Tung Tau Estate, Kowloon

Caritas Lok Him Day Activity Centre
Podium M/F, Verbena Heights, 8 Mau Tai Road
Tseung Kwan O, Sai Kung, New Territories

Caritas Lok Hing Child Care Centre
No. 40–45, G/F Hing Yiu House, Tai Hing Estate
Tune Mun, New Territories

Caritas Lok Kin Workshop
G/F, On Chiu House, Cheung On Estate
Tsing Yi, New Territories

Caritas Lok King Hostel
Podium G/F, Verbena Heights, 8 Mau Tai Road
Tseung Kwan O, Sai Kung, New Territories

Caritas Lok Miu Early Education & Training Centre
1/F, Causeway Bay Community Centre, 7 Fook Yum Road
North Point, Hong Kong

Caritas Lok Ngai Day Activity Centre
M/F, Whampoa Plaza, Whampoa Garden, 7 Tak On Street
Hunghom, Kowloon

Caritas Lok Shing Hostel
G/F, Wah Hau House, Wah Kwai Estate, Hong Kong

Caritas Lok Wo Hostel
1/F, On Chiu House, Cheung On Estate
Tsing Yi, New Territories

Caritas Lok Yau Early Education & Training Centre
Room 102, Caritas House, 2 Caine Road, Hong Kong

Caritas Lok Yin Day Activity Centre
M/F, Whampoa Plaza, Whampoa Garden, 7
Tak On Street, Hunghom, Kowloon

Caritas Morning Star Hostel
58–61, Kai Yue House, Kai Yip Estate,
Kowloon Bay, Kowloon

Caritas Occasional Child Care Services for Disabled Pre-Schoolers
1/F Causeway Bay Community Centre, 7 Fook Yum Road
North Point, Hong Kong

Caritas Occasional Child Care Services for Disabled Pre-Schoolers
Room 102, Caritas House, 2 Caine Road, Hong Kong

Caritas Parents Resource Centre
1/F, Causeway Bay Community Centre, 7 Fook Yum Road
North Point, Hong Kong

Caritas Parents Resource Centre
Room 101, Caritas House, 2 Caine Road, Hong Kong

Caritas Pre-School Education Material Reference Centre
54 Pokfulam Road, Hong Kong

Hong Kong Society for Rehabilitation Community Rehabilitation Network
Web address: http://www.renet.org/crn/

Caritas Pui Man House Social Centre — Ngau Tau Kok
1 On Tak Road, Ngau Tau Kok, Kowloon

Caritas Rotary Women & Family Service Centre — Shaukiwan
Flat 1,1/F, Lee Ga Building, 131 Sai Wan Ho Street
Shaukiwan, Hong Kong

Caritas Social Centre — Kowloon
2/F, 134 Boundary Street, Kowloon

Caritas Social Centre — Sham Shui Po
Wing C, G/F, Yun Tin House, Pak Tin Estate, Sham Shui Po, Kowloon

Caritas Supported Employment Service
5/F, Caritas Social Centre — Yaumatei, 4 Cliff Road, Yaumatei, Kowloon

Caritas Wong Yiu Nam Centre
Tseung Kwan O Post Office, P.O. Box 65274, Kowloon

Equal Opportunity Commission (EOC)
Unit 2002, 20/F, Office Tower, Convention Plaza
1 Harbour Road, Wanchai, Hong Kong
Tel.: 852-2511-8211   Fax: 852-2511-8142
E-mail: eoc@eoc.gov.hk
Web address: http://www.eoc.org.hk/

Haven of Hope Sunnyside School
Website: http://hoh.hkcampus.net/

Hired Vehicle Service for Mentally Handicapped Persons
M/F, Whampoa Plaza, Whampoa Garden, 7 Tak On Street, Hunghom,
Kowloon

Hong Kong Education Department Internet Resource
http://www.ed.gov.hk/

Hong Kong Institute of Education, Department of Special Education
10 Lo Ping Road, Tai Po, New Territories
Hong Kong Red Cross
33 Harcourt Road, Wan Chai, Hong Kong
Web address: http://www.redcross.org.hk/index.html

Po Leung Kuk
Web address: http://www.poleungkuk.org.hk/index_e.htm

Special Education Resource Center, Hong Kong Education Department
特殊教育資源中心
香港九龍何文田巴富街六號特殊教育服務中心地下102–104室
Tel.: 852-2760-6201 or 852-2760-6202   Fax: 852-2761-0976
Email: serc@ed.gov.hk
Web address: http://serc.ed.gov.hk/

Special Education Society of Hong Kong
香港特殊教育學會
Tel.: 852-2320-3452
Web address: http://www.seshk.org.hk/

The Spastics Association of Hong Kong
Room 603, Duke of Windsor Social Service Bldg
15 Hennessy Road, Wanchai, Hong Kong
Web address: http://www.spastic.org.hk/

The University of Hong Kong, Department of Education
Pokfulam Road, Hong Kong

Resources in Taiwan

ArBao's Paradise
E-mail: spe.aide.gov.tw
Web address: http://spe.aide.gov.tw/image/index.asp

教育部特殊教育小組
台北市中山南路五號
Tel.: 886-2-23566051-2
E-mail: mail@mail.moe.gov.tw
Web address: http://spcedu.tkblind.tku.edu.tw/

Special Education Association of Republic of China
台北市和平東路一段162號　中華民國特殊教育學會
Tel.: 886-02-2392-2784
Web address: http://searoc.aide.gov.tw/index.htm

International Resources

The Accreditation Council on Services for People with Disabilities
8100 Professional Place, Suite 204, Landover, MD 20785-225 U.S.A.

American Network of Community Options and Resources
4200 Evergreen Lane, Suite 315, Annandale, VA 22003 U.S.A.

American Orthopsychiatric Association
1775 Broadway, New York, NU 10019 U.S.A.

American Personnel and Guidance Association
Two Skyline Place, Suite 400
5203 Leesburg Pike, Falls Church, VA 20041 U.S.A.

The Association for Persons with Severe Handicaps
29 W. Susquehanna Ave. Suite 210, Baltimore, MD 21204 U. S. A.

Council for Exceptional Children
1110 North Glebe Road, Suite 300, Arlington, VA 22201-5704 U.S.A.
Tel.: 1-888-CEC-SPED or 1-703-620-3660
TTY: 1-703-264-9446 Fax: 1-703-264-9494
Web address: http://www.cec.sped.org/

The Canadian Council on Rehabilitation and Work (CCRW)
500 University Avenue, Suite 302, Toronto, Ontario, Canada M5G 1V7
Tel.: 1-416-260-3060 TTY: 1-416-260-9223   Fax: 1-416-260-3093
Web address: http://www.ccrw.org/

The Disability Net of the United Kingdom
Web address: http://www.disabilitynet.co.uk/

ERIC Clearinghouse on Disabilities and Gifted Education
Web address: http://www.accesseric.org:81/home.html

IBM National Support Center for Persons with Disabilities
P.O. Box 2150, Atlanta, GA 30055 U.S.A.

Information Resources for People with Disabilities in Japan
Web address: http://www.sd.soft.iwate-pu.ac.jp/sensui/

National Association for the Education of Young Children
1834 Connecticut Avenue NW, Washington, DC 20009 U.S.A.

National Association of Rehabilitation Facilities
P.O. Box 17675, Washington, DC 20041 U.S.A.

National Council on Disability
800 Independence Avenue SW, Suite 814, Washington, DC 20591 U.S.A.

National Rehabilitation Association
633 South Washington Street, Alexandria, VA 22314 U.S.A.

People First International
P.O. Box 12642, Salem, OR 97309 U.S.A.

United Nations Educational, Scientific and Cultural Organization
(UNESCO)
Headquarters, 7, place de Fontenoy, 75352 PARIS 07 SP France

U.S. Department of Education
400 Maryland Avenue, SW, Washington, DC 20202-0498 U.S.A.

University of Kansas, Beach Center on Families and Disability
Bureau of Child Research, 4138 Haworth Hall, Lawrence, KS 66045
U.S.A.

REFERENCES

34 C.F.R. (Code of Federal Regulations) Section 300.17.
Aiello, B. (1976). Especially for special educators: A sense of our own history. *Exceptional children, 42*, 244–252.
Ballard, J., Ramirez, B.A., & Weintraub, F.J. (1982). *Special education in America: Its legal and governmental foundations*. Reston, VA: Council for Exceptional Children.
Board of Education. (1996). *Report of the sub-committee on special education*. Hong Kong: Government Printer.

Education Department. (1968). *Education Department: Annual Reports*. Hong Kong: Government Printer.

Education Department. (1986). *Hong Kong Supplement to Guide to the Standard Progressive Matrices*. Hong Kong: Government Printer.

Hardman, M.L., Drew, C.J., & Egan, M.W. (1996). *Human exceptionality: Society, school, and family* (5th ed.). Needham Heights, MA: Allyn & Bacon.

Hong Kong Council of Social Welfare. (1995, May). *White paper on rehabilitation: A better tomorrow for all*. [Online] http://swik.socialnet.org.hk/swik1/C400/c402/hk/ Erehab.htm#C4C37.

Hong Kong Education Department. (2001, September). *Implementation guide for integrated education*. Hong Kong: HKED.

Hong Kong Government. (1981). *Hong Kong — Wechsler Intelligence Scale for Children: Manual*. Hong Kong: Government Printer.

Kanner, L. (1964). *A history of the care and study of the mentally retarded*. Springfield, IL: Thomas.

Lian, M-G.J. (1999). *Getting to know individuals with physical disabilities and health impairments*. Normal, IL: University Communications, Illinois State University.

Lian, M-G.J. (2001, July 21). *Use of technology for students with severe cognitive disabilities*. Paper presented at the Hong Kong School Leadership Network-SEG1 Cross-school Collaboration Project, Hong Kong Institute of Education, Hong Kong.

Marsh, R.M. & Sampson, J.R. (1963). *Report of the Education Commission*. Hong Kong: Government Printer.

Screerenberger, R.C. (1983). *A history of mental retardation*. Baltimore: Brookes.

Smith, D.D. & Luckasson, R. (1995). *Introduction to special education: Teaching in an age of challenge* (2nd ed.). Needham Heights, MA: Allyn & Bacon.

United Nations Educational, Scientific and Cultural Organization and Ministry of Education and Science. (1994, June). *Final Report. World Conference on Special Needs Education: Access and Quality*. Salamanca, Spain.

Wolfensberger, W. (1972). *Citizen advocacy for handicapped, impaired, and disadvantaged: An overview*. [DHEW Publication No. OS 72-42] Washington, DC: Government Printing Services.

Yung, K. K. (1997). Special education in Hong Kong: Is history repeating itself? *Special Education Forum, 1*(1), 1–7.

2

Special Needs Education in Hong Kong

ADVANCED THINKING

Answer the following questions as you read this chapter:

1. Which governmental departments are involved in the administration and funding of education in Hong Kong?
2. Why were there frequent changes regarding the in-charge governing bodies for the provision of special needs education?
3. How is special needs education defined in the Hong Kong education system?
4. How are children with special needs identified in Hong Kong?
5. How are educational assessments conducted for children with special needs in Hong Kong?
6. What are the existing educational service delivery models for children with special needs in Hong Kong?
7. What related services are currently available in Hong Kong?
8. What are the government's strategies to promote integration in Hong Kong?
9. Which group of children with special needs is underserved in Hong Kong?

KEY TERMS AND PHRASES

advisory service
audiological service
boarding school
cost of schooling
curriculum
examination service

funding
governing agency
history
identification
integration
mainstream school

peripatetic
placement
policy
practice school
psychological service
reference
related service
remedial support
resource class
resource teaching service

school-based program
screening
service delivery
skills opportunity school
special school
speech therapy service
system of assessment
tertiary education
training service

INTRODUCTION

Following the common path of development in other parts of the world, the effort to provide special needs education in Hong Kong was initiated by missionaries. The government's active involvement began in late 1970s when compulsory education was implemented and all children had the right to attend school. After a number of turnovers of the power and responsibility in policy making over the last three decades, the Education and Manpower Bureau now has overall authorization and accountability for the formulation, coordination and implementation of education and manpower policies in Hong Kong. Special needs education has become part of the integral education system. In this chapter, we will briefly study the governing and funding of our education system, including special needs education, system of identification, system of educational assessment, service delivery models, related services, and integration of children with disabilities in Hong Kong.

GOVERNING AND FUNDING

There have been a lot of changes regarding the governing and funding for the provision of special needs education in the past three decades, when the pace of the development of special needs education began to speed up. The changes reflected a shift of the concept regarding the provision of education to children with disabilities — from social service or welfare to education. This change of concept followed along the shift from the concept of education for a few privileged to education to a public responsibility. Therefore, when the provision of education in Hong Kong went from an elite system to a mass system, children with disabilities were included in this shift. All children have a right to an education; therefore, teaching children with disabilities is no longer perceived as a gesture of philanthropy, but a civil right.

Governing of Special Needs Education

In the 1970s, the Secretary for Social Services was responsible for making policies for education, including special education in Hong Kong as well as for the manpower, welfare, health, and rehabilitation programs. In 1978, a Rehabilitation Division was established under the Social Services Branch, as recommended by the 1977 White Paper on Rehabilitation, entitled "Integrating the Disabled into the Community: A United Effort," to coordinate the development of rehabilitation services which included special education. The Rehabilitation Division was transferred to the Education and Manpower Branch in 1983, to the Health and Welfare Branch in 1988, and then back to the Education and Manpower Branch in April, 1995. This most recent transfer resulted from concerns regarding resource allocation of various interest groups, professional, and statutory bodies, in particular, the Hong Kong Special Schools Council. Figure 2.1 illustrates organization of current governing agencies related to education. The Education Department now has a Services Section to be responsible for all matters related to the provision of special needs education, except for policy making.

Funding of Special Needs Education

Special schools in Hong Kong are currently funded to provide 9 years of free general education to children with physical disabilities or sensory impairments and 10 years to children with mental retardation. Additionally, a number of blind, deaf, or physically disabled children may be allowed to participate in educational program at the preparatory or preprimary level or at the primary or junior secondary level for 1 to 2 years. The formula for funding special schools has been undergoing continual changes in recent years. At present, each student in special schools is funded up to three times as much as a student in mainstream schools. Anticipating a number of changes that may occur in the near future with the implementation of the educational reform, we are not certain how the funding of special schools will be.

**Figure 2.1   Organizational Chart of the Governing Bodies for Education:
The Education and Manpower Bureau and Other Governmental
Agencies**

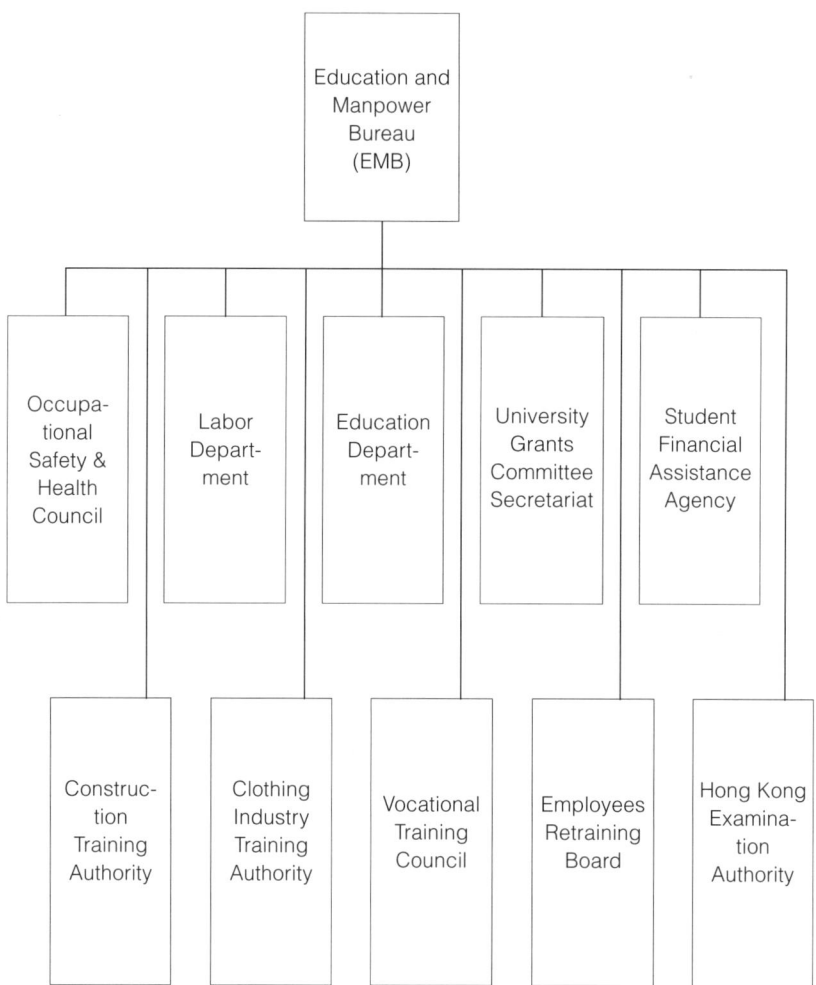

SYSTEM FOR IDENTIFICATION

Before services can be delivered to individuals with special needs, the educational service providers may need to identify their specific disabilities or impairments for eligibility. Developed countries usually have an identification system with legal mandates on the procedures and provisions of services. The Hong Kong government also has a comparatively simplified system of identification of individuals with specific categories of special needs.

From Birth to Preschool

Parents and physicians may play a key role in the identification of disabilities among newly born babies and preschool age children. Neonatal examinations are conducted in public and private hospitals and maternity homes within the first 24 hours to identify physical abnormalities. Children with abnormalities are referred for follow-up treatment. Parents of these infants will be immediately referred to medical social workers for counseling. They will also be referred to parent resource centers for support services and guidance upon discharge.

The Comprehensive Observation Scheme is available to provide developmental screening for all children from birth to the age of five. Such screening is performed in maternal and child health centers for children aged 10 weeks, 9 months, and 3 years. The purpose of this scheme is to ensure that all congenital defects or those acquired after birth are detected and remedial action may be taken as early as possible. The Special Education Services Centers of the Education Department provide a wide range of services for school-age children and preschool children with disabilities. These centers accept referrals from the Department of Health under the Comprehensive Observation Scheme, as well as the nongovernmental organizations and parents. This early childhood identification system primarily assists with the diagnosis of sensory impairments, intellectual disabilities, and physical disabilities.

School Ages

When children reach the school age, the Education Department utilizes the Combined Screening Program to request teachers to identify all Primary 1 children with moderate or severe learning problems and to refer them for a full assessment. This program is intended to identify children at risk of acquiring visual, hearing, speech, or learning problems and provide advice to the schools they attend. If children encounter learning, emotional and behavioral difficulties, parents may approach student guidance officers or student guidance teachers in the primary schools, or school social workers or the guidance teachers in the secondary schools the children are attending. When necessary, students will be referred by these professionals or schools to the Psychological Services Section for assessment and consultation. However, many parents may not know that they could make the request.

SYSTEM OF ASSESSMENT

After a disabling condition is detected in a child, the Child Assessment Centers of the Department of Health provide multidisciplinary teams for a comprehensive assessment so that the appropriate treatment can be provided. The key concern for the Child Assessment Service is the long waiting period.

Children identified through the Education Department's Combined Screening Program are referred to relevant specialists for a thorough assessment. Those who have been identified as having vision problems are referred to appropriate clinics for ophthalmic or optometric assessments. Children identified with hearing difficulties receive an audiological assessment. Children with mental retardation or learning and behavioral problems are given any individual assessment to determine the degree of mental retardation, learning problems, and emotional or behavioral disorders through the Services Division of the Education Department. Results of assessment with recommendations are given to the school principals and parents. Children with speech problems are assessed by speech therapists of the Education Department.

It must be emphasized that children with learning difficulties are only assessed for their intelligence level and general attainment in the three basic subjects of Chinese, English, and Mathematics. Assessments on specific areas of difficulty in language and arithmetic or visual/auditory perceptual difficulties are not routinely conducted. If a child is two grades behind in two of the three basic subjects, the child will be given assistance through remedial type of teaching or tutorial and they are typically expected to take the same examinations as others at the end of the semester or school year.

SERVICE DELIVERY MODELS

Special needs education is now considered education, not rehabilitation in Hong Kong. Rehabilitative services are to support, enhance, or expedite the individualized educational program. To examine the service delivery modes of special needs education in Hong Kong, one must start from the definition of special needs education which is defined within the context of the individuals who qualify for those instructions and services. The official definition of "children with special needs" adopted by the Education Department (Board of Education, 1996) of Hong Kong is:

> Children are considered to have special educational needs if they cannot derive full benefit from the curriculum provided for children of their age cohort and/ or who cannot be catered for adequately in the ordinary educational setting. Children with one or more of the following characteristics can be considered as children with special educational needs: visual impairment, hearing impairment, physical handicap, mental handicap, maladjustment and learning difficulties. (p. 16)

Special Schools

Based on the above definition, children who are clearly diagnosed with the designated categories of disabilities will receive special instruction and services in separate settings designed for those disabilities. Therefore, the majority of services and instructions are delivered to students with disabilities in separate day schools called special schools. There are several types of special schools: schools for children with visual impairments, schools for children with hearing impairments, schools for children with physical disabilities, schools for children with varying degrees of mental retardation, schools for children with physical illness who require a temporary stay at hospitals, and schools for children with maladjustment (called "schools for social development"). Some of the schools of all types have a residential section to minimize traveling required of students who live far from the school campus.

All special schools receive financial support from the Education Department under the Code of Aid for Special Schools. The Education Department also provides subsidy for allied health, social work, nursing and residential care staff of special schools. For example, an annual block grant is made to the Hong Kong Society for the Blind for the operation of the Centralized Braille Production Center, which produces Braille materials for the visually impaired, including textbooks used by students with visual impairments. The residential section of the schools is supported by the Social Welfare Department.

Skills Opportunity Schools and Practical Schools

Two other types of special schools are found in Hong Kong: skills opportunity schools and practical schools. They are discussed separately because of their status as to where they belong. The Education Department considers these schools as mainstream schools (Board of Education, 1996) but they are funded under the Code of Aid for Special Schools. Currently, teachers in these schools are considered teaching in special education settings with monetary incentive. These schools' current status may change as the Education Department has a plan of converting them into mainstream schools and will be funded similar to other mainstream schools.

Skills opportunity schools are junior secondary schools (Secondary 1 to 3) providing a modified curriculum to cater for children who form the bottom 0.9% of the ability range and are of the 12–14 years of age. These students have learning difficulties and cannot benefit from the ordinary curriculum even with the help of the existing intensive remedial services. The curriculum of skills opportunity schools comprises 60% academic subjects and 40% cultural, practical and technical subjects. Through this alternative mode of schooling, education programs containing significant practical skill elements are provided to prepare them for further training in skills centers, technical institutes, or open employment.

Practical schools are junior secondary schools providing a diversified curriculum to cater for the group of secondary school-age children who are more inclined toward a practically oriented curriculum. The curriculum of practical schools comprises 55% academic subjects and 45% cultural, practical, and technical subjects. This alternative mode of provision gives them equal chances for proper schooling and also the necessary facilities to prepare them for either senior secondary educational pursuits or vocational training/apprenticeship training, or employment.

The Subcommittee on Special Education has also completed its review on the future development of practical schools and skills opportunity schools and submitted its report to the Board of Education in March 2000. It has recommended the mainstreaming of all practical schools and the combination of some skills opportunity schools, with a view to mainstreaming in the long run. Its recommendation has been endorsed by the Board of

Education. As such, many teachers in those schools are concerned about losing their status as special education teachers and some are either considering seeking a teaching position in or have already transferred to mainstream schools. The biggest concern, however, should be how the needs of children with severe learning and behavioral difficulties will be adequately met in mainstream schools.

Class Size and Staffing Ratio of Special Schools

The class size of special schools and special education classes in ordinary schools ranges from 8 to 20 per class, depending on the types of children served. The staffing ratio also varies according to the types of special educational provision, ranging from 1 to 2 teachers per class. Besides, there are teacher assistants provided in these schools. To accommodate children's different educational needs, other specialists such as physiotherapists, occupational therapists, speech therapists, and social workers are employed to provide various types of related services.

Duration of Program in Special Schools

While the age of admission to a special school is 6 years, children are admitted to some categories of special schools at 4 years of age. The policy regarding the duration of programs in special schools is that, "Whenever possible, students are transferred from special schools to mainstream schools as soon as they no longer require the special facilities and resources in special schools" (Education Department, October 23, 2000; http://www. info.gov.hk/ed/english/school/eductation_services/index.htm).

Cost of Schooling

All primary and junior secondary classes in aided special schools are free. The School Textbooks Assistance Scheme is also given to needy parents of children attending such classes. For residential students, a boarding fee with substantial government subsidy is charged to those who can afford it. Discount or waiver of boarding fee may be granted to those who qualify.

Curriculum

In general, the mainstream school curriculum is followed as closely as possible. However, to cater for the varied learning needs of students, adapted or extended curricula on different key learning areas, such as programs on daily living skills, are provided. Special schools also offer a wide range of extra-curricular activities aiming at enriching the everyday life experiences of day and residential students. In addition to extra-curricular activities, practical schools and skills opportunity schools also offer complementary studies to provide students with a wide range of experiences and to facilitate them to cultivate interest in further pursuit of the related skills on completion of Secondary Three.

In September 1988, a Special Education Coordinating Committee (SECC) was formed under the Curriculum Development Council (CDC) to formulate policy and oversee curriculum development for children with special educational needs. Work related to curriculum development is the responsibility of the Curriculum Development Institute. With the re-structuring of the CDC in September 1999, the SECC is reorganized into the CDC Committee on Special Educational Needs.

Mainstream Schools

In addition to special schools, the Education Department also offers special education classes in mainstream schools. For the school year of 2001–2002, there were 157 special education classes in mainstream schools (http://www. ed.gov.hk/ednewhp/resource/key_statistics/english/special_education.htm). A few of them are designated for children with hearing impairments and visual impairments while the majority of them are resource classes for children with learning difficulties.

The existing system of identification, assessment, and service delivery models seems to provide better services to children with sensory impairments, intellectual disabilities, and physical disabilities than children with learning difficulties or learning disabilities, though the number of this category of children is a lot greater than the combination of all other categories. Children with learning disabilities are not recognized as having specific disabilities that require intervention. These children are grouped under the term of "children with learning difficulties," and may not be given proper instructional arrangements with properly trained teachers.

The Education Department provides a spectrum of intensive remedial services for students identified with learning difficulties. These services are provided either directly to students inside or outside their schools, or to teachers to enhance their knowledge and skills in curriculum adaptation and remedial strategies. There are four types of services.

Resource Classes

Resource classes are operated in primary schools for students with learning difficulties from Primary 3 to Primary 6. Specialist teachers in the resource classrooms provide intensive remedial teaching to students in the three basic subjects of Chinese, English, and Mathematics. Each resource class can support up to 15 students.

School-based Remedial Support Program

The School-based Remedial Support Program (SBRSP) is operated within secondary schools for junior secondary students who have learning difficulties. To support the junior secondary students with learning difficulties from schools without the SBRSP, intensive remedial teaching in the three basic subjects is also provided at Resource Teaching Centers. Students attend in groups of 15 once every Saturday.

Primary students whose schools are not provided with resource classes or peripatetic teaching service also go to Resource Teaching Centers operated by the Education Department outside their school hours to attend the intensive remedial teaching in the three main subjects. Students attend twice weekly on weekdays or once every Saturday. Specialized teachers conduct teaching sessions in small groups of ten.

Peripatetic Teaching Service

Peripatetic Teaching Service caters itinerant programs for children who require intensive remedial services but whose primary schools are without resource class provision and they could not attend the Resource Centers because of travel distance or escort problem. The peripatetic teachers from the Education Department visit the students in schools to provide remedial teaching in the three basic subjects twice weekly in groups of 6–10 students.

Advisory Service

For schools with a small number of students identified with the need for intensive remedial service but for various reasons do not operate any resource class, inspectors from the Education Department will provide them with consultant and advisory services to enhance school heads' and teachers' awareness of students' special needs, to suggest ways of meeting such needs, to enhance their skills in curriculum adaptation, teaching strategies and classroom management. The service includes school visits, training workshops, and experience sharing seminars.

For schools with a high intake of the bottom 10% students at junior levels. Additional teachers and recurrent grant are provided for the school to conduct supportive programs for the academically low achievers to improve their academic performance. The SBRSP provides intensive remedial teaching in the three main subjects and programs for learning support and developing self-study skills. A team of inspectors from the Education Department also provides advisory support to schools.

While the Education Department has put in place four types of remedial services for children with learning difficulties, the majority of teachers involved in the teaching of these children do not have special education training, much less specific training in dealing with the wide range of learning difficulties or disabilities. Resource classes generally have two grades of students at the same time. In addition to insufficient training, teachers have limited resources in teaching materials to diversify the learning activities to allow for various learning preferences. Teachers and students are also responsible for covering and mastering the standard curriculum for all. It will be beneficial to the public and development of Hong Kong if these students are provided with more assistance in effectively managing their difficulties because they have the greatest potential to cope with their difficulties and to become key contributors of the society. The fact that almost half of the students with disabilities (196,000 out of 428,000 students) are students with learning disabilities in American colleges and universities during the school year of 1997–98 (National Center for Educational Statistics, U.S. Department of Education, 2000) reflects the potential and demands our attention to the provision of proper educational programs.

PROVISION OF RELATED SERVICES

A range of special education services is currently provided by the Education Department for preschool and school children. These services are generally offered at the special education services centers, one in Hong Kong, one in Kowloon and one in Kwai Chung, New Territories. Outreach and peripatetic programs are organized to meet children's special needs in their own schools. The primary purpose for the provision of these services is to facilitate early diagnosis and treatment/intervention in an attempt to prevent a mild impairment from becoming a serious or permanent one (Education Department, 2002). A variety of services have been launched:

Screening, Referral and Placement Services

These services aim at achieving the following:

- Recommendations for appropriate placement for children with special educational needs to Primary One Admission Unit

- Recommendations for allocation of primary six students to practical schools or skills opportunity schools through Secondary School Places Allocation
- Audiometric and eye-sight screening programs
- Programs for identifying children with learning difficulties and speech problems
- Intake and initial screening service for children seeking special help or assessment
- Referral of children suspected of having sensory impairments or learning problems for further assessment and remedial help
- Referral of children to government departments or non-governmental organizations for other services
- Placement of children in special schools, practical schools, skills opportunity schools or special education classes according to their individual needs

Audiological Service

This service aims at achieving the following:

- Audiological assessment and diagnosis
- Prescription, fitting, issue, advice and maintenance of hearing aids and assistive learning systems for its effective use in a learning environment
- Production and issue of ear moulds
- Peripatetic advisory service to hearing impaired children studying in ordinary schools and special schools other than schools for the hearing impaired
- Advisory and training services for preschool hearing impaired children
- Referral to ear, nose and throat specialists for medical treatment
- Parent guidance, review and recommendation of school placement
- Visiting audiological service to special schools and special education classes for the hearing impaired
- Professional support for Integrated Kindergartens and Supportive
- Remedial service for hearing impaired children

Speech Therapy Service

This service aims at achieving the following:

- Assessment and diagnosis of speech and/or language impaired children

- Direct work on speech and language problems in the form of individual/group therapy and parent counseling/training
- Professional support to and supervision of speech therapy personnel in special schools
- Professional support to Regional Education Offices

Psychological Service

This service aims at achieving the following:

- Psychological, intellectual, social and educational assessment for children with suspected learning and/or behavioral problems
- Individual and group counseling for parents and their children with behavioral and emotional problems, including behavior management programs and social skills training groups
- Consultation and support to schools on case management and crisis management
- Short-term learning support group programs for children, and advice for parents on systematic support methods
- Professional support to guidance service in secondary schools
- Professional support to schools which adopt a whole school approach to integration of pupils with special needs
- School-based psychological service for special schools, practical schools and skills opportunity schools
- Regular visits to integrated kindergartens

Resource Teaching Service

This service aims at achieving the following:

- Remedial support to children with learning difficulties and physical handicaps studying in ordinary schools
- Adjustment programs for children with behavior/adjustment problems

Advisory Service

This service aims at achieving the following:

- Professional advice to preschool centers, special and ordinary schools, non-governmental organizations and government departments on the education of children with special educational needs

- Operation of a Teaching Resources Room for special education teachers

School-based Remedial Support Program

This program aims at achieving the following:

- Professional advice to ordinary schools with a high intake of bottom 10% junior secondary students on the implementation of the SBRSP
- Professional support and training to teachers deployed for the SBRSP

Other Services

(a) Examination Service

This service aims at achieving the following:

- Assessment of special needs of handicapped candidates sitting for public examinations
- Recommendation for special arrangements for such candidates

(b) Training Service

This service aims at achieving the following:

- Orientation, introductory, refresher and professional courses/ workshops for teachers
- Lectures and talks on special education requested by educational and other professional institutions
- Supervision of trainee educational psychologists, speech therapy personnel and audiologist, and coordinating field placement for social work students

INTEGRATING CHILDREN WITH SPECIAL NEEDS

As one of the most controversial issues and topics for debate in the field of special needs education, *integration* has gradually made its way into the education system in Hong Kong since the 1970s. This progressive humanistic movement for individuals with disabilities receives general consensus, but disagreements exist as to how integration should be implemented and how far it should go. Much of the argument among educators is based upon this humanistic perspective of "the right to an education like everybody else." Research results only cause more controversies. Nevertheless, Hong Kong has adopted the perspective of right to an education as the foundation for integrating children with disabilities. The present policy aims at placing children with special educational needs whenever possible in ordinary schools so that they receive the fullest benefit of education from mixing and interacting with nondisabled children in an ordinary environment. Such movement toward integration is universally recognized and will gain momentum in future developments.

Integration is now set as the goal of special needs education (Board of Education, 1996). With this goal in mind, the government has set the following objectives in developing educational services (Social Welfare Department, 1995):

1. Providing all children with at least a 9-year free and compulsory general education;
2. Giving children with disabilities appropriate programs to enable them to maximize their abilities;
3. Providing vocational and skills training beyond compulsory school age as required;
4. Making available higher education to individuals with disabilities if they are academically capable;
5. Providing special schools and special education classes in ordinary schools for those who cannot benefit from ordinary classrooms;
6. Giving special preschool educational programs to children with special needs; and
7. Making available adult education for individuals with disabilities who missed the compulsory education.

Strategies to Promote Integration of Students with Special Needs

Enhancing school reforms to support an inclusive education has become a major trend in American schools (Lipsky & Gartner, 1989, 1998; Stainback & Stainback, 1984, 1990, 1992). In the United States as well as a number of other countries, a list of strategies has been developed for schools to include children with special needs in general education programs. Dyches (1995), for example, developed an accommodation planning guide (APG) for teachers to effectively work with the integrated students with disabilities. Clasberry and Lian (1998) disseminated effective strategies for field practitioners to enhance inclusive schooling, including the use of teacher's assistants, instructional adaptations, cooperative learning, material adaptations, team- or co-teaching, itinerant teaching, consultant services, multi-level curriculum, and assistive technology.

The Education Department has implemented a number of strategies in promoting integration of students with disabilities. To enhance teachers' understanding and acceptance of children with special educational needs, there is a component in the initial teacher training for present and future teaching force on working with children with special needs. To promote integration, the Education Department organizes regular seminars for ordinary school teachers on the acceptance and handling of children with disabilities. Pamphlets and leaflets promoting understanding of children with disabilities are made available to teachers. The whole-school approach to guidance and the development of the school-based curriculum is being implemented. Further promotion includes topics relating to individuals with disabilities in the formal curricula for ordinary school children at primary and secondary levels and the optional curricula at the senior secondary and sixth form levels. Schools are also encouraged to organize various extra-curricular activities in the civic and moral education programs to promote integration.

Preschool-level educational services for young children with special needs consist of early education and training centers, special child care centers, integrated child care centers and integrated kindergartens. Families of children with disabilities are supported by relevant community services and parents are encouraged to be involved as full partners in decision-making process.

Special schools for the blind and for the deaf. Special schools for the blind and for the deaf currently function as resource centers for integrators. The possibility of utilizing special schools for children with mental retardation as resource centers is being explored. Accessible facilities are prerequisite for integrating children with physical disabilities. New schools scheduled for completion from 1998 onwards will be wheelchair accessible. Converting existing schools to improve accessibility is also considered.

Visual impairments. Children with visual impairments, if integrated, may receive assistance from resource teachers (from schools for the visually impaired) in preparing supplementary teaching materials such as braille or sounded books, notes, tests, and examination papers, embossed maps and diagrams, and training in the use of technical aids. The Hong Kong Society for the Blind and the Hong Kong Association of the Blind provide supportive educational services at their resource centers, including reading, tutoring, brailling and study rooms. The Education Department subsidizes the Centralized Braille Production Center of the Hong Kong Society for the Blind.

Physical disabilities. In ordinary schools, students with physical disabilities receive remedial teaching, counseling, and advice on rehabilitation aids and resources from the Resource Help Service operated by the Education Department. The Hong Kong Spasticity Association provides resource and support services.

Hearing impairments. Children with hearing impairments in ordinary schools receive peripatetic advisory services or special classes. A special school piloted the Supportive Remedial Service for children with hearing impairments in ordinary schools. It has proven to be effective to improve the performance of these children and is now implemented in all primary schools. The Education Department also provides advice on the use of hearing aids, ear moulds, the special seating arrangements, and resource materials.

Mild mental retardation. If integrated, children with mild mental retardation are provided with intensive remedial support services such as resource classes or peripatetic teaching services, center-based remedial support, and advisory services for teachers.

English-speaking children. English-speaking children with special needs in Hong Kong are provided with services run by the schools of the English Schools Foundation which receives subsidy from the government. English-speaking children with special needs are placed in ordinary schools with support from school-based special units. Children with more severe disabilities receive their educational services at the Jockey Club Sarah Roe School of the English Schools Foundation. Some of the international schools also provide learning specialists and psychologists for children with learning and behavioral difficulties.

Preschool age. For preschool age children with special needs, the policy emphasizes the provision of equal opportunities and full participation through early intervention programs. Families of these children are supported by relevant community services, and parents are encouraged to be involved as full partners in decision-making process. Services consist of early education and training centers, childcare centers, integrated child care centers and integrated kindergartens.

Early education and training centers. Early education and training centers provide center-based programs for children with disabilities from birth to two and those aged between two and five years 11 months who need their service. The primary objective is to support parents in training and caring for the children.

Special childcare centers. Special childcare centers were first established in 1978. These centers provide intensive training and care for children with moderate and severe disabilities between two and five years 11 months of age who cannot benefit from the integrated programs in ordinary childcare centers or in kindergartens. Training at these centers focuses on developing sensory, perceptual, motor, cognitive communication, social, and self-care skills. If a child requires therapy or care services that cannot be provided by a day special childcare center or his/her family, he or she may be admitted to a residential special childcare center. Such centers also take in children with disabilities who are also homeless, abandoned, or whose families cannot care for them adequately.

Integrated kindergarten program. The integrated kindergarten program was first piloted in 1985 and found to be effective in 1988. The program was expanded to 20 kindergartens. It was designed for preschool children with mild disabilities from ages three to five and 11 months. Every nonprofit kindergarten joining the program can employ an additional trained kindergarten teacher to serve as a resource teacher and to conduct remedial programs for up to six children. These children receive individual instruction for half an hour a day and participate in the regular activities with their peers for the rest of the day.

Preparatory classes. Special schools for children with blindness, deafness, and physical disabilities aged 4 to 5 years 11 months provide preparatory classes. These classes are designed to ensure a smooth transition from early education to primary education by developing the children's general learning ability, language proficiency, reading and writing, concept of numbers, and social and motor skills.

Special schools for primary and secondary levels. Special schools are provided for primary and secondary school aged children with special educational needs that cannot be addressed in ordinary schools. Children who require medical attention in hospitals or medical rehabilitation centers may receive instruction in hospital schools. In 1994–95, 15 hospitals offered classes ranging from primary to junior secondary levels. These classes included those run in psychiatric hospitals or children centers for children with psychiatric or behavioral problems, including autism, schizophrenia, depression, and conduct disorder.

Boarding facilities in special school. Boarding facilities are available for children with moderate, severe, and profound mental retardation, blindness, deafness, physical disabilities, and no family; children who live far away from school, who need temporary care or whose families cannot care for them adequately.

Tertiary education. While higher education institutions are aware of the need to serve students with disabilities who have aspiration for advanced studies, services to facilitate the enrollment and learning process of students with various types of disabilities are limited compared to North American and European countries. Inadequate technical devices and the lack of accessibility to or around the various campuses are recurring issues. Some measures have been taken to improve the situation. Needy students may apply for the Local Student Finance Scheme for grants or loans to purchase the technical devices and may continue to use them after graduation. All the new buildings in the higher education institutions funded by the University Grants Committee are wheelchair accessible. However, students with learning disabilities have limited access to tertiary education at present as they are generally sifted out in the lower grades.

At present, integrating children with disabilities in mainstream schools remains restricted to a few categories of disabilities and a number of issues remain unresolved. Some of the key issues include: (a) whether untrained mainstream teachers should continue to work with integrated children without support from the special education personnel; (b) whether special education teachers should be allowed to teach or co-teach in the mainstream schools without losing their salary increment specially designated for special school teachers; (c) whether those students and their teachers are responsible for the standard curriculum; (d) whether they take the same examinations as others and if they do, how their grades will be dealt with in comparison to others; (e) whether related services should be delivered in the mainstream school or elsewhere and if they should be delivered during school hours; and (f) how teachers can provide special assistance to these students in the mainstream classrooms. Clear policies with systemic support must be in place in order to move forward in the direction of integration.

SUMMARY

1. In early years, the missionaries in Hong Kong provided custodial and educational services for children with special needs. The government became more actively involved in 1970 when compulsory education was implemented and, like their nondisabled peers, children with learning difficulties began to be entitled to general school education.

2. After a series of evolutional changes, the Service Section of the Education Department now has the authorization and responsibilities for implementation of all matters relating to the provision of special

needs education. Other governmental agencies serve in the resource and supporting roles.

3. Special schools in Hong Kong are receiving funding to provide 9 years of free general education to students with physical and sensory disabilities, and one additional year to students with mental retardation. Capable students who are deaf, blind, or have physical disabilities may have an opportunity to go on, attending the primary or junior secondary level schools for 1 to 2 years.

4. A system has been developed for identifying and comprehensively assessing children with special needs at the birth-to-preschool and school ages. The identification system includes neonatal examination, referral, the Comprehensive Observation Scheme, the Combined Screening Program, and related services and support. Multidisciplinary teams are organized for children with identified learning difficulties, through which remedial teaching or tutoring and, if applicable, services of audiologists, speech therapists, psychologists, physical/occupational therapists, and other supporting professionals are provided.

5. Special needs education in Hong Kong is provided through special schools, skills opportunity schools/practical schools, and mainstream schools in a centralized service delivery model with corresponding programs.

6. Related services consist of screening, referral and placement services, audiological service, speech therapy service, psychological service, resource teaching service, advisory service, school-based remedial support program, and others (i.e., examination service and training service).

7. Integrating children with special needs in general education programs has become a goal since the past few years, accompanied by a set of government-initiated objectives for schools to carry out. In addition, strategies have been developed and there are increasing supporting agencies and community groups for enhancement of integration. Nevertheless, integrating children with special needs in mainstream schools remains restricted to a few categories of disabling conditions. A number of integration issues remain unresolved.

ACTIVITIES

1. Do a literature search and look into issues related to education of children with sensory impairments. Write a five-page report about what you

think as the most effective way of delivering educational programs and services to children with sensory impairments in Hong Kong, taking into consideration the structure and funding of our education system.

2. Do a literature search and look into issues related to education of children with mental retardation. Write a five-page report about what you think as the most effective way of delivering educational programs and services to children with mental retardation in Hong Kong, taking into consideration the structure and funding of our education system.

3. Do a literature search and look into issues related to education of children with learning disabilities or behavior disorders. Write a five-page report about how you think we can improve in identifying, assessing and delivering educational programs and services to children with learning disabilities in Hong Kong. Discuss your findings with your peers in class.

4. Divide into groups of 4–5 and discuss how integration can be done effectively and the potential groups of children who may benefit from integrated settings in Hong Kong.

RESOURCES

Resources in Hong Kong

Chinese YMCA of Hong Kong
[Kowloon site] 23 Waterloo Road, Kowloon
Tel.: 852-2771 9111 Fax: 852-2771 4096
[Hong Kong Island] Johnston Road, Wo Chung Building,
Wanchai, Hong Kong
Tel: 852-2891-0088 Fax: 852-2893-0858
Web address: http://www.ymca.org.hk/engindex.htm

Equal Opportunity Commission (EOC)
Unit 2002, 20/F, Office Tower, Convention Plaza
1 Harbour Road, Wanchai, Hong Kong
Tel.: 852-2511-8211 Fax: 852-2511-8142
E-mail: eoc@eoc.gov.hk
Web address: http://www.eoc.org.hk/

Fung Hon Chu Gifted Education Center
7 Shing Mun Road, Tsuen Wan, New Territories

Heep Hong Society 協康會
G1-11, Tung Yu House, Tai Hang Yung Estate, Kowloon
Tel.: 852-2776-3111   Fax: 852-2776-1837
E-mail: info@heephong.org
Web address: http://www.heephong.org

Hong Kong Christian Service
33 Granville Road, Tsimsatsui, Kowloon
Tel.: 852-2731-6316
Web address: http://www.hkcs.org/index_e.htm

Hong Kong Education and Manpower Bureau 教育統籌局
香港雪廠街11號中區政府合署 (西座) 9樓
Tel.: 852-2810-2631   Fax: 852-2868-5916
E-mail: embhome@emb.gcn.gov.hk
Web address: http://www.info.gov.hk/emb/prog_high/special_map.html

Hong Kong Education Department 教育署
Web address: http://www.info.gov.hk/ed/english/index.htm

The Parents' Association of Pre-School Handicapped Children
鑽石山鳳德村，紫鳳樓地下1–2A室, Kowloon
Web address: http://www.parentsassn.org.hk/big5/

Po Leung Kok
66 Leighton Road, Causeway Bay, Hong Kong
Tel.: 852-2277 8888   Fax: 852-2576 4509
Web address: http://www.poleungkuk.org.hk/rehab_c.htm

Rehab Power
Power Retail Centre, G/F Lobby, Shatin Hospital,
Shatin, New Territories
Web address: http://www.rehabpower.org.hk/index.html

Special Education Resource Center, Hong Kong Education Department
特殊教育資源中心
香港九龍何文田巴富街六號特殊教育服務中心地下102–104室
Tel.: 852-2760-6201 or 852-2760-6202   Fax: 852-2761-0976
Email: serc@ed.gov.hk
Web address: http://serc.ed.gov.hk/

Special Education Society of Hong Kong
香港特殊教育學會
Tel.: 852-2320-3452
Web address: http://www.seshk.org.hk/

The Society for the Relief of Disabled Children
12 Sandy Bay Road, Pokfulam, Hong Kong
Tel: 852-2819-3050
Web address: http://www.srdc.org.hk/index_e.html

Special Education Society of Hong Kong
Web address: http://www.seshk.org.hk/

Tung Wah Group of Hospitals
12 Po Yan Street, Sheung Wan, Hong Kong
Tel.: 852-2859-7500
Web address: http://www.tungwah.org.hk/

Resources in Taiwan

教育部特殊教育小組
台北市中山南路五號
Tel.: 886-2-23566051-2
E-mail: mail@mail.moe.gov.tw
Web address: http://spcedu.tkblind.tku.edu.tw/

Special Education Association of Republic of China
中華民國特殊教育學會
台北市和平東路一段162號
Tel.: 886-02-2392-2784
Web address: http://searoc.aide.gov.tw/index.htm

International Resources

National Down Syndrome Society
666 Broadway, New York, NY 10012 U.S.A.
Tel.: 1-212-460-9330
Web address: http://www.ndss.org/

Illinois Council on Developmental Disabilities
100 W. Randolph, Suite 10-600, Chicago, Illinois 60601 U.S.A.
Tel.: 1-312-814-2080   Fax 1-312-814-7151
Web address: http://www.state.il.us/agency/ipcdd/

Inclusion Press International
24 Thome Crescent, Toronto, Ontario, Canada M6H 2S5
Tel.: 1-416-658-5363   Fax: 1-416-658-5067
Web address: http://www.inclusion.com/

The National Parent Network on Disabilities (NPND)
1130 - 17th Street, NW, Suite 400, Washington, DC 20036 U.S.A.
Tel.: 1-202-463-2299   Fax: 1-202-463-9403

PEAK Parent Center, Inc.
611 North Weber, Suite 200, Colorado Springs, CO 80903 U.S.A.
Tel.: 1-719-531-9400   Fax: 1-719-531-9452
Web address: http://www.peakparent.org/

Project CHOICES
Tel.: 1-630-778-4508
Web address: http://www.projectchoices.org/

Special Education Resources on the Internet
Hood College, 401 Rosemont Ave, Frederick, MD 21701-8575 U.S.A.
Tel.: 1-301-663-3131
Web address: http://www.hood.edu/seri/serihome.htm

REFERENCES

Board of Education (1996). *Report of the Subcommittee on Special Education.* Hong Kong: Government Printer.

Clasberry, G., & Lian, M-G.J. (1998). *Strategies for an inclusive school: A handbook for teachers & program coordinators.* Project ID# H023B60037, CFDA 84.023B, funded by U.S. Department of Education, Washington, DC

Dyches, T.T. (1995). *Effects of an accommodation planning guide on teachers' recommendations of services, adaptations, and accommodations for students with disabilities.* Unpublished doctoral dissertation, Illinois State University, Normal, Il.

Education Department. (2002). [online] http://www.ed.gov.hk/eng/service.

Lipsky, D.K. & Gartner, A. (Eds.). (1989). *Beyond separate education: Quality for all.* Baltimore, MD: Paul H. Brookes.

Lipsky, D.K., & Gartner, A. (1998). Factors for successful inclusion: Learning from the past, looking toward the future. In S. J. Vitello & D. E. Mithaun (Eds), *Inclusive schooling: National and international perspectives* (pp. 98–112). Mahwah, NJ: Lawrence Erlbaum Associates.

National Center for Educational Statistics. (2000). *Fast facts*. U.S. Department of Education: http://nces.ed.gov/fastfacts/display.asp.

Social Welfare Department. (1995). *White paper on rehabilitation policies and services*. Hong Kong: Government Printer.

Stainback, W., & Stainback, S. (1984). A rationale for the merger of special and regular education. *Exceptional Children, 51*(2), 102–111.

Stainback, W., & Stainback, S. (1990). Rationale for integration and restructuring: A synopsis. In J. W. Lloyd, N. N. Singh, & A. Repp (Eds.), *The regular education initiative: Alternative perspectives on concepts, issues, and models* (pp. 225–240). Sycamore, IL: Sycamore Publishing Co.

Stainback, W., & Stainback, S. (1992). *Curriculum considerations in inclusive classrooms: Facilitating learning for all students*. Baltimore, MD: Paul H. Brookes.

3

Giftedness and Talent

Answer the following questions as you read:

1. How can students with giftedness and talent be in a disadvantaged situation?
2. How can giftedness and talent be appropriately defined for the purpose of special needs education?
3. What are the various types of intelligence and talent?
4. How were persons with giftedness and talent treated and assisted in the history?
5. What are the factors that enhance or inhibit a person's giftedness and talent?
6. What are the general characteristics of children with giftedness and talent?
7. How do school professionals arrange special needs education for students with giftedness and talent?

KEY TERMS AND PHRASES

acceleration
bodily-kinesthetic intelligence
cognition
content of intelligence
convergent thinking
characteristics
creativity
critical thinking skills
curriculum
divergent thinking

egalitarianism
enrichment
evaluative thinking
giftedness
history
insight
intelligence
interpersonal intelligence
intrapersonal intelligence
IQ

knowledge   precocity
linguistic intelligence   product of intelligence
logical-mathematical intelligence   reasoning
musical intelligence   spatial intelligence
operation of intelligence   talent
peer nomination   underachievement

INTRODUCTION

Individuals with superior levels of intelligence, high academic achievement, unique talents, or extreme creativity are not handicapped in the sense of having a disability. Although they usually do not face the limitations or the difficulties that most children who receive special needs education and related services do, many of them appear to be disadvantaged by the society and the educational systems. As Silverman (1988) described:

> Attitudes toward the gifted and talented ... have been on a perpetual roller coaster. This group has been alternatively applauded, attacked, "mined" as a natural resource, and abandoned. We are now riding a new wave of enthusiasm, but our position is fragile. Programs for the gifted are still perceived as unnecessary frills that can be discarded when budgets are cut. These attitudes are costly for the children involved and for society in general.... We cannot know how much talent has been lost for lack of discovery and development, nor can we assess the magnitude of that loss to our society. (p. 264)

The traditional educational approaches can suppress high achieving individuals from expressing their talents and gifts and they may receive direct and indirect discouragement from peers, teachers, and parents to develop their abilities maximally. This may result in significant loss to the individuals and to society in general (Gallagher, 1985).

GIFTEDNESS AND TALENT DEFINED

Traditional definition of *giftedness and talent* may mean, exclusively, those with an IQ score that is three *standard deviations* (i.e., 145) above the *mean* (i.e., 100). This statistical identification is shown on a bell-shaped curve, the *normal curve*. In this curve, the majority of a population falls in the middle of the bell, at or around an intelligence quotient (IQ) score of 100, and fewer and fewer people fall to either end of the distribution. IQ

Figure 3.1 The Normal Curve of Intelligence Quotients

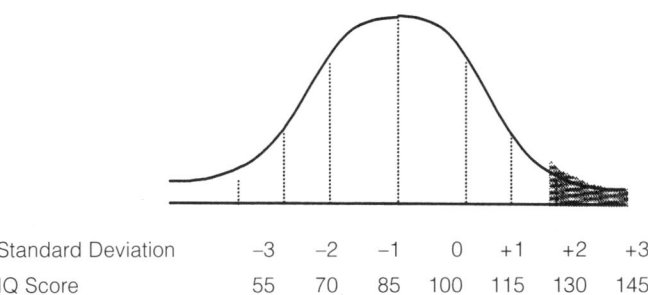

Standard Deviation	−3	−2	−1	0	+1	+2	+3
IQ Score	55	70	85	100	115	130	145

level is determined by the distance a score is from the mean (average) score (see Figure 3.1).

Most definitions of intelligence tend to include one or more of the three basic components (Benner, 1992):

1. the capacity to learn;
2. the sum total of knowledge an individual has acquired; and
3. the ability to adjust to various environments, particularly new situations. (p. 195)

These basic components of intelligence may be similar to, or overlap with, Glick's theory of *cognition* (1975): "The study of cognition is the study of the means by which an individual comes to have organized knowledge of the world, and of the way in which that knowledge is used to guide behavior" (p. 595). His definition of knowledge consists of four overlapping categories of abilities: (1) the ability to detect environmental features, (2) the ability to organize diverse environmental phenomena into categories, (3) the formation of plans of behavior and/or theories about the world, and (4) the organization of thoughts. These abilities may be applied to academic (e.g., mathematics) and other daily living (e.g., religion) forms of thinking.

Heward and Orlansky (1992) pinpointed the problem that "the narrow view of giftedness, dominated by formal measures of intelligence, prevailed for many years and came to be associated with only the white, urban, middle- and upper-class society" (p. 195). In addition, commercially-available intelligence scales are actually general achievement tests that sample a limited of number of behaviors. As Cohen and Spenciner (1998) described, "Performance on a test helps us in our understanding of the examinee's approach to the demands of the tasks that are presented; there are many behaviors that intelligence tests do not sample and our understanding of these is emerging" (p. 378).

A narrow, exclusive definition may identify only a small percentage (e.g., 2–3%) of persons with giftedness and talent, while a broader and more inclusive definition may find over 20% in the general population. Hallahan and Kauffman (1994) indicated that definitions varied primarily due to different opinions expressed in questions such as:

1. In what way do gifted children excel?
2. How is giftedness measured?
3. To what degree must a child excel to be considered gifted?
4. Who should make up the comparison group? (pp. 446–448)

In the early 1950s, Guilford proposed a broader and multifaceted structure of intelligence:

1. The *content of intelligence*, which consists of figure, symbolic, semantic, behavioral.
2. The *operation perspective of intelligence*, which includes evaluation, convergent production, divergent production, memory, cognition.
3. The *product of intelligence*, which include units, classes, relations, systems, transformations.

Giftedness and talent are not necessarily positively correlated. Some highly creative persons do not obtain high scores on intelligence tests, while many individuals who are very bright do not show comparable levels of creativity. The following are definitions of some important terms with related concepts about giftedness, creativity, and different forms of thinking (Smith & Luckasson, 1995):

High intelligence	A composite of human traits, including a capacity for insight into complex relationships, an ability to think abstractly, solve problems, and the capacity to develop more capacity.
High IQ	IQ score to be 1.5 to 2 standard deviations above the mean.
Gifted	A term used to describe children who exhibit evidence of having high levels of intelligence.
Creativity	A form of intelligence that results in advanced

divergent thought, unique products, high levels of intuition, or ability to solve complex problems.

Convergent thinking   Taking apparently unrelated information and moving it toward a common conclusion; requiring memory, classification, and reasoning abilities.

Divergent thinking   Extending information in different directions from a common point; critical for creative behavior (fluency, flexibility, originality, elaboration).

Evaluative thinking   Thinking skills used to make decisions and to allow for comparisons and contrasts between and among items and concepts.

Talented   A term that refers to persons who have superior skills or abilities in just one or a few areas.

Hallahan and Kauffman (1994) had a similar list of terms and definitions relating to giftedness, talent, and creativity:

Precocity   Remarkable early development.

Insight   Ability to separate and/or combine various pieces of information in new, creative, or useful ways.

Genius   A word sometimes used to indicate a particular aptitude or capacity in any area; rare intellectual powers.

Creativity   Ability to express novel and useful ideas, to sense and elucidate new and important relationships, and to ask previously unthought of but crucial questions.

Talent   A special ability, aptitude, or accomplishment.

Giftedness   Cognitive (intellectual) superiority, creativity, and motivation of sufficient magnitude to set the child apart from the vast majority of age-mates and make it possible for him or her to contribute something of particular value to society.

Various psychologists and educational professionals have attempted to define intelligence with different but similar parameters: the ability to understand and to cope with the environment. Gardner and Hatch (1989) asserted that there are seven different types of intelligence:

1. *Linguistic intelligence:* sensitivity to the sounds, rhythms, and meaning of words; sensitivity to the different functions of language.

2. *Logical-mathematical intelligence:* sensitivity to, and capacity to discern, logical or numerical patterns; ability to handle long chains of reasoning.
3. *Spatial intelligence:* capacities to perceive the visual-spatial world accurately and to perform transformations on one's initial perceptions.
4. *Bodily-kinesthetic intelligence:* abilities to control one's body movements and to handle objects skillfully.
5. *Musical intelligence:* abilities to produce and appreciate rhythm, pitch, and timbre; appreciation of the forms of musical expressiveness.
6. *Interpersonal intelligence:* capacities to discern and respond appropriately to the moods, temperaments, motivations, and desires of other people.
7. *Intrapersonal intelligence:* access to one's own feelings and the ability to discriminate among them and draw upon them to guide behavior; knowledge of one's own strengths, weakness, desire, and intelligences.

Table 3.1 shows major components and adult roles which may further describe the seven different types of intelligence:

HISTORY OF THE FIELD

Emphasis on the education of persons with giftedness and talent have been scattered in human history. As early as 618 A.D. in China, gifted and talented children were brought to the imperial court, where they received special education during the Tang dynasty. Such a system was a response to the belief of Confucius (a Chinese philosopher who was recognized as the greatest teacher in Chinese history) that all children should be educated but that education should be tailored to their abilities.

In Western cultures, some attributed attention to people's innate and superior abilities to Charles Darwin and Sir Francis Galton in mid-1800s. Charles Darwin is most famous for his theories about natural selection and the evolution of species. He was the first person to study individual differences among people or issues relating to intelligence and heredity on a broad scale (Clark, 1992). In 1869, Galton proposed his theory that genius is solely attributed to heredity (Callahan, 1981). The notion that genetic factor contributes greatly to giftedness is still prevalent today while the important contributions of the environment are recognized.

Table 3.1 Components and Adult Roles of Different Types of Intelligence

	Components	Adult Roles
Linguistic intelligence	Syntax, semantics, pragmatics, written and oral language	Novelist, lecturer, lawyer, lyricist
Logical-mathematical intelligence	Deductive reasoning, inductive reasoning, computation	Mathematician, physicist
Spatial intelligence	Ability to represent and manipulate spatial configurations, interrelationship of parts	Architect, engineer, mechanic, navigator, sculptor, chess player
Bodily-kinesthetic intelligence	Ability to use all or part of one's body	Dancer, athlete, mime, surgeon
Musical intelligence	Pitch discrimination; ability to hear themes in music; sensitivity to rhythm, texture, and timbre; production of music through performance or composition	Musician, composer, singer
Interpersonal intelligence	Ability to understand and act productively on others' actions and motivations	Teacher, therapist, clergy, politician, salesperson
Intrapersonal intelligence	Understanding of self	

Source: Gardner, J.W. (1984). *Excellence: Can we be equal and excellent too?* (rev. ed.). New York: Norton.

In the United States, the hesitant commitment to the education of students with giftedness and talent reflects the national philosophy about equity and social justice. The popular view that education was best for the elite during the 18th century swung to *egalitarianism* (i.e., the notion that no one should get special treatment) during the 19th century. Gardner (1984) suggests that the concept of equal opportunity was developed from this social philosophy. One legacy of egalitarianism is the attitude that special education for gifted children is elitist, unnecessary, and wasteful.

EDUCATIONAL CONCERNS

Hereditary Factor vs. Environmental Factor

Throughout the history of education for high achieving children, people tended to believe that genetics is the primary cause of giftedness and talent. In the 1920s, Terman's work, which also led to the birth of the *Stanford-Binet Intelligence Scale,* reflected this view as well. Another proponent in the 1940s was Gesell, who emphasized biological perspective (i.e., maturation) of intelligence. Today, however, researchers have recognized the important role the environment plays in the development of children's intellectual abilities (Clark, 1992). As Heward and Orlansky (1992) described:

> Once we are born, we begin interacting with our environment (nurture). We begin learning and changing from these interactions. Research on identical twins raised apart, who behave in similar ways, shows we are strongly influenced by our genetic histories, but does that mean nurture does not play a roles? (p. 195)

Factors That Enhance or Inhibit Giftedness and Talent

Intelligence and talent are not fixed. Terman's research (1925; cited in Smith & Luckasson, 1995) has shown that factors such as values and expectations of the culture, socioeconomic level of the family, birth position in the family (for example, firstborn), and the number of children in the family are related to giftedness. Environmental stimulation correlates to giftedness or creativity but environmental factors can also diminish giftedness. Major environmental factors, such as wars, famines, and social upheavals, can affect the potential of any individual. Certainly, parental malnutrition, isolation, neglect, abuse, insufficient infant stimulation, and poor medical treatment can have devastating effects upon the development of the intellect. Additionally, children whose early experiences are not rich often do not develop outstanding cognitive skills, and children who are not challenged in school do not develop their potential. Today, superior abilities are generally recognized as resulting from the interaction between heredity and the environment. Therefore, programs that help gifted individuals to achieve their potential should be available.

CHARACTERISTICS

Intellectual Characteristics

Smith and Luckasson (1995) indicated that, compared to their peers, students with giftedness and talent are more likely to

1. reason abstractly,
2. conceptualize,
3. process information well,
4. solve problems,
5. learn quickly,
6. show intellectual curiosity,
7. have wide interests,
8. dislike drill and routine,
9. show possible unevenness,
10. generalize learning,
11. remember great amount of material,
12. display high level of verbal ability, and
13. prefer learning in a quiet environment.

Social and Emotional Characteristics

Smith and Luckasson (1995) also indicated that, compared to their peers, students with giftedness and talent are more likely to:

1. criticize self,
2. empathize,
3. play with older friends,
4. persist,
5. be sensitive to others' feelings,
6. exhibit individualism,
7. have strength of character,
8. demonstrate leadership abilities,
9. be concerned about ethical issues,
10. take risks,
11. be independent and autonomous,
12. highly sensitive,
13. have mature sense of humor, and
14. be nonconforming.

Individuals with Disabilities Who Are Gifted

Giftedness occurs in all special education categories, including those with mental retardation or severe developmental disabilities. Unfortunately, disabilities may mask potential and students with disabilities often are not included in educational programs for students with giftedness and talent. They frequently receive falsely low scores on ability and achievement tests (Silverman, 1988). Whitmore and Maker (1985) estimated that 2% of persons with disabilities are also mentally gifted. Yet, society's biases about people with disabilities can overshadow the individuals' strengths. For example, a student with a severe physical disability might require more time to answer questions on a timed, standardized test. Students with visual impairments might need large print reading materials. Students with learning disabilities might need a computer to function in a traditional testing situation. Modifications to the testing situation are seldom provided when qualifying a child for classes of gifted education.

Currently, attention is given to students with learning disabilities who are gifted. Historically, a large number of underserved students with special gifts come from this group. For example, Nielsen, Higgins, and Hammond (1993) found, in a large school district, that 66% of the "*twice-exceptional students*" identified were gifted with a learning disability. These students are extremely bright, but because of their learning disability, many do not achieve their potential and often do not receive any special services. In many states of the U.S., because of their high IQ scores, they do not qualify for educational programs for those with learning disabilities, and because of their low achievement test scores, they do not qualify for educational programs for students with giftedness and talent.

Underachievers Who Are Gifted

Children who are gifted or talented but are underachievers may demonstrate high intelligence but low academic achievement. Often times, these students may be confused with students who are gifted and have learning disabilities, depending on the discrepancy between their scores on intelligence and achievement tests. Teachers and parents often recognize these students' true capabilities, but the students do not do well in school or perform up to their abilities, sometimes for unexplainable reasons. They have been frequently described as disorganized, unmotivated, lacking interest in school, having poor study skills, and lacking in self-confidence (Rimm, 1986). Some of these children are hyperactive, while others are passive. Some present discipline problems to their teachers and families. Some are bored with school; others are frustrated by their experiences. These students, like those who have disabilities and who are gifted, need a strong motivation to succeed.

In fact, it may be motivation that makes the difference between achievers and underachievers. Although these students do not achieve the levels they should, they understand the relationship between effort and success. Unfortunately, they do not make the effort to excel at a task. Therefore, these children need specialized educational services to teach them how to (a) achieve in school, (b) approach learning tasks more meaningfully, and (c) use their talent in a directed fashion.

EDUCATION

Various approaches for successfully working with students who are gifted or talented have been developed. Two of the most common school arrangements are enrichment and acceleration.

Enrichment

Feldhusen and Robinson (1986) suggested the following approaches for providing an *enrichment* program:

1. Interdisciplinary instruction: teaching a topic by presenting perspectives of different disciplines about the issues involved.
2. Independent study: encouraging the student to examine a topic in more depth than is usual in a regular education class.
3. Mentorship programs: pairing students with adults who guide them in applying knowledge to real-life situations.
4. Internship: providing programs that allow students to be placed in a job setting that matches their career goals.
5. Enrichment triad/revolving door model: implementing an inclusive and flexible model for gifted education that changes the entire educational system; students are exposed to planned activities that seek to develop thinking skills, problem solving, and creativity.
6. Curriculum compacting: making additional time available for enrichment activities by reducing time spent on traditional instructional topics.

Acceleration

The following are examples of acceleration provided by Feldhusen and Robinson (1986):

1. Advanced placement: arranging for courses that students take during their high school years and result in college credit.
2. Honors sections: implementing a form of ability grouping where gifted and non-gifted students who demonstrate high achievement in a particular subject are placed together in advanced classes.
3. Ability grouping: clustering students in courses where all classmates have comparable achievement and skill levels.
4. Individualized instruction: delivering instruction on a one-to-one basis, with students moving through the curriculum at their own pace independently.

An example of a program model for students with giftedness and talent in secondary schools is included in Table 3.2.

General Suggestions for Teachers

Smith and Luckasson (1995) gave the following tips for teachers of students with giftedness and talent:

1. Teach a full range of content areas in considerable depth.
2. Vary your instructional approaches.
3. Encourage students to become independent learners.
4. Enrich topics of study with additional activities, such as guest speakers, field trips, demonstrations, videotapes, and interest centers.
5. Allow students to move through the curriculum at their own pace.
6. Watch for signs of boredom.
7. Encourage lively class discussions.
8. Create a safe environment where novel ideas are accepted.
9. Pose important problems to solve so that thinking about present and future dilemmas is considered
10. Teach and foster the use of library and research skills.
11. Develop instructional activities, and use questions that generate the application of different types of thinking skills.
12. Integrate the use of technology into your instruction.

Critical Thinking Skills

The development of critical thinking skills can begin early in children's

Table 3.2   Components of the Purdue Secondary Model for Gifted and Talented Youth

Counseling Services
- Talent identification.
- Education counseling.
- Career counseling.
- Personal counseling.

Seminar
- In-depth study.
- Self-selected topics.
- Career education.
- Affective activities.
- Thinking, research, and library skills.
- Presentations.

Advanced Placement Classes
Open to students in grades 9–12
All subject matter areas.

Honors Classes
- English.
- Social studies.
- Biology.
- Language.
- Humanities.

Math-Science Acceleration
- Begin algebra in 7th grade.
- Continue acceleration and fast-paced math.
- Open science courses to earlier admission.

Foreign Languages
- Latin or Greek.
- French or Spanish.
- German or Asian.
- Russian.

The Arts
- Art.
- Drama.
- Music.
- Dance.

Cultural Experiences
- Concepts, plays, exhibits.
- Field trips.
- Tours abroad.
- Museum program.

Career Education
- Mentors.
- Seminar experience: study of careers, study of self, and educational planning.

Vocational Programs
- Home economics.
- Agriculture.
- Business.
- Industrial arts.

Extra-school Instruction
- Saturday school.
- Summer classes.
- Correspondence study.
- College classes.

Source: Feldhusen, J., & Robinson, A. (1986). *The Purdue Secondary Model for Gifted and Talented Youth.* Mansfield Center, CT: Creative Learning Press, p. 158.

education. Units specifically aiming at developing critical thinking can be incorporated as enrichment activities. McDowell (1989, cited in Smith & Luckasson, 1995) demonstrates that critical thinking can be taught to very young children through an experiential approach. She used an apple as the basis for lessons designed to develop vocabulary, oral language, reading, and thinking abilities. Table 3.3 illustrates how critical thinking skills can be integrated into educational programs for even very young children. The approach involves a slight modification of typical teaching routines, more involvement of the children, and some good questioning from the teacher.

Gifted Students Can Cause Dilemmas

Because of our conservative effort in educating gifted children, children

Table 3.3 An Example of Teaching Critical Thinking Skills

Mrs. Peterson, a preschool teacher, teaches a group of bright children. Because of their young age, their experiential backgrounds are still very limited. On the first day of the unit about apples, she reads the story of Johnny Appleseed to her class. During her reading, she stresses important concepts and language (words) presented in the story. After reading the story, she engages the children in a discussion about the story and their own experiences with apples. How do you get apples? Where do they come from? Are they all alike? What do you do with them?

On ensuing days, Mrs. Peterson creates different lessons to help the children to think about and experience a food they have all eaten. She has the children reenact the story of Johnny Appleseed, with each child taking a turn playing the main character. Then she rereads the story. She stops several times and asks the children to predict what is going to happen next. On another day, the children discuss where apples come from, how they grow on trees, and when they are picked.

Later, the class takes a trip to the store. One by one, Mrs. Peterson tells them to go find the apples. The children meet in the produce section, compare different types of apples, and discuss how they differ (in color, size, texture, taste). The class then goes to find other products in the store that are made of apples. The children identify the following items: cereal, pies, cookies, applesauce, and juice. Before leaving the store, the children and Mrs. Peterson buy several sacks of apples to use at school later in the week.

At school the next day, the class studies the apples they purchased. They slice one open and talk about the various parts (seeds, stem, peel). The children create a story about apples through a language experience approach and then role-play their story.

One day, Mrs. Peterson writes "Foods with Apples" on the board. The children have to think of all the foods they can that are made with apples. They talk about how these foods were packaged (in boxes, bottles, jars). They discuss how many apples it would take to make these foods. Since the children seem to have no concept of the number of apples it takes to make various foods, the next day Mrs. Peterson helps them make applesauce. Beforehand, the children take turn guessing how many apples it will take to fill the two jars that Mrs. Peterson has brought to school. They all participate fully in making the applesauce, and they enjoy eating their culinary creation the next day during snack time.

Source: Smith, D.D., & Luckasson, R. (1995). *Introduction to special education: Teaching in an age of challenge* (2nd ed.). Needham Heights, MA: Allyn & Bacon.

with certain giftedness and talents tend to be under-identified in many occasions. Parents have to be advocates for these children in order to bring appropriate education and related services for them. Table 3.4 shows a typical example.

Table 3.4 From a Parent

Robin Bayer

Robin Bayer said "kie-kie" for "cookie" at five months old. She spoke in complete sentences when she was a year old. She was reading books like *Wuthering Heights* when she was in 2nd grade. Robin was obviously different from most other children, for her IQ was over 150. However, Robin's excitement about school fainted soon after she started kindergarten at age five. After a few weeks of coloring the letters of the alphabet and circling triangles with color markers, she became bored and disillusioned with school. Her mother decided to teach her at home for the following year and, then, moved to another community, where Robin entered 3rd grade. Now she is 10 and placed with 6th graders for most of her subjects and studies English with 8th graders instead of attending 5th grade. Robin is reportedly happy at school and has many friends, even though they are older.

According to her mother, Robin is now studying in accelerated programs and has the support of her family. Decisions about education and related services for gifted children and what is the best for these children are difficult and subject to criticism by professionals who are also concerned about what is best for gifted children. Gifted education leader Treffinger (1993) and his associates itemized "tough questions" that a thoughtful program planner should ponder:

1. How does the child learn best? How does the school program take into account students' characteristics and learning preference?
2. In what areas (academic and general) does the child display strengths and special interests? What provisions can we make for these to be expressed and developed in school?
3. What specific provisions are made for students to learn at their own pace rather than being limited to a rigid, "lock-step" curriculum? That is, what provisions are made to insure that students receive instruction suitable for their *real* instructional needs?
4. What provisions are made for advanced content or courses for students whose achievement warrants them? How are the students' needs determined and reviewed?
5. What enrichment opportunities are offered that are not merely "busywork" or "more of the same" assignments?

6. How do you help students to become aware of their own best talents and interests and to appreciate those of others as well?

7. How do teachers provide opportunities for students to learn and apply critical and creative thinking and problem-solving skills?

8. How do you help students learn to plan and investigate everyday real problems, rather than contrived, textbook exercises? How do they create and share the products or results of those investigations?

9. What specific steps do you take to insure that learning is exciting and original rather than boring and repetitious?

10. What provisions are made to create opportunities for students to explore a variety of motivating and challenging topics outside the regular curriculum?

11. How do you provide opportunities for students to interact regularly with others who share similar talents and interests?

12. How do you help students learn to set goals, plan projects, locate and use resources, create products, and evaluate their work?

13. How do you use community resources, parents, and mentors to extend students' learning in areas of special talents and interests?

14. What resources and materials are available to expose students to the newest ideas and developments in many fields and to the people whose work creates those ideas?

15. How do you help students to consider future career possibilities and to cope with rapid changes in our world?

16. How do teachers inspire students to ask probing questions, examine many viewpoints, and use criteria to make and justify decisions?

17. What provisions do you make to help students feel comfortable and confident in expressing and dealing with their personal and academic goals and concerns?

18. How do you insure that children are challenged to work toward their full potential and "at the edge of their ability"?

19. How does the school program help students learn social or interpersonal skills without sacrificing their individuality?

Locating Students with Giftedness and Talent

Table 3.5 includes a sample peer nomination form for locating students with giftedness and talent.

Table 3.5   A Sample Peer Nomination Form

Think about classmates. Everyone is different! Read the questions below. In each space write the name of a classmate who best fits the description. You may write a name more than once and you may write your own name where you feel it fit.

1. If you were forming a committee to work on a project, whom would you choose to lead it:

    Language arts _____ Math   _____

    Science _____ Social Studies _____

    Art _____ Other   _____

2. If you need somebody to help you with your homework, which one of your classmates would you ask?

    _____

3. If your class was on a trip and became separated from the teacher, which one of your classmates would lead you back safely?

    _____

4. Whose stories do you enjoy listening to?

    _____

5. Who is the most exciting person in class?

    _____

6. Who has the best ideas for games and activities in and out of school?

    _____

7. Who is the best problem solver?

    _____

8. Who is the best person to tell a story to?

    _____

9. Who is the best reader?

    _____

10. Who is the best writer?

    _____

11. Who likes to try new things?

    _____

12. Who uses good judgments?

    _____

13. Who would be a good friend?

    _____

14. Who has a good imagination?

    _____

15. Who has many interests?

    _____

    Name   _____

    School _____

    Date   _____

Source: Eisenberg, D., & Epstein, E. (1982). *The special gifted student.* New York: Special Education Training and Resource Center.

Summary

1. Although persons with giftedness and talent are not handicapped in a sense of having a disability, they may face discouragement, limitations, and difficulties in society or educational systems.
2. Giftedness and talent used to be defined as an exceptionality among high IQ students. Today's definition may include a broader and multifaceted structure of intelligence.
3. Gardner and Hatch's seven different types of intelligence include linguistic, logical-mathematical, spatial, bodily-kinesthetic, musical, interpersonal, and intrapersonal talent.
4. Teaching children with giftedness and talent took place in ancient China as well as Western countries.
5. There has been debate regarding biological and environmental factors in the study of giftedness and talent. School practitioners need to be aware of factors that may enhance or inhibit giftedness and talent.
6. With possible individual differences, children with giftedness and talent may have tendency to perform intellectual tasks, or respond to social-emotional situations, in a unique way.
7. There are persons with physical, mental, sensory, emotional/behavioral, and learning disabilities who also have giftedness and talent.
8. Due to certain factors, students with giftedness and talent may be found as underachievers in school.
9. Teachers are encouraged to utilize observation, referral, and peer nomination in order to identify students with exceptional giftedness and talent.
10. Two most common educational arrangements for students with giftedness and talent are enrichment and acceleration. Other related services may include counseling, seminar, honor programs, foreign language, cultural experiences, art programs, career education, and vocational programs. It is recommended that critical thinking skills be taught at young age through an experimental approach.

Activities

1. Assign small groups to review websites relating to programs for students with giftedness and talent in Hong Kong, Taiwan, Singapore, Australia, the United Kingdom, and the United States. Schedule each study group to report to the class.
2. Arrange the class to visit and observe in schools with enrichment or

acceleration programs and follow-up with a discussion with the in-charge teacher or program coordinator.

3. Invite students with various talents to speak to class regarding their personal experience, concerns, and suggestions for educators.

4. Have a class discussion on the statement, "Johnny is gifted and talented, but he happens to be an academic underachiever in school." The discussion may address the concerns of finding out why it happened and give suggestions for how the situation can be improved.

5. Assign small groups to develop a program for students with giftedness and talent, including mission/goals, conceptualization framework (e.g., for enrichment or acceleration) and rational, classroom arrangement, and teacher's instructional approaches.

6. Assign each student to design a lesson for enhancing children's critical thinking skills, including the objective statement, teaching materials needed, methods (i.e., motivation, introduction, explore, and practice), and procedure to evaluate the child's progress.

RESOURCES

Resources in Hong Kong

Chinese University of Hong Kong
Program for the Gifted and Talented (PGT)
Tel.: 852-2603-7444   Fax: 852-2603-7436
E-mail: pgt@fed.cuhk.edu.hk
Web address: http://www.fed.cuhk.edu.hk/%7Epgt/index_c.htm

Fung Han Chu Gifted Education Center
新界荃灣城門道7號
Tel.: 852-2490-4019   Fax: 852-2490-6858
Web address: http://www.cdccdi.hk.linkage.net/cdi/SEN/Gifted/fhc/
    indexfhc.htm

Hong Kong Baptist University, Centre for Child Development
Room 720 David Lam Building, Shaw Campus
34 Renfrew Road, Kowloon Tong, Kowloon
Tel.: 852-2339-7260 or 852-2339-7249   Fax: 852-2339-8902
E-mail: ccd@hkbu.edu.hk
Web address: http://www.hkbu.edu.hk/~ccd/

Hong Kong Education Department, Special Educational Needs Curriculum
Development/Fung Hon Chu Gifted Education Center
7 Shing Mun Road, Tsuen Wan, New Territories
Tel.: 852-2490-4241   Fax: 852-2490-6858
Web address: http://www.cdccdi.hk.linkage.net/cdi/sen_2/cindex_cmain.
htm

Hong Kong Association of Parents for Gifted Children
香港資優兒童家長會
Web address: http://www.gifted.org.hk/index_e.htm

Puiching Education Center
香港培正教育中心
香港九龍培正道20號
Tel.: 852-2713-9111   Fax: 852-2713-9112
Web address: http://www.puiching.edu.hk/centre/advance.htm

Resources in Singapore

Gifted Education Branch Home Page
Web address: http://socrates.moe.edu.sg/gifted/gep.htm

Gifted Education Department in Anglo-Chinese School (Independent)
Web address: http://www.acs.sch.edu.sg/acs_indep/departments/gep/

Gifted Education Program
Web address: http://members.tripod.com/~DHSGEP/

Gifted Education Program of RGS
Web address: http://www.rgs.edu.sg/dept/dgep/gepmain.html

Gifted Education Program in Rosyth
Web address: http://www1.knowledge.com.sg/t41/index.html

Nanyang GEP Website
Web address: http://www.moe.edu.sg/gifted/nanyang/

Raffles Institution of Gifted Education Department
Web address: http://www.ri.sch.edu.sg/Departments/GEP/Home/

Talent Development Programme, National University of Singapore
Web address: http://www.nus.edu.sg/NUSinfo/TDP/

Resources in Taiwan

大榮中學資訊資優班簡介及重點課程內容
Web address: http://www.dystcs.kh.edu.tw/act/19980519.htm

台北市敦化國民小學資優班
Web address: http://w7.dj.net.tw/~THESBC/

金城國中數理資優班
Web address: http://www.chinmen.edu.tw/kin3301.htm

科教處科學資優計劃
Web address: http://www.nsc.gov.tw/sci/stud.html

建國中學高中資優生物理補充教材之研討及編輯
Web address: http://www.ck.tp.edu.tw/~phytea/ckhs0115.html

資賦優異組網頁
Web address: http://www.ntnu.edu.tw/spe/WWW/gt/

資優教育研習中心
Web address: http://www.kh.edu.tw/kh/ymps/gc/default.htm

資優教育濃縮課程
Web address: http://www.iest.edu.tw/j1/v13n3/40.htm

資優數學平和教室
Web address: http://www.geocities.com/Tokyo/Bay/8623/index.html

資優暨特殊才能學生甄輔計劃
Web address: http://www.ntsh.ntct.edu.tw/音樂班/page10.htm

應用數學系高中資優班
Web address: http://www.math.nsysu.edu.tw/highschool/index.html

International Resources

California Association for the Gifted
Mailing address: 5777 West Century Blvd., Suite 1670
Los Angeles, CA 90045 U.S.A.
Tel: 1-310-215-1898   Fax: 1-310-215-1832
Web address: http://www.cagifted.org/

The Connie Belin and Jacqueline N. Blank International Center for Gifted
    Education and Talent Development, U.S.A.
Web address: http://www.uiowa.edu/~belinctr/

Gifted and Talented Children
Austega Pty Ltd, 10 Lascelles Rd, Narraweena NSW 2099, Sydney, Australia
Tel: 0415 715 743
Email: education@austega.com
Web address: http://www.austega.com/gifted

Gifted Canada
Web address: http://www3.bc.sympatico.ca/giftedcanada
Email: David_Shepherd@bc.sympatico.ca

Gifted Child Society
190 Rock Road, Glen Rock, New Jersey 07452-1736 U.S.A.
Tel: 1-201-444-6530
E-Mail to: admin@gifted.org
Web address: http://www.gifted.org/

Gifted Education in a Multicultural Australia
Web address: http://www.nexus.edu.au/teachstud/gat/becherv1.htm

Gifted World, U.S.A.
Web address: http://www.gtworld.org/

International Centre for Gifted Education and Talent Development
U.S.A.
Tel: 1-800-336-6463 or 1-319-335-6148   Fax: 1-319-335-5151
Web address: http://www.uiowa.edu/~belinctr/bbc/index.html

National Association for Gifted Children
1707 L Street, NW Suite 550, Washington, DC 20036 U.S.A.
Tel.: 1-202-785-4268   Fax: 1-202-785-4248
Web address: http://www.nagc.org

NEAG Centre for Gifted Education & Talent Development
Mailing address: 2131 Hillside Road, Unit 3007, Storrs, CT 06269-3007
    U.S.A.
Tel: 1-860-486-4826   Fax: 1-860-486-2900
Web address: http://www.gifted.uconn.edu/

Pennsylvania Association for Gifted Education (PAGE)
3026 Potshop Road, Norristown, PA 19403 U.S.A.
Tel.: 1-215-616-0470
Web address: http://www.penngifted.org/index.html

Queensland Association for Gifted and Talented Children
Australia
Web address: http://www.bit.net.au/~qagtcinc/

Selected Internet Resources for Gifted Education
U.S.A.
Web address: http://ericec.org/faq/gt-urls.htm

Selected Readings for parents and Educators of Gifted Children
U.S.A.
Web address: http://www.cec.sped.org/minibibs/eb6.htm

Selected Readings: Gifted Students and Educational Reform
U.S.A.
Web address: http://ericec.org/minibibs/eb8.htm

State Resources for Gifted Education, U.S.A.
Web address: http://www.cec.sped.org/fact/stateres.htm

Talnet Development Programme,National University of Singapore
Singapore
Web address: http://www.nus.edu.sg/NUSinfo/TDP/

The Support Society for Children of High Intelligence
United Kimdom
Web address: http://www.users.dircon.co.uk/~tutorcom/chi/

World Council for Gifted and Talented Children, U.S.A.
Web address: http://www.worldgifted.org/

REFERENCES

Benner, S.M. (1992). *Assessing young children with special needs.* New York: Longman.
Callahan, C.M. (1981). Superior abilities. In J.M. Kauffman & D.P. Hallahan (Eds.), *Handbook of special education* (pp. 48–86). Englewood Cliffs, NJ: Prentice-Hall.

Clark, B. (1992). Growing up gifted. New York: Merrill-Macmillan.

Cohen, L.G., & Spenciner, L.J. (1998). *Assessment of children and youth.* New York: Longman.

Eisenberg, D., & Epstein, E. (1982). *The special gifted student.* New York: Special Education Training and Resource Center.

Feldhusen, J., & Robinson, A. (1986). *The Purdue Secondary Model for Gifted and Talented Youth.* Mansfield Center, CT: Creative Learning Press.

Gallagher, J.J. (1985). *Teaching the gifted child* (3rd ed.). Boston: Allyn & Bacon.

Gardner, J.W. (1984). *Excellence: Can we be equal and excellent too?* (rev. ed.). New York: Norton.

Gardner, H., & Hatch, T. (1989). Multiple intelligence go to school: Educational implications of the theory of multiple intelligences. *Educational Researcher, 18*(8), 4–10.

Glick, J. (1975). Cognitive development in cross-cultural perspective. In F.D. Horowitz (Ed.), *Review of child development research* (vol. 4). Chicago: University of Chicago Press.

Hallahan, D.P., & Kauffman, J.M. (1994). *Exceptional Children: introduction to special education* (6th ed.). Needham Heights, MA: Allyn and Bacon.

Heward, W.L., & Orlansky, M.D. (1992). [Study guide to accompany] *Exceptional children: An introductory survey of special education* (4th ed.). New York: Merrill.

McDowell, L. (1989). *Prepackaged program experimentation assignment.* Unpublished manuscript, University of New Mexico, Albuquerque.

Rimm, S.B. (1986). *Underachievement syndrome: Causes and cures.* Watertown, WI: Apple.

Silverman, L.K. (1988). Gifted and talented. In E.L. Meyen, Skrtic, T.M. (Eds), *Exceptional children and youth: An introduction* (3rd ed.) (pp. 263–291). Denver CO: Love Publishing Co.

Smith, D.D., & Luckasson, R. (1995). *Introduction to special education: Teaching in an age of challenge* (2nd ed.). Needham Heights, MA: Allyn & Bacon.

Treffinger, D.J. (1993). *The mentor kit: A step-by-step guide to creating an effective mentor program in your school.* Waco, TX: Prufrock Press.

Treffinger, D.J., & Sortore, M.R. (1992a). *The programming for giftedness series. Volume I: Programming for giftedness — A contemporary view.* Sarasota, FL: Center for Creative Learning.

Treffinger, D.J., & Sortore, M.R. (1992b). *Programming for giftedness series. Volume II: A process approach to planning for contemporary programming.* Sarasota, FL: Center for Creative Learning.

Treffinger, D.J., & Sortore, M.R. (1992c). *Programming for giftedness series. Volume III: Leadership guide for contemporary programming.* Sarasota, FL: Center for Creative Learning. ,

4

Mental Retardation

ADVANCED THINKING

Answer the following questions as you read:

1. How is mental retardation defined?
2. How did the concept of mental retardation evolve over time?
3. Who are the key players that contributed a great deal to the historical development of education for children with mental retardation?
4. What are the possible causes of mental retardation?
5. What are the prevention strategies or measures for mental retardation?
6. What are the six areas of learning identified for children with mental retardation in Hong Kong?
7. What are the main strategies used in teaching children with mental retardation?

KEY TERMS AND PHRASES

AAMR	intellectual functioning
academics	IQ
adaptive behavior	language and communication
aesthetics and creative activities	memory
ARC	mental handicap
attention	mental retardation
characteristics	modeling
communication	normal curve
developmental period	normalization
generalization	perceptual training
grouping	perinatal cause
history	physical prompt

postnatal cause   shaping
prenatal cause   social/personal development
prevention   standard deviation
record keeping   verbal prompt

INTRODUCTION

This chapter concentrates on individuals whose intellectual and social/
adaptive capabilities may differ significantly from the norm. Their lowered
capabilities may range from mild to severe/profound levels and affect every
aspect of their life. Some of the school-age children may also have multiple
disabling conditions with sensory, emotional, and physical difficulties. In
school, the developmental delays among children with mental retardation
("mental handicap" is the common synonym in Hong Kong) make apparent
impact on their academic learning, social skills, and other adaptive behavior
development.

In spite of impairments in intellectual abilities and other areas among
individuals with mental retardation, we must keep in mind that mental
retardation is only one of the many attributes that make up who they are.
Like us, these individuals are members of families, have friends and
neighbors, and have personalities shaped by their innate characteristics and
by their unique life experiences. They experience joy, sadness, pride, love,
disappointment, and all other emotions that are simply part of living.

Mental retardation is, however, a serious disability. Individuals with
this disability must make special efforts to learn and need the special
assistance of teachers in order to enhance general successful performance
in cognitive, language/communication, perceptual-motor, social/emotional,
and/or self-help/independent living activities. The impaired ability to learn
creates obstacles in their lives. Some of these obstacles can be overcome
with support from their families, friends, teachers, and others. With
appropriate assistance and supports, people with mental retardation can
lead lives that are productive and satisfying.

In this chapter, we are going to discuss the definition of mental
retardation, history of the field of mental retardation, possible causes and
prevention, characteristics of children with mental retardation, and
curriculum and instruction for these children.

MENTAL RETARDATION DEFINED

Over the years, mental retardation has been defined in many different ways.

Before we look at the two most widely recognized definitions, we will discuss the concept of intelligence and its measurement.

The question of what intelligence is has challenged philosophers, scientists, and educators for ages. On IQ tests, intelligence is considered a human trait that is distributed among humans in a predictable manner. This statistical distribution is generally represented as a bell-shaped curve, the normal curve (see Figure 4.1). In this curve, the majority of a population falls in the middle of the bell, at or around an intelligence quotient (IQ) score of 100, and fewer and fewer people fall to either end of the distribution. IQ level is determined by the distance a score is from the mean (average) score. An individual with an IQ level of approximately 70 (or 75 for some intelligence scales) or below, which is about 2 standard deviations below the mean score, is generally considered to have mental retardation.

Figure 4.1   The Normal Curve of Intelligence/IQ

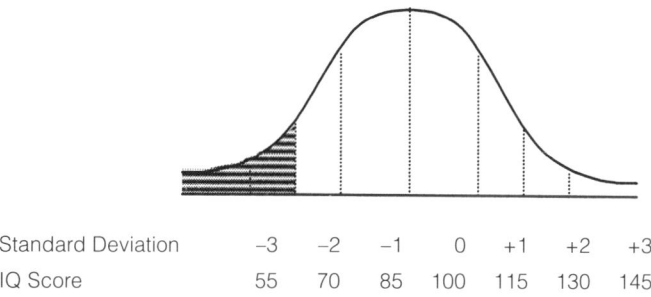

| Standard Deviation | −3 | −2 | −1 | 0 | +1 | +2 | +3 |
| IQ Score | 55 | 70 | 85 | 100 | 115 | 130 | 145 |

Doll's Definition

Edgar Doll (1941) proposed a then widely accepted definition:

> Mental deficiency is a state of social incompetence obtaining at maturity, or likely to obtain at maturity, resulting from developmental mental arrest of constitutional (hereditary or acquired) origin; the condition is essentially incurable through treatment and unremediable through training except as treatment and training instill habits which superficially or temporarily compensate for the limitations of the person so affected while under favorable circumstances and for more or less limited periods of time. (p. 217)

Today, professionals believe that an individual might have mental retardation even if there is no "constitutional" or bodily basis for the retardation. We also know that it is possible to cure some cases of mental retardation — for instance, through prenatal surgery (such as correcting fetal hydrocephalus) and to prevent many more cases — for instance, through early intervention programs. As such, Doll's requirement that mental retardation be "essentially incurable" is no longer true.

The AAMR Definition

The currently widely accepted definition of mental retardation comes from the American Association on Mental Retardation (AAMR). Its manual, *Mental Retardation: Definition, Classification, and Systems of Supports* (Luckasson, Coulter, Reiss, Schalock, & Snell, 1992), defines the term as follows:

> *Mental retardation* refers to substantial limitations in present functioning. It is characterized by significantly subaverage intellectual performance, existing concurrently with related limitations in two or more of the following applicable adaptive skill areas: communication, self-care, home living, social skills, community use, self-direction, health and safety, functional academics, leisure, and work. Mental retardation manifests before age 18. (p. 1)

The application of this definition is based on the following essential assumptions:

1. Valid assessment considers cultural and linguistic diversity as well as differences in communication and behavioral factors;
2. The existence of limitations in adaptive skills occurs within the context of community environments typical of the individual's age peers and is indexed to the person's individualized needs for supports;
3. Specific adaptive limitations often coexist with strengths in other adaptive skills or other personal capabilities; and
4. With appropriate supports over a sustained period, the life functioning of the person with mental retardation will generally improve. (Luckasson et al., 1992, p. 1)

The AAMR had an earlier definition (Grossman, 1983) that, to date, has been adopted in Hong Kong as the official definition of mental retardation and is still in use:

Mental handicap (retardation) refers to significantly subaverage general intellectual functioning existing concurrently with deficits in adaptive behavior and manifested during the developmental period. (p. 1)

There are three major themes in this definition:

1. *Intellectual functioning*: "significantly subaverage intellectual functioning" was defined as an IQ score below approximately 70–75 on an individually administered intelligence period. Wechsler Intelligence Scale for Children remains the most widely used IQ test in the world and, in Hong Kong, the Hong Kong–Wechsler Intelligence Scale for Children was developed for such purposes.
2. *Adaptive behavior*: Adaptive behavior was defined as "the effectiveness or degree with which individuals meet the standards of personal independence and social responsibility expected for age and cultural group." Professionals have developed standardized tests to assess an individual's adaptive behavior, yet assessing an individual's adaptive behavior, even using commercially available behavior scales, remains imprecise.
3. *Developmental period*: The impairments in intelligence and adaptive behavior must be "manifested during the developmental period" (Grossman, 1983, p. 1).

HISTORY OF THE FIELD

Mental retardation has always been a part of human history. It did not become a focus of study by professionals until late 1700s. In 1798, Jean-Marc-Gaspard Itard, a French physician, began working with the boy Victor who had lived all his life in the wild with animals (translated by G. Humphrey & M. Humphrey, 1962). Itard's reports on his work provided substantial evidence for the possibility to improve mental ability through skilled teaching.

In Switzerland, Johann Guggenbuhl created Abendberg, the first mental retardation residential rehabilitation program around 1840. This institution was built in the mountains and, along with fresh mountain air, provided good diet, baths, massages, physical exercises, sensory stimulation, structured routine, memory exercises, and speech training. Guggenbuhl believed that both education and medical care were important. However, Abendberg was closed in 1867 after allegations of financial and medical malpractice (Kanner, 1964; Scheerenberger, 1983, 1987).

Nevertheless, the idea of residential institutions had taken root by the mid-nineteenth century. Residential institutions were built throughout Europe. In 1848, Samuel Gridley Howe established the first American mental retardation institution, which was initially part of the Perkins Institute for the Blind and later became a separate institution known as the Walter E. Fernald State School.

Howe saw the danger of residential institutions in isolating people with disabilities both geographically and socially and warned to keep the number of institutions down and keep them small. Yet institutions spread over the United States and all but four states had institutions for people with mental retardation by 1917. Widespread abuses developed in these institutions and the court ordered many of them to close in the 1970s and 1980s because of the inhumane conditions and the standards that were far below minimum requirements and violated residents' constitutional rights.

Organizations of professionals and parents began to form powerful forces at about the same time of residential institutions being started. The American Association on Mental Retardation (AAMR) was founded in 1876 and is still the largest interdisciplinary organization of professionals in the field of mental retardation. In 1954, a group of parents founded the Association for Retarded Citizens (ARC) (formerly the National Association for Retarded Children, or NARC) which exerted great influence in the battle for rights of these citizens.

In the 1960s, the philosophy of *normalization* from Scandinavia began to influence the field of mental retardation. The principle of normalization stressed the availability of "patterns of life and conditions of everyday living which are as close as possible to the regular circumstances and ways of life of society" (Nirje, 1985, p. 67). This principle helped provide a foundation for the civil right cases tried in the courts and the court actions subsequently led to widespread deinstitutionalization of people with mental retardation. Today most children with mental retardation live with their families and most adults live in integrated community living arrangements.

The first American special class for "defective children" was opened in Providence, Rhode Island in 1896 and soon followed in large cities. These classes were generally segregated in that the students spent their entire school day with other students who had mental retardation. The Individuals with Disabilities Education Act (IDEA), signed into law in 1975, allowed all children with mental retardation to attend public schools in their neighborhood if there was no other factor to cause a placement otherwise.

POSSIBLE CAUSES

Mental retardation is caused by many factors, the understanding of which can be helpful as the cause can be associated with treatable health-related problems and may itself be treatable. Various groupings are used to organize the causes of mental retardation. There are currently two major groupings.

The AAMR organizes the causes of mental retardation into three groups by time of onset:

1. prenatal causes, e.g., chromosomal disorder[1], syndrome disorders, maternal health conditions such as malnutrition or diabetes, infections such as cytomegalovirus (CMV), and consumption of alcohol and other drugs;
2. perinatal causes, e.g., intrauterine disorders[2], infection during birth, Rh incompatibility, and neonatal disorders; and
3. postnatal causes, e.g., head injuries, toxic substances, and environmental deprivation.

Another major grouping of possible causes of mental retardation includes four categories (Smith & Luckasson, 1995):

1. socioeconomic and environmental factors, e.g., prenatal and postnatal malnutrition, unsafe housing;
2. injury, e.g., deprivation of sufficient oxygen at birth, car accidents before the age of 18, and child abuse/neglect;
3. infections and toxic substances, e.g., measles, encephalitis, fetal alcohol syndrome, lead poison; and
4. biological, e.g., Down syndrome, phenylketonuria (PKU).

---

1. Disorders related to problems with chromosomes, the microscopic rod like structure that carries the genes
2. The main intrauterine disorder that causes mental retardation is intrauterine growth retardation or restriction (IUGR) which denotes the condition of intrauterine stunting of the fetus due to poor infant nutrition and general life support, or intrinsic factors in the fetus itself. The most common identifiable causes of IUGR are of course maternal smoking, high blood pressure, poor diet, maternal substance abuse, or serious medical disease during pregnancy. Rare causes include growth restriction in one of the twins who receives much less than his fair share of nutrients while the bulk of blood flow is shunted to his luckier sibling. This occurs through accidents of placental malformation, and can lead to very striking differences in size between twins. (source: http://www.sleeptight.com/EncyMaster/I/IUGR.html)

Prevention of Mental Retardation

Examining the causes of mental retardation allows us to see that many cases of mental retardation could be prevented. Many preventive strategies are simple and can target at women before and during pregnancy, babies, children, and society as a whole.

For Women Before and During Pregnancy

- Maintain good health,
- Avoid alcohol,
- Avoid smoking,
- Avoid sexually transmitted diseases,
- Obtain prenatal medical care,
- Obtain good nutrition,
- Take precautions against injuries and accidents, and
- Receive genetic counseling and prenatal tests.

For Infants

- Screen for Phenylketonuria (PKU) at birth,
- Drain excess fluid around the brain, i.e., implant of a shunt,
- Receive neonatal intensive care services,
- Provide immunizations,
- Prevent infections, and
- Thorough screening and examinations on growth and development.

For Children

- Provide proper nutrition,
- Test lead level as a routine,
- Provide proper medical care,
- Provide immunizations,
- Prevent infections,
- Keep household chemicals out of reach,
- Ensure the use of automobile seat belts, safety seats, and cycle helmets, and
- Eliminate child abuse and neglect.

For Society

- Assure proper health care of children and pregnant women,
- Assure the provision of proper nutrition for pregnant women and young children,

- Educate parents,
- Improve sanitation and safety,
- Eliminate environmental toxic substances (e.g., lead),
- Eliminate child poverty, and
- Educate the public on prevention of fetal alcohol syndrome and communicable diseases.

CHARACTERISTICS

Approximately 90% of children with mental retardation are functioning at the mild levels and can benefit from mainstream schooling. On the other hand, the less than 4% of children with severe mental retardation and other disabilities have complex and intense needs (Smith & Luckasson, 1995). Within the wide range of abilities and disabilities of mental retardation, field practitioners and service providers may witness many drastically different characteristics as well as some common characteristics in the following aspects: learning, communication, attention, memory, and generalization.

Learning Characteristics

Communication

Children with mental retardation may have problems in communication. Delayed speech is common. Other speech problems and hearing impairment are more frequently found among children with mental retardation as well. In turn, these communication problems may affect a child's ability to learn. Children with severe mental retardation may not acquire speech at all or most people around them cannot understand their speech.

Attention

Students with mental retardation often have problems attending to tasks. Teachers need to adapt curricular activities to enhance the students' attention to learning. Task analysis is a useful strategy for helping a student with attention problems to learn a new skill because the job is broken down into several steps which are taught in sequence.

Memory

Students with mental retardation are often challenged in memory, especially short-term memory. As for long-term memory, correctly remembering events or the proper sequence of events may be difficult. Teachers can assist students to develop memory strategies, such as a picture notebook that sequences a checklist of things to do before leaving home for school.

Generalization (Transfer of Learning)

Individuals with mental retardation are frequently less able than their nondisabled peers to acquire knowledge through incidental learning. That is, unplanned learning resulting from their ordinary daily experiences. Direct instruction is required to ensure that learning takes place. It is crucial that teachers plan to teach for generalization of skills to enable students to use what they learn in school, at home, or in the community environment. Smith and Luckasson (1995) suggested the following strategies for improving generalization:

1. Have the students' attention before talking or starting a lesson.
2. Select learning goals and objectives that are functional for the students' lives.
3. Teach in the environment in which students will be required to use the skills.
4. Use different teachers to teach the skill.
5. Use actual materials (rather than symbols or representations) when teaching new skills.
6. Use different materials and examples.
7. Repeat the teaching over a period of time.
8. Make certain that students actively participate in the learning.
9. Make certain that students practice the new skills.
10. Gradually phase out the teacher's role.

EDUCATION

Curriculum Used in Hong Kong

Children with mental retardation typically learn at a slower pace than their non-disabled peers. They have prominent difficulties in language and motor coordination. Often times, they require training in daily independent and social skills. One of the most useful skills students with mental retardation can be taught is the ability to make and express decisions and choices — the ability that allows them to function independently. It is obviously impossible to use the same curriculum at the same pace for children with mental retardation. Flexibility must be built in to allow for optimal and effective learning.

In Hong Kong, six areas of learning are identified for children with mental retardation (Curriculum Development Council, 1994) and schools for those children are required to follow with flexibility:

1. Academics: e.g., functional mathematics, use of computers and calculators, basic reading, writing, and functional reading;
2. Language and communication: e.g., verbal communication, comprehension, and expressive skills;
3. Social and personal development: e.g., self-help skills, growth and sex education, interpersonal social skills, and use of leisure;
4. Perceptual training: e.g., sensory training and motor coordination;
5. Motor development: e.g., rhythm and movement, physical training; and
6. Aesthetics and creative activities: e.g., music, art and craft.

Academics

Academic subjects should concentrate on functional mathematics, use of computers and calculators as well as basic reading and writing. Functional mathematics aims at enabling the children to cope with their daily life. Knowledge of numbers, basic weights and measurement, time concept, money concept, interest rate, payment by installments, and concept of percentage should be taught to them with plenty of real-life practice in natural settings. They can be taught to use computers and calculators for some of the calculations and other tasks in their everyday life.

Children with mental retardation should also acquire the basic vocabulary and expressions required for social and survival purposes. Examples include words like "male," "female," "toilets," "danger," "exit," "fire alarm," and so on. For functional reading, they should learn to read addresses, simple notices, instructions, and newspapers. For functional writing, they need to learn to fill in forms and write simple correspondence required in their everyday life.

Language and Communication

Language and communication skills here refer to the ability to use speech for communication and to interpret and use nonverbal and graphical means of communication. The development of language and communication skills is essential for children to grasp concepts, organize their thinking, understand speech and express their thoughts and feelings. Children with varying degrees of mental retardation should learn language and communication skills to the maximum level possible.

Social and Personal Development

The curriculum in this area addresses four aspects: self-help skills, growth and sex education, interpersonal social skills, and use of leisure time.

Self-help skills. Schools need to teach these skills to help children achieve independence. Some of the main skills include cooking, self-feeding, taking a bath, managing a home, attending to one's belongings, and observing safety rules.

Growth and sex education. Like their nondisabled peers, children with mental retardation need to be taught about their physical growth, changes at puberty, personal hygiene, environmental cleanliness, sex roles, and the correct attitude toward the opposite sex and family life.

Interpersonal social skills. This area of training involves the development of skills to behave in socially acceptable ways in different situations. These skills in turn enable the children to participate in teamwork and group activities.

Use of leisure time. Children with mental retardation should be taught to play games and sports and to develop hobbies as much as possible to assist them to communicate with other, cooperate in group work, develop good habits, and spend their leisure time meaningfully for their physical, mental, and social/emotional well-being.

Perceptual Training

This area of curriculum focuses on sensory training and motor coordination. Such training helps a child to develop the ability to use the senses, to concentrate and discriminate, gather relevant information for concept formation, to coordinate their motor skills with perception, to help them increase awareness of their environment, and to respond to relevant stimuli in the environment.

Motor Development

Two aspects of training are essential in motor development: (a) rhythm and movement and (b) physical training. Rhythm and movement refer to teaching a child to explore the types of movement they can make with various parts of his/her body. The ultimate goal is to enable him/her to gain better control of movements. Physical training refers to the introduction of a great variety of sports and recreational activities to children, through which they develop socially acceptable behaviors in situations when cooperation is needed and an appreciation of the effect of body mechanics on their postures during movement and when motionless.

Aesthetics and Creative Activities

Curriculum for this area has two essential components: (a) music and (b) arts and craft. *Music* helps to stimulate children's perception and enhance their ability to discriminate. Children should be taught to listen to music, play musical instruments, sing, and participate in other music-related activities, all of which help children to acquire self-discipline and develop abilities to cooperate with others in a group. *Arts and craft* are activities that encourage creativity and imagination, improve children's capacity to respond emotionally and intellectually to sensory experiences, and help develop keener senses of observing their environment.

In addition to Curriculum Development Council's main areas of learning described above, there have been a number of curriculum guide or training packages developed for specific needs and situations of persons with mental retardation in Hong Kong. The training package developed by the Working Group on Home-based Training Programme for Persons with Mental Handicap (Crawford & Tse, 1988), for example, is for teaching children and adults in core areas of learning that are closely related to daily life: motor (gross and fine motor), self-care (eating and drinking, toileting, dressing and undressing, personal hygiene), domestic (cleaning, cooking, laundering), community living (number, concept of time, buying and shopping, using public transport, road safety, using public facilities, identification of signs and symbols, home safety), communication (receptive language, reading, writing), social/interpersonal (interpersonal relations, greeting/conversation), recreational (indoor, outdoor) (pp. 19–21).

In 1992, the Working Group on Curriculum Development for Day Activity Centres and Hostels prepared another training package (Crawford, 1992) to further fulfill the need for enhancing life-oriented skills among individuals with mental retardation. In this training package, detailed component behaviors are developed for enhancement of motor skills, self-help skills, communication skills, domestic skills, community living skills, work skills, social and interpersonal skills, and leisure and recreation skills (p. 1). Both training packages were sponsored by Hong Kong Social Welfare Department.

Instructional Strategies

The cognitive abilities of children with mental retardation are affected; therefore, abstract thinking becomes more difficult for them. Practicality should be the main thrust behind all curricular activities. Using familiar situations that children have experienced and can experience in everyday life, activities that can be applicable to real-life situations, and multisensory approaches with ample opportunities for direct sensory contacts are fundamental to teaching children with mental retardation. As such, teaching goals and objectives should be set in observable behavioral terms. Each teaching objective should consist of the following elements:

1. Target behavior — the behavior children are expected to achieve after learning or mastering the task
2. Entry skills — required skills before children can learn a new task
3. Instruction and materials required — how the lesson will be delivered and materials needed to assist with the achievement of learning objectives
4. Criteria of mastery — the number or percentage of successful performances of a target behavior before the children are considered to have mastered the target skill

Several general teaching principles are effective and frequently employed when working with children who have mental retardation: task analysis, shaping, verbal and physical prompts, grouping, and ongoing record keeping.

Task Analysis

This strategy refers to the breakdown of a task into simple steps in a logical sequence. It is a popular and effective strategy used to teach skills to children with mental retardation is task analysis. The following is an example of task analysis for tooth brushing:

1. Go to sink.
2. Pick up toothbrush.
3. Turn water on.
4. Wet toothbrush.
5. Put toothbrush down on sink.
6. Pick up toothpaste.
7. Unscrew cap of toothpaste.
8. Pick toothbrush up.

9. Squeeze small amount of paste on toothbrush.
10. Brush outside surface of teeth in up-and-down directions.
11. Brush biting surfaces of teeth in circular directions.
12. Rinse mouth out.
13. Rinse mouth out.
14. Wipe mouth.
15. Turn water off.
16. Put cap on toothpaste.
17. Put toothbrush away.
18. Put cup away.

Task analysis of a skill or performance is particularly essential in teaching daily living skills to children with moderate to severe mental retardation. Within this framework, teachers may teach a skill through *chaining*, a strategy that teaches the steps of skills that have been task-analyzed either first step first (*forward chaining*) or last step first (*backward chaining*). In forward chaining, students are taught to perform the first step in the chain first. In the task of zipping a jacket, for example, students would be taught to engage the tab first. Once that step is mastered, students are taught to slide the tab up the zipper accurately. Each step up the chain of steps is taught and mastered before the next step in the chain is taught and mastered. In some cases, the teacher might want to teach the steps in reverse order, which is called backward or reverse chaining.

Table 4.1 shows an example of using the strategy of task analysis to teach daily living skills.

Shaping

This strategy stresses the need to teach the target behavior at an appropriate pace to increase the precise performance of the target behavior. It involves successive approximation of the target behavior. Shaping is especially helpful for the development of a behavior the child has never learned or displayed (Lian, 2000). In a shaping approach, small steps are taken toward a goal. Each step is a little more modified than the previous step until the child consistently and efficiently displays the target behavior. In other words, the teacher or parent takes a child's behavior and changes it gradually or teaches a novel response by reinforcing closer and closer approximation to that behavior (Mandell & Gold, 1984). In shaping approach, all steps are not to be chained. The child moves from one step to another to work on more advanced behavioral task. For instance, the teacher can teach the skill

Table 4.1   Task Analysis for Daily Living Skills

Mrs. Smith chose chaining when teaching Mak how to zip his coat.

Mak is 6 year old with mental retardation and extensive needs for supports in most areas. His fine and gross motor skills are not yet well developed, but he has the ability to use both his index fingers and thumbs to pinch and grasp with sufficient strength to be able to pull up a tab of a zipper. Mrs. Smith has decided that Mak must learn to put on and zip up his jacket by himself as winter is coming. Dressing skills are part of his IEP, but Mrs. Smith had planned to target this skill a little later in the school year. Until now, Mrs. Smith or the class aide has prepared Mak to go outside for recess or to go home after school. At home, Mak's mother dresses him.

Mrs. Smith decides to use task analysis for zipping, with backward chaining of the instructional sequence. Mrs. Smith schedules time to work with Mak alone on the skill of zipping 10 minutes before recess. On the first day of instruction, Mrs. Smith tells Mak that he is going to learn to zip up his jacket by himself. She tells him that for several days she will help him do the task, but fairly soon, he will be responsible for doing the job himself. She also tells him that he will learn how to zip in small steps. Each day, they will work on a different step. If he can show her that he can do the step being taught that day correctly three times, he can go out to recess early. Mrs. Smith stands behind Mak with her arms around him. She slides the tab into the slider and pulls the zipper up about halfway. She then tells Mak to finish zipping his jacket three times and leaves for recess early.

On the next day, 10 minutes before recess, Mrs. Smith works with Mak again. Standing behind him and putting her arms around him, she tells Mak to watch her as she zips his jacket. Mrs. Smith slides the tab into the zipper and moves it up approximately an inch. She then tells Mak to finish zipping him jacket, which he does. She unzips his jacket and repeats the process until Mak has completed the task correctly three times. She then dismisses him for recess.

On the third day, Mrs. Smith asks Mak if he is ready for the hard part. She repeats the steps she has followed on the two previous days, and for the first time, she helps Mak slide the tab into the slider. She guides him several times; each time, he finishes the last steps by himself. She then asks Mak to zip his coat by himself. She offers him some assistance by holding the sides of his jacket firmly. Mak then zips his jacket. When he does so three times correctly, she praises him for his good work and excuses him to go to recess. Mrs. Smith plans to instruct Mak on putting on his jacket next week.

Source: Smith, D.D., & Luckasson, R. (1995). *Introduction to special education: Teaching in an age of challenge* (2nd ed.). Needham Heights, MA: Allyn & Bacon.

of threading a needle by initially using a needle with a big eye and thick thread and can gradually increase the precision by using an ordinary needle and sewing thread.

Verbal and Physical Prompts

Prompts can be used at any stage of skill teaching and development but should only be used when necessary and should be faded out as soon as the children demonstrate certain degree of mastery. Prompts break down steps of performing a task even smaller. Various types of prompts commonly used include verbal prompts, physical guidance (e.g., hand-over-hand, hand-over-wrist, and hand-over-elbow prompting), gestures, and eye pointing.

Modeling the Target Behavior

Modeling is another effective teaching strategy. Children frequently learn by copying other people's behavior. For children with impaired intellectual functioning, modeling skills or behaviors to be learned is even more important. The teacher can model the target behavior or have some children perform it to encourage other children to imitate.

Grouping

Teachers tend to find various levels of abilities among children with mental retardation who are already grouped by degrees of severity, i.e., mild, moderate, and severe. In other words, children with mild mental retardation do not all function at the same level or have the same interests. Grouping based on needs and interests with occasional individual teaching time may enhance learning. Small group arrangements can facilitate modeling among the children, increase generalization of skills for use in other situations, and encourage the children to help one another by prompting and by reinforcing task completion. Individual teaching is necessary for teaching certain skills to children with mild to severe mental retardation. Nevertheless, teachers should be reminded that children with mental retardation also need opportunity to interact and learn together with nondisabled peers, which may also be effective in enhancement of cognitive, language/communication, social/emotional, and other adaptive behaviors and skills.

Ongoing Record Keeping

Ongoing assessment and a clear record of progress are important in educating children with disabilities. Keeping records ensures consistent and continuous teaching procedure and objectives as well as programming planning based on the actual progress of the children.

SUMMARY

1. Mental retardation may impact a student's academic learning, social skills, and other adaptive behavior development. Nevertheless, children with mental retardation, like their nondisabled peers, are members of

    families, have friends and neighbors, and have personalities shaped by their innate characteristics and by their unique life experiences.

2. AAMR defines mental retardation as substantial limitations in present functioning due to significant subaverage intellectual performance, along with related limitations in two or more adaptive skill areas of communication, self-care, home living, social skills, community use, self-direction, health and safety, functional academics, leisure, and work.

3. The historical development in the field of mental retardation includes pioneers' efforts, clinical treatment and training in isolation, formation of parent groups and professional organizations, concept of normalization and deinstitutionalization, and right to a free, appropriate, public education.

4. Possible causes of mental retardation may exist during the prenatal, perinatal, and postnatal stages. Prevention of mental retardation needs to be engaged through women before and during pregnancy, babies, children, and the society.

5. Children with mental retardation have unique learning characteristics in communication, attention, memory, and generalization.

6. The curriculum for children with mental retardation in Hong Kong includes 6 areas of learning: academics, language and communication, social and personal development (self-help skills, growth and sex education, interpersonal social skills, and use of leisure time), perceptual training, motor development, and aesthetics and creative activities.

7. Teaching objectives for students with mental retardation should include the elements of target behavior, entry skills, instruction and materials, and criteria of mastery.

8. Instructional strategies may include task analysis, chaining, shaping, verbal and physical prompts, modeling, grouping, and ongoing record keeping.

ACTIVITIES

1. Using the definition references cited in the chapter, research the evolution of the definition of mental retardation and share this information in class.

2. Contact the Hong Kong Social Service Department to obtain information on supported independent living housing, supported housing, and group homes. Interview a social worker or relevant professionals and

examine the details of various types of living conditions for individuals with mental retardation in Hong Kong. If possible, schedule a visit to the different types of community-living arrangements. Compare and contrast different living arrangements. Suggest areas for improvement. Write a five-page short paper based on the information you have found and recommendations you make.

3. Research how individuals are classified as having mental retardation in other countries and report your findings to the class.
4. Design a one-minute public service announcement advertising ways to prevent mental retardation.
5. Work in small groups to design brochures to present to a primary school health class documenting causes of and ways to prevent mental retardation.
6. Hold a prevention debate on the following issues: (a) Why has our society not taken more aggressive steps to prevent mental retardation? (b) Are prevention strategies too expensive? (c) Is the connection between a prevention strategy and the birth of a healthy baby too obscure? (d) Would the imposition of strategies put a clamp on many cherished freedoms of our society? (e) What strategies has the government implemented to prevent mental retardation?
7. Research social trends and how these trends influenced treatment and attitudes of persons with mental retardation. How did living conditions evolve? How did involvement in public education evolve? How did attitudes change? Write a short paper on what you have researched.
8. Form small groups of 4–5. Design a task analysis for the following: (a) creating and caring for a window box of flowers, (b) telephoning an emergency number, (c) getting a written birthday greeting for someone in another country, and (d) making changes for sums less than ten dollars.

RESOURCES

Resources in Hong Kong

Hong Chi Association
Pinehill Village, Chung Nga Road, Nam Hang, Tai Po, NT, Hong Kong
Tel.: 852-2661-0709
Web address: http://www.hongchi.org.hk/

The Hong Kong Sports Association for the Mentally Handicapped
Unit No. 2, LG/FL, Lek Yuen Community Hall, Shatin, N.T., Hong Kong
Tel: 852-2697-3731   Fax: 852-2601-2509
Web address: http://www.hksam.org.hk/index.html

Lai Yiu Adult Training Centre
70 Level 204, Shopping Block, Lai Yiu Estate, Kwai Chung, N.T.
Mental Handicap Teaching & Learning Services Website:
http://www.socialwork.com.hk/swtheroy.htm

New Life Psychiatric Rehabilitation Association
332 Nam Cheong Street, Kowloon, Hong Kong.
Tel: 852-2332-4343   Fax: 852-2770-9345

[Service Centres/Units]:

Hong Kong Island	Tel:	Fax:
Lei Tung Halfway House	852-2874-7770	
Jockey Club New Life Hostel	852-2524-1447	
Wong Chuk Hang Sheltered Workshop	852-2552-4202	852-2814-7577

Kowloon		
New Life Building Long Stay Care Home	852-2776-2820	852-2779-7431
New Life Building Halfway House (I)	852-2776-7318	
New Life Building Halfway House (II)	852-2776-8072	
New Life Building Halfway House (III)	852-2776-1086	
New Life Building Sheltered Workshop	852-2778-6023	852-2776-7612
New Life Building Activity Centre	852-2319-2103	852-2351-7871
Chuk Yuen Halfway House	852-2327-4926	
Aftercare Service	852-2325-9733	
Chuk Yuen Sheltered Workshop	852-2324-9974	852-2328-5178
Supported Employment Service	852-2327-4931	852-2351-7871

N.T. (Kwai Chung)		
Shek Lei Halfway House	852-2426-7577	
Kwai Shing Sheltered Workshop	852-2428-8711	852-2485-1833

New Territories (Shatin)		
Sun Chui Halfway House	852-2606-7456	
Pok Hong Halfway House	852-2646-1884	

New Territories (Tuen Mun)

Shan King Halfway House	852-2462-6481	
Tuen Mun Halfway House	852-2459-8080	
Jockey Club Farm House	852-2461-2818	
Tin King Hostel	852-2461-7115	
New Life Jubilee Hostel	852-2463-7190	
Tuen Mun Long Stay Care Home	852-2454-3866	852-2454-0980
Tuen Mun Activity Centre	852-2450-2172	852-2441-5625
New Life Farm	852-2461-8385	852-2456-3201
Tin King Sheltered Workshop	852-2466-0068	852-2464-6960

SHH Service Centers:
Father Tapella Home
30 Units 201–209, Shek Fong House, Shek Wai Kok Estate, Tsuen Wan, N.T.

Social Welfare Department
Tel.: 852-2343-2225
Email: swdenq@swd.gov.hk
Web address: http://www.info.gov.hk/swd/html_tc/index.html

The Society of Homes for the Handicapped (Services for Moderate and Severe Mental Handicap):
Ground Floor, No 2A, Cronin Garden, Shamshuipo, Kowloon, Hong Kong.

Wo Che Adult Training Centre
35 G/F, High Block, Tai Wo House, Wo Che Estate, Shatin, N.T.

Resources in Taiwan

Children Are Us 喜憨兒文教基金會
Tel.: 02-2325-7383   07-726-6096
Web address: http://www.careus.org.tw/index1.htm

Parent' Association for Persons with Intellectual Disability
台北市建國南路一段285號3樓
Tel.: 02-2701-7271   Fax: 02-2754-7250
Web address: http://www.papmh.org.tw/

財團法人向陽文教基金會
台南市北區北門路二段237巷31弄5之1號
Tel.: 06-282-6632   Fax: 06-282-9170
Web address: http://www.shiang-yang.org.tw/

International Resources

American Association on Mental Retardation (AAMR)
Web address: http://207.201.142.179/index.shtml

The Arc of the United States
Web address: http://www.thearc.org/

The Association for Persons with Severe Handicaps (TASH)
Web address: http://www.tash.org

Council for Exceptional Children-Division on Mental Retardation and
    Developmental Web address: Disabilities (ECE-MRDD)
http://www.mrddcec.freeservers.com/

People First International
P.O. Box 12642, Salem, OR 97309 U.S.A.

Voice of the Retarded, Inc.
5005 Newport Drive, Suite 108
Rolling Meadows, IL 60008 U.S.A.
Tel.: 1-847-253-6020   Fax: 1-847-253-6054
Web address: http://www.vor.net/

Yahoo! Health
Web address: http://health.yahoo.com/health/Diseases_and_Conditions/
Disease_Feed_Data/Mental_retardation/

REFERENCES

AAMR Ad Hoc Committee on Terminology and Classification. (1992).
    Classification in mental retardation (9th ed.). Washington, DC: American
    Association on Mental Retardation.
Crawford, N. (Ed.) (1992). *Skills for life for mentally handicapped persons.* Hong
    Kong: The Working Group on Curriculum Development for Day Activity
    Centres and Hostels, Social Welfare Department.
Crawford, N., Tse, J. (Eds). (1988). *Home-based training package for persons
    with mental handicap.* Hong Kong: The Working Group on Home-based
    Training Programme for Persons with Mental Handicap, Social Welfare
    Department.
Doll, E. (1941). The essentials of an inclusive concept of mental deficiency.
    American Journal of Mental Deficiency, 46, 214–219.
Grossman, V. (Ed.). (1983). *Classification in mental retardation.* Washington, DC:
    American Association on Mental Deficiency (now Retardation).

Hardman, M.L., Drew, C.J., & Egan, M.W. (1996). *Human exceptionality: Society, school, and family.* Needham Heights, MA: Allyn & Bacon.

Hong Kong Curriculum Development Council. (1994). *Guide to curriculum for mentally handicapped children.* Hong Kong: Curriculum Development Institute, Education Department.

Itard, J.M.G. (1806). *Wild boy of Aveyron.* (G. Humphrey & M. Humphrey, Trans.). (1962). Englewood Cliffs, NJ: Prentice-Hall. Originally published Paris: Gouyon (1801).

Kanner, L. (1964). *A history of the care and study of the mentally retarded.* Springfield, IL: Charles C. Thomas.

Lian, M-G.J. (2000). *Teaching students with physical and multiple disabilities.* Normal, IL: University Communications, Illinois State University.

Luckasson, R., Coulter, D.L., Polloway, E.A., Reiss, S., Schalock, R.L., Snell, M. E., (1996). The 1992 AAMR Definition and Preschool Children: Response from the Committee on Terminology and Classification. *Mental Retardation, 34*(4), 247–253.

Mandell, C.J., & Gold, V. (1984). *Teaching handicapped students.* St. Paul, MN: West Publishing Co.

Nirje, B. (1985). The basis and logic of normalization principle. *Australia and New Zealand Journal of Developmental Disabilities, 11,* 65–68.

Scheerenberger, R.C. (1983). *A history of mental retardation.* Baltimore: Brookes.

Scheerenberger, R.C. (1987). *A history of mental retardation: A quarter century of promise.* Baltimore: Brookes.

Smith, D.D., & Luckasson, R. (1995). *Introduction to special education: Teaching in an age of challenge* (2nd ed.). Needham Heights, MA: Allyn & Bacon.

Spitalnik, D.M., & Stark, J.A. (1992). *Mental retardation: Definition, classification, and systems of supports.* Washington, DC: American Association on Mental Retardation.

Learning Disabilities

ADVANCED THINKING

Answer the following questions as you read:

1. How is "learning disabilities" defined?
2. What are the controversies surrounding the definition of learning disabilities?
3. What are potential causes of learning disabilities?
4. What are common characteristics of individuals with learning disabilities?
5. Identify the "learning-to-learn strategies" that can be taught to children with learning disabilities?
6. Identify strategies that may facilitate learning among children with learning disabilities?
7. What is attention deficit hyperactivity disorder? How is it related to learning disabilities?
8. What are the behavioral characteristics of a child with attention deficit hyperactivity disorder?
9. What school and home interventions can be helpful to children with attention deficit hyperactivity disorder?
10. How can computer technology be used in the instruction of children with learning disabilities?

KEY TERMS AND PHRASES

academic achievement
ADHD
attention deficit
auditory perception

behavior modification
characteristics
children with learning difficulties
cognitive processing

cognitive training
computer-assisted instruction
creative drama
curriculum
direct instruction
discrimination
environmental influence
genetic cause
history
home intervention
HOW
hyperactivity
hyperactivity learning disabilities
impulsivity
information processing
intelligence
learning characteristics
learning-to-learn strategy
maturational delay
medication

mnemonics
neurological cause
NJCLD
PCCT
perception
psycholinguistic ability
reading comprehension
scaffolding
self-determination skills
self-instruction
self-monitoring
simulation
social emotional characteristics
specific learning disabilities
spell/grammar check program
TARGETS
use of technology
visual perception
word predict
word processing

INTRODUCTION

Most of us have had the experience that, no matter how hard we try, we have trouble understanding some of the information presented in the elementary, secondary, and college classrooms. Sometimes we find it difficult or impossible to organize our thoughts to write a coherent essay or report; sometimes we are unable to convey our thoughts, feelings, and knowledge; sometimes we forget things we need to do; occasionally, we feel uncomfortable working with other people. For persons with learning disabilities, having one or more of these situations is common.

Children with learning disabilities have rather diverse or heterogeneous difficulties but share a common problem: they do not learn in the same way or as efficiently as their nondisabled peers. Although they have normal intelligence, they generally perform significantly behind their peers in academics. Some have great difficulty in learning mathematics, but the majority of them find reading and writing to be their greatest challenge (Mercer, 1991).

Compared to visual disabilities, deaf and hard-of-hearing conditions, and mental retardation, the field of learning disabilities is one of the youngest among various categories of special needs identified worldwide. Of all the types of special needs, education for children who have learning disabilities is possibly inadequately addressed in the current Hong Kong education system.

This chapter will discuss and examine the issues surrounding the definitions of learning disabilities, history, possible causes, characteristics, instructional strategies, and technology for persons with learning disabilities.

LEARNING DISABILITIES DEFINED

More controversy and confusion have been generated by the specific category of learning disabilities than any other exceptionality. Educational services for students with learning disabilities were practically nonexistent prior to the 1960s. Many of these children would have been labeled as slow learners, emotionally disturbed, or even mentally retarded. Today, learning disabilities represent the largest single program for exceptional children in the United States. The latest figures show that 5.3% of the total student population is labeled with learning disabilities in the United States.

Like children with other exceptionalities, children with learning disabilities must meet specific criteria to be eligible for special education services. These criteria are based on definitions adopted by a region, state, or nation. The definition of *specific learning disabilities* (SLD) may exclude primary causes of mental retardation, motor disabilities, sensory (hearing, visual) impairments, emotional disturbance, as well as social-economic, environmental, and cultural disadvantages (Baechle & Lian, 1990).

The education system in Hong Kong has not adopted a definition for learning disabilities since this category is not yet recognized for special education services. Children with reading/writing or mathematics disabilities are grouped under the category of "children with learning difficulties," which includes academically low achieving students who may or may not have learning disabilities.

In the U.S., two definitions of learning disabilities are most frequently used in the education systems. One is the federal definition and the other is from the National Joint Committee on Learning Disabilities (NJCLD). The federal definition is as follows:

"Specific learning disability" means a disorder in one or more of the basic psychological processes involved in understanding or in using language, spoken or written, that may manifest itself in an imperfect ability to listen, think, speak, read, write, spell, or to do mathematical calculations. The term includes such conditions as perceptual disabilities, brain injury, minimal brain dysfunction, dyslexia, and developmental aphasia. The term does not apply to children who have learning problems that are primarily the result of visual, of hearing, of motor disabilities, of mental retardation, of emotional disturbance, of environmental, cultural, or economic disadvantages. (U.S. Department of Education, 1992).

The NJCLD's definition is as follows:

"Learning disabilities" is a general term that refers to a heterogeneous group of disorders manifested by significant difficulties in the acquisition and use of listening, speaking, reading, writing, reasoning, or mathematical abilities. These disorders are intrinsic to the individual, presumed to be due to central nervous system dysfunction, and may occur across the life span. Problems in self-regulatory behaviors, social perception, and social interaction may exist with learning disabilities but do not by themselves constitute a learning disability. Although learning disabilities may occur concomitantly with other handicapping conditions (for example, sensory impairment, mental retardation, serious emotional disturbance) or with extrinsic influences (such as cultural differences, insufficient or inappropriate instruction), they are not the result of those conditions or influences. (1988, p. 1)

This definition is important in the current discussion for three reasons. First, it describes learning disabilities as an umbrella term for a heterogeneous group of disorders. Second, a person with learning disabilities must manifest significant difficulties which is an obvious attempt to eliminate the connotation of a mild problem. Third, this definition stresses that learning disabilities are lifelong problems and should not be mixed with other disabilities. These fundamental elements serve as guideposts for educators to identify, assess, and design instructions for children with learning disabilities.

HISTORY OF THE FIELD

The field of learning disabilities is relatively new. The late Samuel Kirk coined this term in 1963 when he had a meeting with parents and other professionals in Chicago. At that time, children with learning difficulties were labeled in various ways. Robinson and Deshler (1988) indicated that "some labels referred to cause of specific learning problems (e.g., brain injury, minimal brain damage, psychoneurological disorder), [while] other labels referred to behavioral manifestations (e.g., perceptual disorder, dyslexia, hyperkenetic behavior, Strauss syndrome)" (p. 110).

Because of Kirk and other pioneers' work, the number of children with identified learning disabilities grew exponentially. Programs for teacher training and the scope of related services continued to expand at all stages of education.

Professionals supported visual perceptual approaches in the early learning disabilities programs (e.g., Marianne Frostig's *Developmental Test of Visual Perception*, or DTVP). Throughout the history of the field, various fads have become popular with the media and the public. One of the fads suggested teaching students with learning difficulties to crawl again, regardless of their age. Others included various diets and placing plants on students' desks to improve students' academic and behavioral performances. The 1970s witnessed heated debate over the validity issue of the learning disabilities theories and the best approaches, namely perceptual training (or process) and direct instruction with behavior modification, to use in the remediation of students' academic deficits. Hammill and Larsen (1974), for example, questioned the effort of enhancing psycholinguistic abilities in students with learning disabilities. The 1980s saw the development of a number of learning strategies following the information-processing theory and metacognition. Self-management techniques are found to help students to remember what they are taught, to think, to organize their study, and to solve other problems. Research studies continue to identify ways how these students should be taught while debate over who should be included as having learning disabilities continues.

POSSIBLE CAUSES

Learning disabilities are manifested in different ways and at different levels of severity. The behaviors of individuals with learning disabilities have been explained in a number of ways and a number of causes have been suggested. However, determining precise causation is still a difficult task.

Neurological Causes

For a number of years, the cause of learning disabilities has been attributed to structural neurological damage or some kind of neurological activation abnormality. A number of professionals of the field have supported this view. However, neurological damage causation must be largely inferred, since direct evidence tends not to be available (Bender, 1995; Drew, Hardman, & Logan, 1996).

Maturational Delay

It is also suggested that a maturational delay of the neurological system may result in the difficulties experienced by individuals with learning disabilities. The behavior and performance of children with learning disabilities, in many ways, resemble that of much younger individuals (Smith, 1994). They often exhibit delays in slower development of language skills, problems in the visual-motor area and several academic areas. However, maturational delay is not likely considered a causative factor in all types of learning disabilities but as one of the many factors.

Genetic Causes

Genetic abnormalities are thought to cause or contribute to one or more of the problems categorized as learning disabilities. Some of the past research, including studies of identical and fraternal twins, has suggested an inheritance linkage (Bonnet, 1989; Eme, 1992). However, these findings must be viewed with caution due to the well-known difficulty in separating the influences of heredity and environment.

Environmental Influence

Environment influences are often suggested as a cause of learning disabilities. Factors such as dietary inadequacies, radiation stress, smoking, drinking, drug consumption, and inappropriate/poor school instruction are being investigated and sometimes blamed for learning disabilities. Findings linking to environmental causation remain inconclusive.

CHARACTERISTICS

In spite of the diverse types of learning disabilities, educators have identified some common characteristics among these individuals.

Intelligence

According to the exclusive definition, individuals with learning disabilities are expected to have average, above-average, or near-average intelligence.

Hyperactivity

Hyperactivity is a behavioral characteristic commonly found among children with learning disabilities, but not a criterion. Findings of some research studies indicated that as many as half of the children with learning disabilities are not hyperactive and it is not a universal characteristic (e.g., Faraone, Biederman, Lehmman, & Keenan, 1993).

Learning Characteristics

The learning characteristics of individuals with learning disabilities may include perceptual, discrimination, cognitive and information processing, academic, and social/emotional perspectives:

Perception

Perception difficulties in individuals with learning disabilities portray a pattern of behavior abnormalities. Visual perception difficulty, excluding impaired vision, is closely associated with learning disabilities. This type of abnormality is evident when a child sees a visual stimulus as unrelated parts instead of an integrated pattern. For example, the child may not be able to identify an alphabet because he or she perceives only unrelated lines rather than a letter as a meaningful whole. Obviously, such situation causes severe performance problems in school, especially during the early years (Smith, 1994).

Discrimination

Individuals with difficulties in visual discrimination may find it impossible to distinguish one visual stimulus from another (e.g., between words such as *dig* and *dug* or letters such as *V* and *W*). Therefore, they commonly reverse letters such as *b* and *d*. While this type of error is common among young children, most normally developed children show few reversal or rotation errors on visual images by about 7 or 8 years of age.

Individuals with auditory discrimination difficulty may be unable to distinguish between the sounds of different words or syllables or even to identify certain environmental sounds (e.g., ringing telephone) and differentiate them from others. Those with auditory blending problems may be unable to blend word parts into an integrated whole as they pronounce the word; those with auditory memory difficulty may be unable to recall information presented verbally; and those with auditory association problems may be unable to associate ideas or information presented verbally.

Haptic perception (touch, body movement, and position sensation) is another area of perceptual difficulty associated with learning disabilities. This is relatively uncommon but important in some areas of school performance. For instance, handwriting requires haptic perception because tactile and kinesthetic information about the grasp of a pen or pencil must be transmitted to the brain. Children with learning disabilities are often described by teachers as having poor handwriting, with difficulties in spacing letters and staying on the lines of the paper. Such problems, however, could be due to visual perception abnormalities. It is therefore difficult to attribute some behaviors to a single factor.

Cognitive/Information Processing

Research suggests that children with learning disabilities have different rather than deficient cognitive abilities (Kraker, 1993; Swanson, 1993). Attention problems are also associated with learning disabilities. Children with learning disabilities are often found to have difficulty in sustaining attention for more than a very short time and some have considerable daydreaming and high distractibility (Leviton, Bellinger, & Allred, 1993). Some research has indicated that these children have difficulty in certain types of attention problems and in attending selectively (Zentall & Ferkis, 1993).

Academic Achievement

Individuals with learning disabilities have many academic problems despite having normal or above-average intelligence. These problems generally persist throughout the formal schooling, including college (Yanok, 1993). Among the academic problems, reading difficulty is the most prominent one. Some estimates suggest that 85 to 90 percent of all students with learning disabilities have reading disabilities (Bender, 1995). The specific reading problems of these children vary as much as the many elements involved in the reading process. Often times they also have difficulty in writing and spelling which are closely related to reading. Arithmetic is another major difficulty found in individuals with learning disabilities. They often have difficulty in counting, writing numbers, and mastering other simple math concepts (Fuchs, Fuchs, & Bishop, 1992; Zentall & Ferkis, 1993). Intelligence-achievement discrepancy is almost always a major criterion for identifying the existence of a learning disability.

Social/Emotional Characteristics

In addition to academic difficulties, children with learning disabilities often encounter emotional and interpersonal difficulties (de la Cruz, Lian, & Morreau, 1998; Pearl & Bryan, 1992). They frequently experience low self-esteem due to their learning problems (Bender, 1995) and may not be able to interact effectively with others due to a distorted perception of social cues or an inability to discriminate or interpret the fine distinction of normal interpersonal association. Researchers have identified a number of areas where the social behavior of children with learning disabilities is inferior to that of their nondisabled classmates (e.g., Bender & Smith, 1990). Examples are as follows:

1. They choose less socially acceptable behavior.
2. They cannot predict the consequences of their behaviors.
3. They misinterpret social, nonverbal cues.
4. They make poor decisions.
5. They use social conventions (manners) improperly.
6. They do not pay close enough attention during classroom assignments.
7. They are shy, withdrawn, distractible, or hyperactive.
8. They are socially naïve and unable to determine when other people are sincere, deceptive, or sarcastic.

Overall, possible characteristics of persons with learning disabilities include the following:

1. Significant discrepancy between potential and academic achievement,
2. Distractibility or inability to pay attention for as long as peers do,
3. Disorganized approach to learning,
4. Evidence of poor language and/or cognitive development,
5. Hyperactive behavior, exhibited through excessive movement,
6. Immature social skills,
7. Impulsiveness,
8. Inability to solve problems,
9. Inattentiveness during lectures or class discussions,
10. Over-reliance on teacher and peers for class assignments,
11. Poor motor coordination and spatial relation skills,
12. Poor motivation and little active involvement in learning tasks, and
13. Substantial delays in academic achievement.

EDUCATION

Instructional approaches for students with learning disabilities may include learning-to-learn strategies, strategies for academic subjects, and creative drama.

Learning-to-learn Strategies

One of the most effective approaches in working with students with learning disabilities is to teach them strategies they have not learned — strategies that nondisabled students seem to learn without specific instruction. For example, some students use contextual and graphic clues to understand words and ideas they do not grasp immediately, or they may reread and question. Strategic learners know the purpose of their study and summarize and integrate information with that purpose in mind. In contrast, many individuals with learning disabilities do not have a repertoire of strategies and/or do not understand how to use strategies flexibly.

Cognitive Training

Two of the most common difficulties students with learning disabilities face are (1) not knowing how to plan, monitor, and check their performance and (2) being unable to remediate the problems they experience in learning. Cognitive training has been found to be effective in improving these difficulties. Cognitive training involves three components: (1) changing thought processes, (2) providing strategies for learning, and (3) teaching self-initiative. Cognitive training is concerned with modifying unobservable thought processes, prompting observable changes in behavior. Cognitive training has proven successful in resolving a variety of academic problems for many students with learning disabilities (Borkwowski, 1992).

At least two reasons are given as to why cognitive training is particularly appropriate for students with learning disabilities (Hallahan & Kauffman, 1997):

1. Cognitive and metacognitive problems by providing them with specific strategies for solving problems, and
2. Motivational problems of passivity and learned helplessness by stressing self-initiative and involving them as much as possible in their own treatment.

Several strategies have been created to teach metacognitive processes.

The *TARGETS* (Ellis & Lenz, 1987) is a problem-solving strategy that incorporates a first-letter mnemonic to help students recall each of the seven steps:

T = Task specified in a question
A = Answer question
R = Review past performance
G = Goal written
E = Enter planned behaviors
T = Try planned behaviors
S = Step evaluated

This strategy can be used to help a student solve the problem of not completing his homework. He can complete the following plan using TARGETS:

T = How can I finish my homework?
A = I can do it as soon as I get home, before I watch TV or go out with my friends.
R = I wait until late at night and don't have enough time to do my homework, and I don't know how to do some of it
G = I will finish my homework.
E = I will do my homework before I watch TV or see my friends, and I will ask my study buddy if I can call him for help when I don't understand my homework.
T = I tried my plan.
S = It worked. The only problem was that when I called my study buddy, he was not home.

PCCT is a strategy that helps students complete independent assignments during class, Archer (cited in Salend, 1994) developed the following procedure:

Plan it.	Read the directions and circle the words that tell you what to do.
	Get out the material you need.
	Tell yourself what to do.
Complete it.	Do all items.
	If you can't do an item, go ahead or ask for help.
	Use HOW (see below)
Check it.	Did you do everything?

Did you get the right answer?

Did you proofread?

Turn it in.

This procedure assists students in monitoring their own performances by providing prompts for specific actions. In order to help students recall all the steps in this procedure, you may suggest that each student write the steps on an index card, which he or she then tapes to the inside of a notebook or individual assignment folder.

HOW is a procedure that specifies the formats of assignments that students turn in to teachers. It outlines how students' papers should look. Teachers can adapt the HOW procedure to include the specific information and structures they prefer. An example of requesting students to format their papers is as follows:

H = Heading	O = Organized	W= Written neatly
1. Name	1. Write on the front side only.	1. Write on the lines.
2. Date	2. Leave one blank line at the top	2. Make neat erasures.
3. Subject	3. Leave one blank line at the bottom	3. Do not cross out anything.

Self-determination Curriculum

Test, Karvonen, Wood, Browder, and Algozzine (2000) reviewed 60 curricula which were designed to enhance *self-determination skills* of children with disabilities. They listed the main curricular components as follows:

1. Choice and decision-making.
2. Goal setting and attainment.
3. Problem-solving.
4. Self-evaluation, observation, and reinforcement.
5. Self-advocacy.
6. Inclusion of student-directed individualized educational programs (IEP).
7. Relationships with others.
8. Self-awareness. (p. 48)

Teachers need to be encouraged to teach students with learning disabilities the above self-determination skills, while nondisabled peers and other school personnel and service providers need to be prepared to "encourage and respect the decisions made by self-determining individuals with disabilities" (Test et al., 2000, p. 50).

Self-Monitoring. One important strategy for enhancing self-determination skills of students with learning disabilities is to teach students to self-monitor their thinking and behavior. *Self-monitoring strategies* provide students with new ways of thinking about their performance and reinforce the idea that students control their own behavior. An example of the steps used in self-monitoring are as follows (Hallahan & Kauffman, 1997):

- *Select the behavior.* Begin by selecting a behavior that is specific, observable, and appropriate to the student's cognitive and developmental levels and to the classroom setting. For example, Ms. Wong was concerned with the high percentage of errors Ted made on his math assignments because he seemed to rush through the problems. She selected accuracy of math performance as an appropriate behavior for Ted to self-monitor.
- *Collect baseline data.* To have both an objective measure of the extent of the problem and a point of comparison from which to assess the effectiveness of this strategy, Ms. Wong gathered information about the accuracy of Ted's math computation. Five days prior to introducing self-monitoring, she collected and scored Ted's math assignments. The average for this period was 12.6 problems correct of the 20 problems assigned each day
- *Obtain willing cooperation from the student.* Because the student will be responsible for monitoring, he or she must "buy into" the procedure. To "sell" self-monitoring, Ms. Wong emphasized outcomes that would be meaningful to Ted: reducing the number of problems he would have to correct, thereby increasing the time he would have to spend playing the sports he enjoyed.
- *Instruct the student in the procedure.* Training involves defining precisely the selected behavior for the student, teaching the specific steps in the procedure, and teaching the student how to record his or her behavior. Ted was taught these steps:
  (1) Work the problem.
  (2) Ask myself, do I think my answer is correct?
  (3) Check for accuracy.
  (4) Mark the square on the tally sheet with an X.

(5) Make corrections, if necessary.

(6) Continue until all the problems have been worked.

(7) Count the number of Xs and write the number by the day's total.

(8) Graph the number.

Ms. Wong taught Ted to record his behavior on a self-monitoring form. He was instructed to record an X each time he checked a math problem for accuracy; to count the Xs at the end of math period and write the number in the box labeled "Total"; and then to graph the daily total on a separate form entitled "Problems Checked for Accuracy."

• *Have the student independently perform the self-monitoring procedure.* Ms. Wong placed the strategy steps and a self-monitoring form inside Ted's math folder, and for the first few days, she monitored his accuracy closely. She also put the answer key for the day's math problems in a folder on the worktable near her desk, so that Ted would have access to it to check the accuracy of his problems. As. Ms. Wong circulated around the classroom, monitoring students' progress in math, she also checked to see that Ted was using the self-monitoring form and graphing the results. She provided prompts as needed. With these supports, Ted was able to self-monitor and to improve his percentage of correct responses.

• *Evaluate the effectiveness of the intervention.* After Ted began to self-monitor independently, Ms. Wong collected samples of his math assignments as she had done during baseline collection. She compared the average number correct after self-monitoring with that before self-monitoring. She found that Ted had completed 17.4, 14.9, and 18.1 problems correct during the three weeks he had used self-monitoring, which represented an improvement over the 12.6 problems correct during baseline.

Self-Instruction. Self-instruction is to make students aware of the various stages of problem-solving tasks while they are performing them and to bring behavior under verbal control (Meichenbaum, 1975). Typically, the teacher first models the use of the verbal routine while solving the problem. Then he or she closely supervises the students using the verbal routine while doing the task, and then the students do it on their own.

Case, Harris, and Graham (1992) conducted a study involving 5th and

6th graders with learning disabilities to use self-instruction as an integral feature of instruction in solving math and word problems In this study, the students learned to use a five-step strategy of saying the problem out loud, looking for important words and circling them, drawing pictures to help explain what was happening, writing the math sentence, and writing the answer. Additionally, students were prompted to use the following self-instructions:

- problem definition: *"What do I have to do?"*
- planning: *"How can I solve this problem?"*
- strategy use: *"The five-step strategy will help me look for important words."*
- self-evaluation: *"How am I doing?"*
- self-reinforcement: *"Good job. I got it right."*

Kosiewicz, Hallahan, Lloyd, & Graves (1982) provided an example of self-instruction used for spelling (1) say the word out loud, (2) say the first syllable of the word, (3) name each of the letters in the syllable three times, (4) say each letter as he wrote it, and (5) repeat steps 2 through 4 for each succeeding syllable.

Strategies for Academic Subjects

Students with learning disabilities also need to learn strategies in academic areas. Most of the strategies discussed here include components that teach specific skills and the metacognitive procedure students need to use them successfully.

Mnemonics for all Subjects

This method can be applied for various academic areas and is designed to help students with memory problems to remember information by associating the first letters of items in a list with a word, sentence, or picture. For example, many people remember the names of Great Lakes by the mnemonic HOMES (Huron, Ontario, Michigan, Erie, and Superior).

Reading Comprehension

Several strategies have been developed to facilitate students' understanding of text through promoting learning by activating students' prior knowledge, establishing a purpose for reading, directing attention to important features of the text and vocabulary, and checking for problems in comprehension.

For example, Think-Aloud (Davey, 1983) teaches students to think of questions that help them monitor their understanding while they read by observing a good reader (e.g., teacher) verbalize the strategies he or she uses. The process a teacher models in Think-Aloud sessions includes the following self-questioning strategies (Wisconsin Department of Public Instruction, 1989):

Before Reading

"Before I read I ask myself several questions": Why am I reading this selection (purposes)? What will I do with this information? What do I already know about this topic? What do I think I'll learn about this topic?" (predictions)

During Reading

"As I read I ask myself: Am I understanding? Does this make sense to me? Is this what I expected? What parts are similar to and different from my predictions?"

After Reading

"When I finish reading, I wonder: What are the most important points? Which part of the text supports them? How do I feel about this information?" What new information did I learn and how does it fit with what I already know? Do I need to go back and reread the part so I can understand better?" (p. 158)

After every self-question the teacher poses he or she talks through his or her answers aloud. Consequently, Think-Alouds model not only the strategy of self-questioning but also the thought processes used to monitor and regulate comprehension.

Scaffolding

In scaffolding, students receive help when they are first learning tasks and help is gradually reduced, so that eventually, students do the tasks independently. The types of supports provided can vary. For example, *reciprocal teaching* is an approach that uses scaffolded instruction because the teacher and students take turns teaching the content to one another. In this method, students (1) see cognitive strategies modeled by the teacher and (2) try out those strategies while being monitored by the teacher. The idea is for the teacher's monitoring to become less vigilant as the students become more capable of learning. An example of reciprocal teaching is given as follows:

The teacher assigned a segment of the passage (usually a paragraph) to be read and either indicated that it was her turn to be the teacher or assigned one of the students to teach the segment. The teacher and the students then read the assigned segment silently. After reading the text, the assigned teacher (student or adult) for that segment summarized (reviewed) the content, discussed and clarified any difficulties, asked a question that a teacher or test might ask on the segment, and finally, made a prediction about future content. All these activities were embedded in as natural a dialogue as possible, with the teacher and other students giving feedback to one another.

Direct Instruction

This method focuses specifically on the instructional process and emphasizes a systematic analysis of the concept to be taught. A variety of Direct Instruction programs is available for reading, math, and language (e.g., Englemann, Carnine, Englemenn, & Kelly, 1991). These programs consist of precisely sequenced, fast-paced lessons for small groups of four to ten. There is a heavy emphasis on drill and practice. The teacher teaches from a well-rehearsed script, and students follow the teacher, who often uses hand signals to prompt participation. The teacher offers immediate corrective feedback for errors and praise for correct responses.

Direct Instruction programs are among the most well-researched commercial programs available for students with learning disabilities. Use of these programs not only results in immediate academic gains but may also bring long-term academic gains.

Creative Drama

De la Cruz, Lian, and Morreau (1998) recommended creative drama activities for children with learning disabilities. Table 5.1 shows an example of a drama lesson. Results from the de la Cruz et al. study with control group indicated positive effects of creative drama in improving social skills and expressive language skills of children with learning disabilities.

Children with Attention Deficit Hyperactivity Disorder

As mentioned earlier, many children with learning disabilities also have attention deficit disorder (ADD) or attention deficit hyperactivity disorder (ADHD). Children with only significant attention difficulties are diagnosed

Table 5.1 An Example of a Creative Drama Lesson

Saying an Apology

Objective: For students to apologize when their actions have injured or infringed on another peer.

Session I: A picture of a child crying after playing with other children was shown and, then, five questions were asked for discussion: "What is happening in the picture?" "Why is the child crying?" "What happened before the child cried?" and "What happened after the child cried?" Pantomime was explained and demonstrated when the class was divided into small groups. Students pantomimed what happened after the child in the picture cried. They later put words into their actions.

The conclusions of the first session were that (1) hurting the feelings or body of another person should be avoided, and (2) if another person was hurt, an apology would have to be made.

Session II: The picture of a child crying was reviewed and, then, four questions were asked for discussion: "What is an apology?" "What are the words that you say in an apology?" "When do you say an apology?" and "How do you say an apology?" Students were divided into small groups. They practiced ways of saying an apology by performing improvisations based on three given situations (i.e., cutting in front of somebody for lunch, dropping a bag on the foot of another child, and forgetting to say hello to friends).

Session II led to the following conclusions: (1) to avoid hurting other people, keep your hands, feet, and objects to yourself, (2) be careful of what you say and do not say unkind words to other people, and (3) when an apology is needed, you say it nicely and gently.

Source: de la Cruz, R., Lian, M-G.J., & Morreau, L.E. (1998). The effects of creative drama on social and oral language skills of children with learning disabilities. *Youth Theatre Journal, 12*, 89–95.

to have ADD while children with both attention and motor hyperactivity difficulties are diagnosed to have ADHD. Educators do not always agree whether these diagnoses belong to learning disabilities, behavioral disorders, or a category of their own. Most frequently, ADD or ADHD is discussed alongside the learning disabilities or emotional/behavioral disorders.

Teachers can quite easily identify a number of children being perceived as not paying attention or not having sufficient attention in class. They keep getting out of seat, talking without raising their hands, touching others or someone's property when they should not, having difficulty in waiting for their turn and so on. They seem to have adequate intelligence to do well in school but they generally do not perform to their potential. Teachers do not like them because they are typically disruptive. Teachers may also find some who are quiet and non-disruptive but they frequently daydream. While there are some commonalities in their behaviors, these children may exhibit varying degrees of attention and behavioral difficulties and may require different types of accommodations.

General Characteristics

Our discussion attempts to be inclusive and will therefore focus on ADHD which includes characteristics or traits of ADD. The three core symptoms or traits that characterize ADHD are: (1) difficulties with sustained attention; (2) impulsivity; and (3) hyperactivity. In Addition, children with ADHD may exhibit the following characteristics: emotional over-arousal; difficulties in delaying gratification; and difficulties with rule-governed behavior.

Difficulties with Sustained Attention. Children with ADHD have difficulties sustaining their attention on tasks perceived as routine, tedious, and repetitive. In order to sustain attention, activities need to be of high interest or have high severe negative consequences. The diagnosis of ADHD does not suggest that the child has generalized attention disorder; however, the disorder may be situation specific in relation to the environment and to the task. Consequently, children with ADHD may appear one day to be very attentive and persistent while the next day to be very distractible depending upon the environment and/or the task.

Impulsivity. Children with ADHD tend to act without considering the consequences of their actions. They seem to have difficulties with inhibiting their behavioral responses to stimuli. Children with ADHD are likely to respond at the moment rather than delaying their responses in order to consider the consequences of their actions. Impulsivity, according to some researchers, is the most defining characteristics of this disorder. ADHD is not a skill-based deficit, but a performance deficit. In other words, children with ADHD may understand how to plan and organize their home, but they may lack the behavioral control to use such a plan.

Hyperactivity. Due to their difficulties with behavioral inhibition and sustained attention (persistence of effort), children with ADHD appear to be hyperverbal or hyperactive. This characteristic may appear given a certain context (environment or task) such as completing an essay or doing paperwork. Their work or academic performance will appear to have a significant amount of variability. Not only does hyperactivity relate to physical movement, it may also appear in their thoughts and conversations. In the classroom, living room, or school cafeteria, children with ADHD may appear to be fidgety, squirmy, day dreamy, overly verbal and socially intrusive.

Educational Methods

William Cruickshank developed an educational program for students with learning disabilities that stressed three principles (Hallahan & Kauffman, 1997): (a) structure, (b) reduction of environmental stimulation, and (c) enhancement of intensity of teaching materials. This program is also suitable for children with ADHD. This structured program is heavily teacher directed and the rationale is that children with attention problems cannot make their own decisions until carefully educated to do so. Because children with attention problems are vulnerable to distraction, irrelevant stimuli should be reduced so that these children can focus on relevant stimuli. For instance, what the teacher wants the child to attend to is increased in intensity (e.g., through the use of bright colors). On the other hand, *stimulus reduction* can be achieved by carpeting, enclosed bookcases, limited use of colorful bulletin boards, opaque windows, and/or soundproofed walls and ceilings.

Behavior Modification. Behavior modification has been a popular way of controlling inattentive behavior. The use of reinforcement (e.g., verbal praise, extra time on the computer) to increase attentive behaviors and punishment (e.g., reduced time for recess) to reduce them can have powerful effects on behavior. Joining special education teachers, regular education teachers increasingly use behavior modification in ordinary classrooms in recent years.

Cognitive Training. Cognitive training is also considered to be a way of getting students with attention deficit hyperactivity disorder to take control over their own behavior. The basis of this belief is that if students can think about their behavior more carefully, they can regulate their impulsive and inattentive behavior. Self-monitoring, procedures that require the person to keep track of his or her behavior, is an example of a cognitive training technique. In self-monitoring of attention, students monitor whether they are paying attention while engaged in academic work. The procedure is simple (Hallahan & Kauffman, 1997): The teacher places a tape recorder near the child. While the child is engaged in some kind of academic activity, a tape containing tones is played. (The time between tones varies randomly.) Whenever he or she hears a tone, the child is to stop work and ask, "Was I paying attention?" He or she then records on a separate score sheet a "yes" or "no," depending on his or her own assessment of attention behavior.

Medication. For years, physicians have been prescribing medication for children with attention deficit hyperactivity disorder. Although antidepressants are sometimes used, psycho-stimulants, such as Ritalin, are most common.

Teachers and school personnel are obligated to provide the "best and most appropriate" education for children. However, there are some basic principles that "excellent" teachers should apply in the education of children with ADHD. The following is a list which describes these general responsibilities of teachers:

1. Designing a classroom environment in which the child can learn.
2. Providing instruction which is interactive and enjoyable.
3. Selecting classroom materials which are of high interest for all children.
4. Designing and posting classroom expectations, rules, consequences, and rewards.
5. Developing a behavior management system which is accepting and understanding of the child's disability.
6. Testing the child's understanding of the material rather than disability. Timed test in noisy environments are inappropriate for the child with ADHD.
7. Praising the child's efforts. Concentrate on the "good" rather than criticizing the "bad."
8. Centering instruction so it meets all the children's needs rather than the needs of the one.
9. Avoiding statements which bring attention to the child's disability: "Did you take your medication today?"
10. Accepting and understanding the child's disability.
11. Providing appropriate accommodations for the child within the classroom.

Home Intervention for Children with ADHD

Parenting a child with ADHD could be compared to managing a tornado. The child with ADHD, acting on the impulse, may cause turmoil and chaos within even the most stable home. At times the parents may be in conflict over discipline and management of the child. Attempting to correct the child's behavior, parents may enter an ineffective cycle of feedback, such as the following: 1) reasoning with the child, 2) persuading the child, 3) yelling at the child, and 4) hitting the child. This cycle often leads to breakdowns in communication between child and parent. The child and the parent develop a negative relationship which is grounded in anger and punishment. The child may become oppositional and defiant against the parent and, in turn, the parent may become harsh and hateful with the child. Teachers may provide the following suggestions for parents to help manage a child with ADHD at home:

1. The 1-2-3 behavior management system (Phelan, 1992) has been found effective for children with ADHD. The purpose of the 1-2-3 behavior management system is to avoid arguing about the child's behavior and debating the punishment. It is designed to provide immediate behavioral consequences that have proven to be effective in child management. If the behavior is inappropriate, state the behavior and why it is inappropriate. If behavior continues, say to the child "that's 1"; if the behavior continues, "that's 2"; if the behavior continues, "that's 3 and take a five minute time-out". If the initial inappropriate behavior is serious (fighting), state, "that's 3 and take a five (or possibly ten) minute time-out". The time out center should be a place in the home which is removed from the traffic pattern free of distractions, such as the laundry room or bathroom (assuming that both of these rooms are child proof). A timer is set for the time-out period once the inappropriate behavior has ceased and the child is quiet and calm. After time-out is served, avoid talking about the incident.

2. Design, with the child, the rules, expectations, and consequences of behavior at home. This list should be posted in a visible place. A contract system with reward menus may assist the parents and child in defining appropriate expectations. Rewards may need to be real, substantial, and frequent in order to insure the child's compliance.

3. Provide an appropriate and consistent study area. This space should be designed to allow the child to study in an area of the house which is away from distractions, such as TV or family members.

4. Implement a daily homework time. With the child's input, parents set a homework time (for example, 4:00 p.m.–5:00 p.m.) each day for the child. During this time, a timer should be set for fifteen to thirty minutes of study, then a five-minute break. This will help the child pace his study efforts.

5. Provide assistance, when necessary, with class assignments.

    6. Assist the child in the organization of the child's materials prior to school and after school, such as helping with school bags or back packs.
    7. Support the teacher's rules and consequences for the child.
    8. Work cooperatively and positively with the school, teachers and administrators, in designing and implementing an educational and behavioral program which provides appropriate and reasonable accommodations (listed in the following School Interventions section).
    9. Reinforce the usage of age-appropriate social skills at home, such as no swearing or fighting.
  10. Provide the school, teachers and administrators, with testing or documentation concerning the child's diagnosis and treatment recommendations.
  11. Provide the school personnel with information from the child's physician concerning medication: usage, dosage, and side effects. Assure that the school has an ample amount of medication for the child.

Working with their child, the parents may foster the foundation of respect and discipline which improve the communication and reinforce appropriate behavior with the child. Consequently, the parents and the child develop a supportive relationship that will provide the basis for school success.

Use of Technology

Today, microcomputers and PCs are increasingly common in classrooms or computer labs in schools. They can assist regular and special needs students as they study, learn new information, write essays and reports, and do practice and drill in simulated situations. For students with disabilities, computers will continue to change the content and the mode of their instruction.

Many applications of computer technology benefit students with disabilities and their teachers. For students with learning disabilities, the applications of *computer-assisted instruction* (CAI), word processing, some new innovations in videodisc instruction, and simulation play an increasingly important role.

Computer-Assisted Instruction

Breakthroughs and improvements in both hardware and software are occurring almost daily in the computer field. For students with learning disabilities, advances in software are most important and far reaching. For example, the effectiveness of CAI to supplement or replace traditional instruction and of *computer-enhanced instruction* (CEI) for drill and practice depends on the quality of the software available and selected (Lewis, 1993).

Word Processing

The writing process is difficult for students with learning disabilities because this complex task requires the application of many different skills and cognitive abilities. Students need to select their topic, generate and organize the content of their paper, revise it, proofread and edit it, and produce a final copy (MacArthur & Schwartz, 1991). However, the combination of special writing instruction and the use of a computer with a good word processing program improves both the quality and quantity of these students' writing.

The computer system supports the writing process naturally. It is physically less tiring for some; the print on a computer screen is easier to see and read than the print on paper for some; the results of the word-processing program can also be exceptionally attractive to others. Most word processing software programs have spelling-check and grammar-check functions, which are especially helpful for students with learning disabilities. A number of assistive technology software publishers may provide *word-predict* and *"write-out-loud"* programs which simplify writing tasks for these students. In addition, the computer can facilitate collaboration, making it easier for two or more students to work together and merge their components of a writing task.

Simulation

Computer software programs can be arranged to create hypothetical situations such as grocery shopping, vocational tasks, and electronic table games for students' simulation experiences. Through these experiences, children with learning disabilities get to do decision-making, problem-solving, and practice and drill assignments. Once they are skilled in responding to the simulation programs, they may become competent and efficient in real-life activities.

Table 5.2   An Example of a Teaching Technique

The Demonstration Plus Permanent Model Technique

The demonstration plus permanent model technique uses the principles of direct instruction, task analysis, and individualized instruction to help students learn how to solve complex computational arithmetic problems. Although this technique works best with individuals, it has proven effective with small groups of children who need to learn exactly the same type of problem at the same time. While this individualized instruction requires some teacher time, experience indicates that no more than two minutes of a teacher's or instructional assistant's time is required each day during the instructional phase. Let us look at an example of how this method is applied in the classroom.

Brad is 12 years old, has a severe learning disability, and has great difficulties learning academic subjects. Brad's IEP indicates that computational arithmetic is one of several areas that need very special attention. Brad has recently demonstrated mastery of all the subtraction facts (9–5), of two- and three-digit subtraction problems that do not require borrowing (or regrouping) (479–125), but he does not know how to solve problems that require borrowing (611–429). For several days, Mrs. Tang, Brad's teacher, has assigned him subtraction worksheets that contain 15 problems all of the same type: two-digit problems that require borrowing in the unit's column.

Mrs. Tang had assigned Brad a different version of these worksheets each day for several days. In this way, she could assess the types of errors Brad was making and be certain that she really needed to spend instructional time teaching Brad to solve this kind of subtraction problem. When it became clear that Brad did not know how to solve this type of problem and needed direction in problem solving, Mrs. Tang decided to implement the demonstration plus permanent model technique.

Using this technique, each day before Brad solves the problems on his worksheet, Mrs. Tang comes to his desk and solves the first problem on his worksheet for him. As she does so, she verbalizes the steps she is following to arrive at the correct solution. Then, she asks Brad to solve another problem on the worksheet. She asks him to tell her the steps he follows to solve the problem. On the first day, he cannot correctly solve the problem, and Mrs. Tang re-demonstrates the correct process to use on another problem. Each day of the instructional phase, she reminds Brad that if he forgets how to compute these problems, he is to look at the problems on his worksheet that have just solved.

Before leaving to work with another student, Mrs. Tang tells Brad to do the best he can, not to make careless errors, to use her answer key to correct his worksheet when he is done, and to calculate a correct percentage score for this part of the day's arithmetic assignment. This instructional phase lasts five days; it concludes after Brad receives three consecutive correct percentage scores above 90 percent.

For the next three school days, Mrs. Tang assigns Brad the same types of worksheets, but she does not provide any instruction before Brad solves the problems. She wants to be certain that Brad has mastered problems of this type and can calculate them accurately while working independently. She finds, however, that Brad cannot correctly answer problems where a zero appears in the minuend (70–27). This type of problem becomes the next target for instruction.

Source: Smith, D.D., & Luckasson, R. (1995). *Introduction to special education: Teaching in an age of challenge* (2nd ed.). Needham Heights, MA: Allyn & Bacon.

Summary

1. Remedial instruction of students with learning disabilities is in one of the youngest fields in special needs education. Systematic educational services for these students were practically nonexistent prior to the 1960s.

2. Today, the category of learning disabilities represents the largest single program for exceptional children in the United States.

3. At present, students with learning disabilities in Hong Kong are likely to be labeled as "children with learning difficulties (CWLD)."

4. In the U.S., two definitions of learning disabilities are most frequently adopted by the school system: the federal definition, and the definition of the National Joint Committee on Learning Disabilities (NJCLD).

5. Persons with learning disabilities are in a heterogeneous group of various disorders. They manifest significant, lifelong difficulties as an obvious attempt to eliminate the connotation of a mild problem.

6. A variety of visual-perceptual and psycholinguistic theories and approaches to intervene in children's learning disabilities were developed in the 1960s, which led to the heated debate on the validity of these theories and approaches. More recent remedial strategies of the 1980s and 1990s include the information-processing theory, metacognition, and the self-management techniques.

7. Learning disabilities may possibly be caused by neurological, maturational, genetic, and environmental factors.

8. By an exclusive definition, learning disabilities are not caused by sensory impairments, mental retardation, and racial/cultural and social-economic disadvantages.

9. Children with learning disabilities may have specific characteristics of hyperactivity; difficulties in perceptual, discriminative, cognitive (i.e., attention) and academic performance; and special social/emotional patterns.

10. Instructional approaches include learning-to-learn strategies (e.g., cognitive training, self-monitoring, self-instruction), and the strategies for academic subjects (e.g., mnemonics for all subjects, reading comprehension, scaffolding, directive instruction), and creative drama.

11. General characteristics of children with ADD or ADHD are difficulties with sustained attention, impulsivity, and hyperactivity. Education for these children includes behavior modification, cognitive training, medication, and home intervention.

12. Technology for students with learning disabilities include computer-assisted instruction (CAI), word processing, and simulation.

ACTIVITIES

1. Compare and contrast the components of two definitions of learning disabilities: the one used by the federal government of the United States and the one developed by the National Joint Committee on Learning Disabilities. (Consider the following components: perceptual-processing deficits, information-processing deficits, exclusion clause, academic discrepancies, social skills deficits, philosophical orientation, and reference to age.)
2. Discuss reasons for the government not to recognize learning disabilities as a legitimate category of disability that requires proper assessment and appropriate educational intervention. Then discuss in small groups what can be done to lobby for changes to improve the education of children with learning disabilities.
3. Interview teachers of resource classes or skills opportunity schools who are likely to have students with learning disabilities to determine the types of learning problems they see most frequently and the strategies they use to teach these students. List and rank-order the types of academic and social problems. Compare and contrast your individual lists with your classmates and compile results. Discuss the adequacy of educational intervention for these children in Hong Kong and make recommendations. Write a short paper of five pages on this topic.
4. Do library and online research on attention deficit hyperactivity disorder. After reviewing the literature, lead class discussion on specific issues pertaining to these students. Should this group of students be served within the special education category of behavioral disorders and emotional disturbance? Should they be served within the learning disabilities category? Is ADHD a disability? Should it be considered a separate special education category? What are the pros and cons of serving these students in special education? What role should mainstream education play in the education of these children? What accommodations do they require to succeed in mainstream schools?
5. Each learner of the course selects a country and conducts a study on the prevalence rate of students with learning disabilities worldwide,

why they might be identified as having learning disabilities, and educational interventions available to them. Write a short paper based on the findings and compare your findings with others'.

6. Interview members of local advocacy and parent organizations and ask them how they view the current services and resources for children with learning disabilities and their recommendations on how the situation can be improved.

7. Review journal articles about the latest technology and how it is being used with this population of learners. Share the information with the class or write a short paper.

RESOURCES

Resources in Hong Kong

The Boys and Girls' Club Association of Hong Kong
Tel: 852-2527-9121   Fax: 852-2865-4332
3 Lockhart Road, Wanchai, Hong Kong
Web address: http://www.bgcahk.org/

Dyslexia Association
Third Floor, 8 Crown Terrace, Pokfulam, Hong Kong
Fax: 852-2872 5489
Web address: http://home.netvigator.com/~dhtallon/

Focus on Children's Understanding in School [F.O.C.U.S.]
Tel: 852-2817-8773   Fax: 852-2855-0254

Hong Kong Junior Chamber
60 Bonham Strand East, 1/F, Sheung Wan, Hong Kong.
Web address: http://ajc.org.hk/

International Dyslexia Association, Specific Learning Disabilities
Website of Hong Kong
Web address: http://sld2000.com/index.html

Pang's Music Therapy Center
Web address: http://www.musictherapy.com.hk/Home/Eng.%20AIT.htm
1403 Loon Kee Building, 275 Des Voeux Road Central
Sheung Wan, Hong Kong
Tel: 852-2815-0688

Resources in Singapore

Dyslexia Association of Singapore
Block C Unit C2 Kallang Singapore 397994
Tel.: 475 9535   Fax: 476 2957

Resources in Taiwan

中華民國過動兒協會
台北市建國南路二段151巷30號3樓
Tel.: 886-02-8663-7393   Fax: 886-02-709-0062
Web address: http://www.taconet.com.tw/iceterry/

中華民國學習障礙協會
Web address: http://www.dale.nhctc.edu.tw/

International Resources

The British Dyslexia Association
98 London Rd, READING RG1 5AU
Tel.: Helpline 44-0118-966-8271 Administration 44-0118-966-2677
Fax: 44-0118-935-1927
E-mail(Helpline): info@dyslexiahelp-bda.demon.co.uk
E-mail(Admin): admin@bda-dyslexia.demon.co.uk
Web address: http://www.bda-dyslexia.org.uk/

The Frostig Center
971 N. Altadena Drive, Pasadena, CA U.S.A.
Tel.: 1-626-791-1255   Fax: 1-626-798-1801
Web address: http://www.frostig.org

International Dyslexia Association
8600 LaSalle Road, Chester Building, Suite 382
Baltimore, MD 21286-2044 USA
Web address: http://www.interdys.org/

The Self-determination Synthesis Project (SDSP)
9201 University City Blvd., Charlotte, North Carolina 28223-0001
U.S.A.
Tel.: 1-704-547-3736   Fax: 1-704-547-2916
Web address: http://www.uncc.edu/sdsp

REFERENCES

Baechle, C.L., & Lian, M-G.J. (1990). The effects of direct feedback and practice on metaphor performance in children with learning disabilities. *Journal of Learning Disabilities, 23*(7), 451–455.

Bender, W.N. (1995). *Learning disabilities: Characteristics, identification, and teaching strategies* (2nd ed.). Boston: Allyn & Bacon.

Bender, W.N., & Smith, J.K. (1990). Classroom behavior of children and adolescents with learning disabilities: A meta-analysis. *Journal of Learning Disabilities, 23*, 298–305.

Borkwowski, J.G. (1992). Metacognitive theory: A framework for teaching literacy, writing, and math skills. *Journal of Learning Disabilities, 25*(4), 253–257.

Davey, B. (1983). Think-Aloud — Modeling the cognitive processes of reading comprehension. *Journal of Reading, 27*, 44–47.

de la Cruz, R., Lian, M-G.J., & Morreau, L.E. (1998). The effects of creative drama on social and oral language skills of children with learning disabilities. *Youth Theatre Journal, 12*, 89–95.

Drew, C.J., Hardman, M.L., & Logan, D.R. (1996). *Mental retardation: A life cycle approach* (6th ed.). Columbus, OH: Merrill.

Ellis, E. S., & Lenz, B. L. (1987). A component analysis of effective learning strategies for LD students. *Learning Disabilities Focus, 2*, 94–107.

Faraone, S.V., Biederman, J., Lehmman, B.K., & Keenan, K. (1993). Evidence for the independent familial transmission of attention deficit hyperactivity disorder and learning disabilities: Results from a family genetic study. *American Journal of Psychiatry, 150*, 891–895.

Fuchs, L.S., Fuchs, D., & Bishop, N. (1992). Instructional adaptation for students at risk. *Journal of Educational Research, 86*(2), 70–84.

Hallahan, D.P., & Kauffman, J.M. (1997). *Exceptional learners: Introduction to special education* (7th ed.). Needham Heights, MA: Allyn and Bacon.

Hammill, D.D., & Larsen, S.C. (1974). *The Effectiveness of psycholinguistic training on exceptional children, 41*(1), 5–14.

Illinois State Board of Education. (1997). *Title 23 Illinois Administrative Code 226*, Springfield, IL: ISBE.

Jones, B. F., Palincsar, A., Ogle, D. S., & Carr, E. G. (Eds.). (1987). *Strategic teaching and learning: Cognitive instruction in the content areas.* Alexandria, VA: Association for Supervision and Curriculum Development.

Kraker, M.J. (1993). Learning to write: Children's use of notation. *Reading Research and Instruction, 32*(2), 55–75.

Leviton, A., Bellinger, D., & Allred, E. (1993). The Boston teacher questionnaire: III. A reassessment. *Journal of Child Neurology, 8*, 64–72.

Lewis, R. B. (1993). *Special education technology: Classroom applications.* Pacific Grove, CA: Brooks/Cole.

MacArthur, C.A., & Schwartz, S.S. (1991). An integrated approach to writing instruction: The computers and writing instruction. *LD Forum, 16*, 35–41.

Meichenbaum, D.H. (1975, June). *Cognitive factors as determinants of learning disabilities: A cognitive-functional approach.* Paper presented at the NATO Conference on The Neuropsychology of Learning Disorders: Theoretical Approaches, Korsor, Denmark.

Mercer, C.D. (1991). *Students with learning disabilities* (4th ed.). Columbus, OH: Merrill.

Pearl, R., & Bryan, T. (1992). Students' expectations about peer pressure to engage in misconduct. *Journal of Learning Disabilities, 25*, 582–585, 597.

Robinson, S.M., & Deshler, D.D. (1988). Learning disabled. In E.L. Meyen, & T. M. Skrtic (Eds), *Exceptional children and youth: An introduction* (3rd) (pp. 109–138. Denver, CO: Love Publishing Co.

Smith, C.R. (1994). *Learning disabilities: The interaction of learner, task, and setting* (3rd ed.). Boston: Allyn & Bacon.

Smith, D.D., & Luckasson, R. (1995). *Introduction to special education: Teaching in an age of challenge* (2nd ed.). Needham Heights, MA: Allyn & Bacon.

Swanson, H.L. (1993). Working memory in learning disability subgroups. *Journal of Experimental Child Psychology, 56*, 87–114.

Test, D.W., Karvonen, M., Wood, W.M., Browder, D., & Algozzine, B. (2000). Choosing a self-determination curriculum: Plan for the future. *Teaching Exceptional Children, 33*(2), 48–53.

Wisconsin Department of Public Instruction (1989). *Strategic reading in the content areas*. Madison, WI: Author.

Yanok, J. (1993). College students with learning disabilities enrolled in developmental education programs. *College Student Journal, 27*(2), 166–174.

Zentall, S.S., & Ferkis, M.A. (1993). Mathematical problem solving for youth with ADHD, with and without learning disabilities. *Learning Disability Quarterly, 16*, 6–18.

6

Emotional and Behavior Disorders

ADVANCED THINKING

Answer the following questions as you read:

1. How is "emotional and behavior disorders" defined?
2. What are the controversies surrounding the definition of emotional and behavior disorders?
3. Describe how the field of emotional and behavior disorders was developed.
4. What are possible causes of emotional and behavior disorders and how some of these causes can be prevented?
5. What are common characteristics of individuals with emotional and behavior disorders?
6. Compare and contrast different conceptual models in treating children who have emotional or behavior disorders.
7. What are general recommendations for teachers to efficiently and successfully working with students who have emotional or behavior disorders.

KEY TERMS AND PHRASES

academic performance
adaptive skill
behavior disorder
behavioral approach
behavioral characteristics
biogenic approach
biological cause
classification

conceptual models
curriculum
ecological approach
emotional disorder
environment factor
externalizing behavior problems
family factor
history

humanistic education   psychoanalytical approach
intelligence   psychoeducational approach
learning characteristics   punishment
low-incidence behavior disorders   social-cognitive approach
maintaining discipline   social skills
maladjusted   teaching strategy
prevention

INTRODUCTION

Everyone in a society is expected to conform to certain standards of behavior. Norms of behavior change as children grow and move through the various stages of their lives. Certain behaviors, such as communicating hunger through crying, may be appropriate for a certain age (i.e., infancy) but not for all (e.g., adolescence). A society provides norms of behavior for different stages of development and for specific environments. For instance, children are expected to be generally quiet, orderly, cooperative, and attentive to learning in school. Children are expected to be loving, helpful, and obedient to their parents at home. Children whose behavior is inconsistent with their society's expectations tend to be regarded as having problems. Some behavioral problems are expressed in distinctly behavioral ways, while others are basically emotional or psychological. Thus, the terms *behavioral disorders* and *emotional disturbance*, have come to be used interchangeably for these disabilities or frequently combined in one term: *emotional/behavioral disorders* (EBD). This is the term adopted in this chapter.

EMOTIONAL/BEHAVIORAL DISORDERS DEFINED

Though the terms adopted slightly vary from one nation to another, their references may be similar. In the United Kingdom, the term *emotional and behavioral difficulties* is widely used. In the United States, *emotional/behavioral disorders* or *emotional disturbance* and *behavioral disorders* is widely used. Because of the need to determine whether a child is eligible for special education services, various nations have official or legal definitions to avoid confusions or conflicts.

In the United States, children with difficulties whose characteristics match the concept of the terms mentioned above are classified under *serious emotional disturbance* in the Individuals with Disabilities Education Act (IDEA) of 1990, which defines the term as follows:

    i. The term means a condition exhibiting one or more of the following characteristics over a long period of time and to a marked degree that adversely affects a child's educational performance:

        A. An inability to learn that cannot be explained by intellectual, sensory, or health factors;

        B. An inability to build or maintain satisfactory interpersonal relationships with peers and teachers;

        C. Inappropriate types of behavior or feelings under normal circumstances;

        D. A general pervasive mood of unhappiness or depression; or

        E. A tendency to develop physical symptoms or fears associated with personal or school problems.

    ii. The term includes children who are schizophrenic. The term does not include children who are socially maladjusted, unless it is determined that they have a serious emotional disturbance. (34 C.F.R. 300.7 [B] [9] [1992])

This definition originally included children with autism, which became a separate category in the 1990 IDEA legislation. The IDEA definition has come under criticism by a number of professionals, especially on the exclusion of individuals described as socially maladjusted. Responding to the criticism, 17 organizations formed a coalition, the National Mental Health and Special Education Coalition. This coalition and the Council for Exceptional Children have drafted a new definition for the Congress to consider (Council for Exceptional Children, 1991; Forness & Knitzer, 1990):

> Emotional or Behavior Disorders (EBD) refers to a condition in which behavioral or emotional responses of an individual in school are so different from his/her generally accepted, age-appropriate, ethnic, or cultural norms that they adversely affect educational performance in such areas as self-care, social relationships, personal adjustment, academic progress, classroom behavior, or work adjustment ... EBD is more than a transient, expected response to stressors in the child's or youth's environment and would persist even with individualized interventions, such as feedback to the individual, consultation with parents or families, and/or modification of the educational environment ... The eligibility decision must be based on multiple sources of data about the individual's behavioral or emotional functioning. EBD must be exhibited in at least two different settings, at least one of which must be school related ... EBD can coexist with other handicapping conditions as defined elsewhere in this law [IDEA] ... This category may include children or youth with schizophrenia, affective disorders, or with other sustained

disturbances of conduct, attention, or adjustment. (Council for Exceptional Children, 1991, p. 10)

This newly proposed definition has some advantages over the federal definition: (a) it includes impairments of adaptive behavior as evidenced in emotional, social, or behavioral differences; (b) it uses normative standards of assessment from multiple sources, including consideration of cultural and/or ethnic factors; (c) it examines pre-referral intervention and other efforts to assist children prior to formally classifying them as disabled; and (d) it has the potential to include children previously labeled socially maladjusted.

The pressure to include children considered to be socially maladjusted in the federal definition of serious emotional disturbance continues to be a topic of debate. Many professionals believe that more young children with behavioral disorders will receive preventative treatment if the more inclusive definition is adopted. The rationale is to decrease the need for more intensive and expensive services later in children's lives.

As for Hong Kong, there is not a definition or a category for emotional and behavior disorders. Instead, children who exhibit similar behavioral or emotional characteristics as described in the U.S. definition may potentially be classified under "the maladjusted" and are generally placed in special schools, which used to be called schools for the maladjusted. They were subsequently renamed as schools for social development, due to the negative connotation of the term "maladjusted" and the fact that parents refused to send their children to these schools.

Classification of the characteristics of maladjusted children in Hong Kong includes four aspects: school, family, personal, and social. School-related behaviors include attention-seeking behavior, breaking school regulations, disruptive behavior, poor school attendance (truancy), and poor teacher-student relationship. Family-related behaviors include abscondence from home and poor parent-child relationship. Personal problem behaviors include emotional problems with impulsive behaviors, obsessive acts, phobic reaction, suicidal tendency/symptoms, and withdrawn and moody behaviors. As for the social aspect, acts of physical violence against people/ property, cult involvement, pseudo-triad involvement, sexual promiscuity, stealing/shoplifting, and taking soft drugs and substances.

HISTORY OF THE FIELD

Emotional and behavior disorders have long been recognized in history but the causes of these disorders have often been misinterpreted. In the past, it was believed that individuals with emotional and behavior disorders were possessed by the devil or were just lazy. People also believed that these disorders were contagious; therefore, common treatments for these individuals included imprisonment, placement in poorhouses, beatings, abandonment, and other cruel actions perceived as inhumane by today's standard.

The first institution for people with such disorders, the St. Mary of Bethlehem, was established in London in 1547. Residents in this institution were beaten, chained, and starved. In 1792, Philippe Pinel, a French psychiatrist, ordered humanitarian reform. In the 1800s, reformer efforts started in the U.S. Many states had established institutions for people with emotional and behavior disorders by 1844. Public school classes for children with behavioral disorders began to appear during the late 1800s. In 1909, William Healy founded the Juvenile Psychopathic Institute in Chicago to conduct studies of juvenile offenders (Healy & Bronner, 1926). Meanwhile, Sigmund Freud's theory of psychoanalysis began to influence the education and treatment of children with emotional and behavior disorders both in Europe and in the United States. In the twentieth century, professionals realized that children with emotional and behavior disorders needed special teachers, programs, and teaching techniques. In the 1940s and 1950s, residential treatment centers for troubled youth began to appear (Redl & Wineman, 1957). The 1960s and 1970s were the blooming period for developing educational programs for children with emotional and behavior disorders. Many new textbooks, publications, and research results about educating these children became available. Scientific work on biological causes such as genetic indicators, chemical imbalances, and brain abnormalities provided new insight into diagnosis and treatment in the 1980s and 1990s (Peschel, Peschel, Howe, & Howe, 1992).

POSSIBLE CAUSES

The precise cause(s) of emotional and behavior disorders in an individual are usually unknown because of the number of variables involved. We are seldom able to pinpoint any one variable with sureness as the cause of emotional and behavior disorders. Nevertheless, four general areas are identified as having contributed to the occurrence of emotional and behavior disorders: biology, environment or family, school, and society (see Figure 6.1).

Figure 6.1   Potential Causes of Emotional and Behavioral Disorders

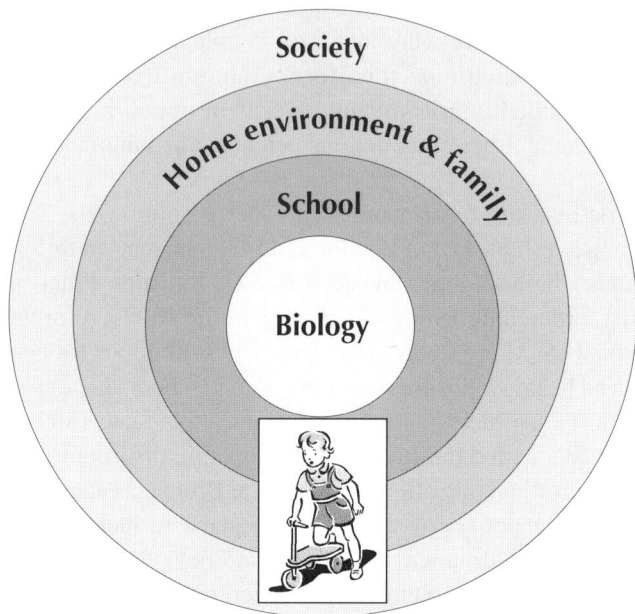

Biological Factor

Some biological causes have been found to be associated with certain emotional and behavioral disorders. Examples include children born with fetal alcohol syndrome, who exhibit problems in impulse control and interpersonal relations that result from the brain damage.

Malnutrition may also cause a behavior change in reasoning and thinking (Ashem & Janes, 1978). In addition, disorders such as schizophrenia may have a genetic foundation.

Environment or Family Factor

Families are extremely important in the development of children. Negative or unhealthy interactions in the family such as abuse and neglect, lack of supervision, interest, and concern, may result in or aggravate existing emotional and/or behavioral difficulties. On the other hand, healthy interactions such as warmth and responsiveness, consistent discipline with modeling, and rewarding desired behaviors can greatly promote positive behaviors in children (Anderson, 1981).

School Factor

Teachers have tremendous influence in their interactions with students. Positive and productive teacher-student interactions can promote student learning and appropriate school behavior as well as provide support when students are experiencing difficult times. Unhealthy academic environments with an unskilled or insensitive teacher may cause or aggravate existing emotional and behavioral disorders.

Society Factor

Societal problems, such as extreme poverty accompanied by poor nutrition, dysfunctional families, dangerous and violent neighborhood, and feelings of hopelessness, can lead to or aggravate emotional or behavioral disorders.

We must not forget examples of youngsters who have survived horrible situations and grown into healthy adults. We learn from these resilient individuals that adverse environments do not unavoidably lead to emotional or behavioral difficulties.

Prevention of Emotional and Behavioral Disorders

Some emotional and behavioral disorders can be prevented by eliminating the major causes or correcting the symptoms. For example, educating pregnant women not to drink to prevent the behavioral effects of fetal alcohol syndrome. In the classroom, teachers may use behavior management techniques to prevent problem behaviors from developing into serious problems. As a society, general strategies to prevent emotional and behavioral disorders include the following:

1. Providing individual and family therapy,
2. Teaching the family new ways of interaction,
3. Promoting and providing character training,
4. Moral education,
5. Promoting health of infants and children, and
6. Providing medical interventions.

CHARACTERISTICS

Emotional and behavioral disorders do not only affect a student's functioning in emotions and behaviors, but they also affect the student's academic performance and social interactions with peers and teachers. We will take a look at these students' learning and behavioral characteristics.

Learning Characteristics

Intelligence

Early studies (e.g., Morse, Cutler, & Fink, 1964) found that the majority of students with emotional and behavioral disorders exhibited above-average intelligence. More recent studies (e.g., Rubin & Balow, 1978; Coleman, 1986) have revealed that these children have a lower average IQ score than children without emotional and behavioral disorders. For children with some type of psychosis, research revealed that their IQ is in the retarded range of functioning. As Kauffman (1996) indicated, "The IQs of disturbed children appear to be the best single predictor of academic and future social achievement" (p. 245).

Lower Academic Performance

Students with emotional or behavioral disorders commonly have low academic performance for their age (Kauffman, 1996). Some studies (Gottlieb, Alter, & Gottlieb, 1991) show that 74% of youth classified with these disorders have academic difficulties.

Deficits in Social and Adaptive Skills

Students with emotional or behavioral disorders typically have deficits in social skills which adversely affect their ability to cooperate with teachers, function in classrooms, and get along with other students (Williams et al., 1989).

Behavioral Characteristics

There are three general types of behavioral disorders: externalizing behavior problems, internalizing behavior problems, and low-incidence disorders.

Externalizing Behavior Problems

Table 6.1 lists several examples of externalizing behavior problems. We will discuss three general categories of problems: hyperactivity, aggression, and delinquency.

Like children with learning disabilities, one of the most common complaints about children referred for evaluations as having emotional and behavioral disorders is hyperactivity. It is difficult to define hyperactivity because both the nature and the type of the activity must be considered. Ross and Ross (1982) defined hyperactivity as "a class of heterogeneous behavioral disorders in which a high level of activity is exhibited at inappropriate times and cannot be inhibited upon command" (p. 14). Basically, a working definition for hyperactivity is that a child engages in too many activities that are troublesome.

Many children with behavioral disorders have aggressive acts toward objects, self, or others. Educators and professionals have more success in teaching children healthy ways of dealing with frustration by recognizing, accepting, and tolerating those feelings of frustration as well as building coping resources.

Delinquency, rather than the medical or educational system, is defined by the criminal justice system (Berdine & Blackhurst, 1985). When juveniles commit illegal acts such as theft, they become delinquent. While more children with emotional or behavioral disorders seem to be in trouble with the law, not all of them are delinquent.

Internalizing Behavioral Problems

There are several types of internalized behavioral problems: depression, anorexia and bulimia, elective mutism, fears and phobias, and withdrawal. Our discussion will focus on the most common types found among school children: depression and anxiety/withdrawal.

It is difficult to recognize depression in children. Components of depression, such as guilt, feelings of rejection, lethargy, and low self-esteem, are often overlooked or may be mistaken as a completely different problem. Some children may also have anxiety disorders that are unnoticed. Anxiety disorders may result from intense anxiety on separation from family and friends or familiar environment. Symptoms may include excessive shrinking from contact with strangers, unfocused, excessive worry and fear, and a very low level of positive interactions with their peers. Many children with anxiety disorders remain untreated because of the difficulty in recognizing its existence.

Low-incidence Behavioral Disorders

There are two familiar, serious but infrequent behavioral disorders: schizophrenia and autism. In the United States, one percent of the general population has been diagnosed with schizophrenia but it is extremely rare among children. As a form of psychosis, schizophrenia includes behaviors such as bizarre delusions (e.g., believing one's thoughts are controlled by the police), hallucinations (e.g., voices telling the child what to do or think), and incoherence. Children with schizophrenia have serious difficulty in schoolwork and often times have to live in hospitals or special educational settings during part of their childhood. These children also require multidisciplinary team members to provide treatment and services.

The prevalence rate of autism is about 4 in every 10,000 (Batshaw & Perret, 1986). This disorder severely affects one's thinking, communication, and behavior. Often times, these individuals seem isolated with severe difficulty in building satisfactory interpersonal relationships, abnormal language or no language, ritualistic movements, and self-injurious behaviors.

It is often difficult to identify behavioral and emotional disorders in young children unless it is a severe disability such as psychosis. School age children with internalized emotional disorders such as can also be difficult to identify. Family members and teachers must be sensitive to detect emotional or behavioral difficulties among children by the following signs:

1. Aggression toward self or others.
2. Anxiety or fearfulness.
3. Distractibility or inability to pay attention for a length of time comparable to peers.
4. Expressing thoughts of suicide.
5. Feelings of depression and unhappiness.
6. Few or no friends.
7. Hyperactive behavior.
8. Immature social skills expressed in inappropriate social interactions.
9. Impulsivity.
10. Problems with family relationships.
11. Problems with teacher-student relationships.
12. Suicidal.
13. Withdrawal into self.

EDUCATION

Conceptual Models

The treatment and education of school-age children with emotional or behavioral disorders can take many modes. The selection of approaches depends greatly on the conceptual model of treatment and education a professional uses when working with these children. Table 6.1 lists major conceptual models of treatment and education for children with emotional or behavioral disorders. These models are the most widely used in the field. Many teachers find the combination of behavioral approach and two or

Table 6.1   Conceptual Models in Treating Children with Emotional or Behavior Disorders

Behavioral approach	Is based on the work of B. F. Skinner (1953) and other behaviorists. Focuses on providing children with highly structured learning environments and teaching materials. The student's behaviors are precisely measured. Interventions are designed and implemented to increase or decrease behaviors. Progress toward goals is measured carefully and frequently.
Ecological approach	The problems of the child are seen as a result of interactions with the family, the school, and the community. The child or youth is not the sole focus of treatment. The family, school, neighborhood, and community also are changed in order to improve the interactions.
Social-cognitive approach	The child is taught the interaction between the effects of the environment and his/her behavior.
Psychoeducational approach	The psychoanalytic view is combined with principles of teaching, with treatment measured primarily in terms of learning. Meeting the individual needs of the child is emphasized, often through projects and creative arts.
Psychoanalytic approach	Is based on the work of Sigmund Freud and other psychoanalysts. Views the problems of the child as having a basis in unconscious conflicts and motivations. Long term individual psychotherapy designed to uncover and resolve these deep-seated problems is the general treatment.
Humanistic education	Love and trust in teaching and learning are emphasized. Children are encouraged to be open and free individuals. A non-authoritarian atmosphere in a non-traditional educational setting is developed.
Biogenic approach	Is based on biological theories of causation and treatment. Physiological interventions such as diet, medications, and biofeedback are used.

Source: Kauffman, J.M. (1996). *Characteristics of behavioral disorders of children and youth* (4th ed.). Columbus, OH: Merrill, pp. 80–82.

three other approaches most effective for educating these children (Smith & Luckasson, 1995).

General Guidelines for School Personnel and Teachers

Children with severe emotional or behavioral difficulties can be the most challenging group of students to school personnel and teachers. In many countries, these children are educated in segregated locations, even in countries such as the United States, the breeding ground for the movements of integration and inclusion. While students with even severe/profound mental retardation or multiple disabilities are integrated into the mainstream schools, students with moderate to severe emotional or behavioral difficulties are largely kept in special schools in the United States. One main reason for this situation is that these children frequently display dangerous behaviors harmful to others and themselves.

In Hong Kong, children with pronounced emotional or behavioral difficulties or the maladjusted children are also educated in special schools. This category of children is further classified into mild, moderate, and severe types according to the nature of their problems. The special schools for this group of children provide a range of additional learning programs in the form of activities both inside and outside the school premises, involving parents and even other family members. The activities target at the promotion of personal and social development, betterment of the students' social integration, parent-child relationship, home-school cooperation, and the re-establishment of family and community support. Examples of activities include training camps, recreational and cultural visits, social skills training, parent-child programs and workshops, and community services. General guidelines for school personnel and teachers in promoting a conducive learning environment for these children are provided below.

General Recommendations for Teachers

- Communicate regularly with the student's family.
- Establish clear and appropriate rules for discipline and practice them with the class.
- Reinforce students when they follow a rule.
- Consequences for abiding and abiding by the rules must be fair and realistic.
- Cultivate cooperation and friendship by teaching students how to work in small groups.

- Teach students how to negotiate and mediate conflict.
- Keep records on behavior changes during changes in medication.

Recommendations Specifically for Primary School Personnel

- Use same-age or cross-age peers to provide tutoring, coaching, and other kinds of assistance in developing the academic and social skills of children with behavior disorders.
- Adopt a school wide management plan that reinforces individual and group accomplishments.
- Collaboratively do problem solving when dealing with chronic and difficult behaviors.
- Help all children in the school develop an understanding of how they should respond to students with behavior problems.
- Work at creating a positive and caring school environment.

Recommendations Specifically for Primary School Teachers

- Provide a structured classroom environment (e.g., clearly stated rules, helpful positive and negative consequences, and carefully taught classroom routines).
- Teach social skills (e.g., dealing with teasing and accepting criticism) to all of the children in collaboration with other teachers.
- Teach self-management skills (e.g., goal selection, self-monitoring, etc.) to all children with help from other teachers.
- Use cooperative learning strategies to promote the learning of all children and to develop positive relationships among students.

Recommendations Specifically for Secondary School Personnel

- Collaboratively create a positive and supportive school climate.
- Help students understand their own roles and responsibilities toward their peers with behavioral disorders.
- Provide social skills training, job coaching, and academic tutoring through peers.
- Adopt school wide procedures for dealing quickly and efficiently with particularly difficult behavior.

Recommendations Specifically for Secondary School Teachers

- Promote positive relationships within the classroom by cooperative learning teams and group-oriented assignments.
- Gain all students' support in creating standards for conduct as well as consequences for positive and negative behaviors.

- Develop positive relationships with students with behavioral disorders by greeting him/her regularly, informally talking with him/her, and becoming aware of his/her interests or preferences.
- Solicit help from other teachers to have unified and consistent reinforcement of appropriate behaviors.

Teaching Social Skills

A teacher may improve the social skills of students through the use of several strategies: (1) implement a commercially available social skills curriculum such as the Walker Social Skills Curriculum, called the ACCEPTS Program (Walker et al., 1988); (2) develop and implement an individualized program of teaching and reinforcement for a student; (3) set up cooperative learning situations such as peer tutoring; and (4) post rule statements related to specific skills (Fad, 1990). In addition to helping the child function in the immediate environment, Hollinger (1987) suggests that improving a student's social skills will improve his or her chances for later life satisfaction.

Maintaining Discipline

If schools are to be safe and predictable environments for all students and teachers, discipline must be maintained. Discipline means training to follow the rules of proper conduct. The critical aspects of maintaining discipline are (1) to make clear the expectations for proper behavior; (2) to teach the students how to achieve the expected behavior; and (3) to implement a system of responses to violations of the rules (Smith & Rivera, 1993). Discipline does not necessarily mean punishment.

Many students with behavioral disorders and emotional disturbance need special help to maintain self-discipline. For example, the teacher may have to spend much more time discussing the school and classroom rules so that students have a clear idea of the behaviors required. The teacher may also need to explicitly teach the proper behaviors and personal strategies for the individual to use to control the behaviors. The teacher may also have to help the student understand the consequences of any actions that violate the rules.

Some of the requirements students must meet in academic environments are obvious, such as keeping quiet when the teacher is talking or joining the other students in the line to leave for recess. But some demands are more subtle. For example, the student is expected to make eye contact with the teacher when speaking in the hallway, take turns in group games, or sit with good posture when school administrators visit the classroom. Violations of setting-related demands such as these can lead to students' being perceived as lacking in discipline. Problems can be prevented, however, by specifically teaching the child to meet the demands of the environment. An example of using a strategy to improve students' self-discipline is provided in Table 6.2.

General Guidelines for Humane and Effective Use of Punishment

- Use only after positive correction methods have failed and when allowing the behavior to continue will result in more serious negative consequences than the proposed level of punishment.
- Institute only in the context of ongoing classroom management and instructional programs that emphasize positive consequences for appropriate conduct and achievement.
- Punishment should be used only by people who are warm and loving toward the individual when his or her behavior is acceptable and who offer ample positive reinforcement for non-aggressive behavior.
- Administer matter-of-factly, without anger, threats, or moralizing.
- Punishment should be fair, consistent, and immediate.
- Punishment should be of reasonable intensity. Relatively minor misbehavior should mean mild punishment.
- Whenever possible, punishment should involve *response cost* (loss of privileges or rewards or withdrawal of attention) rather than aversive treatment.
- Whenever possible, punishment should be related directly to the misbehavior, enabling the youngster to make restitution and/or practice a more adaptive alternative behavior.
- Do not give positive reinforcement immediately after punishment; the child may learn to misbehave and endure the punishment to obtain reinforcement.
- Discontinue punishment if it is not immediately effective.
- Written guidelines for refusing specific punishment procedures should be known to all-students, parents, teachers, and school administrators.
- All punishment procedures should be approved by school authorities.

Treatment and education modes for children with emotional or behavioral disorders can vary greatly, depending on the individual child's

Table 6.2   An Example of a Teaching Strategy

Timer Game

Behavior games, created by Barrish, Saunders, and Wolf in 1969, have gained in popularity throughout the years. There are many variations. Behavior games allow teachers to deal with negative behavior in a positive way that emphasizes peer cooperation and friendship. Because the other team members want to win, they assist their teammates to control their own behavior. Let us look at an example of a behavior game, the timer game, in action.

Mr. Choi's Form 2 world history period, scheduled right after lunch, has always been a bit rowdy. The boys have a difficult time settling down to work. Mr. Choi is beginning a unit on Central America and wants their full attention for lectures and their work in small groups.

Mr. Choi arranges the class in six groups at six tables so that they can have small-group discussions, sharing maps and other information. This world history class comprises 40 students. Two are students with special needs, and one of them, Paul, has a great deal of difficulty controlling his behavior. Sitting still for over 7 minutes, listening when he is supposed to, and generally following directions are all difficult for Paul. The other child with special needs does not present behavior problems. They do, however, need some additional assistance with the academic tasks. Mr. Choi pairs each of these students with a classmate who is doing well in the class. These students help the others take notes, read maps and tables, and understand the homework assignments.

Paul's tutor-friend has an extra assignment. He is to help Paul with the academic work, but he is also to assist Paul's efforts to control his behavior. He is to gently remind Paul about what is necessary in order to accomplish the work throughout class time.

Although these arrangements work well, the class still has problems changing from one activity to another. They are too noisy, and many do not pay attention while the teacher presents important information. They are not all working on their assignments during group time.

Mr. Choi decides to try a timer game to improve class behavior. He explains the rules of the game to the students. Whenever the kitchen timer he has on his desk rings, each group working quietly on a task receives a point on the blackboard. Every member of the group has to be meeting this behavioral standard if the group is to receive a point. The trick is that no one knows when the bell will ring. Sometimes, it is almost 5 minutes between rings; other times, only a few seconds. Mr. Choi does arrange it so that the bell rings, on the average, about every 5 minutes. At the end of the period, all teams with over six points win for the day. (If Mr. Choi feels that Paul needs some practice by himself before joining a team, he can make Paul a team of one, with a goal of earning fewer points in order to qualify as winning for the day.)

Mr. Choi is pleased with the results of the timer game. He does not have to constantly remind the class about the behavior he expects or reprimand students who are not following the rules. The outcome is that the class enjoys the game and behaves according to the teacher's expectations.

needs. Rewards, consequences, or punishment must be effectively used to increase appropriate behaviors and to decrease inappropriate behaviors. Sometimes a number of professionals may be necessary to provide services that can effectively help the child. Intervention plans must be thorough and inclusive of all relevant parties, particularly family members.

SUMMARY

1. Children with emotional and behavioral disabilities may demonstrate behaviors or specific characteristics which are persistently different from their age-appropriate norms according to their social, ethnic, and cultural standards. In Hong Kong, these children may be placed in specific schools for the maladjusted.

2. Before the 1790s, persons with emotional/behavioral disabilities were likely to be locked up, neglected or abandoned, mistreated, or institutionalized. There were efforts for humanitarian reform in the late 1700s and early 1800s and, as a result, classes for students with emotional and behavior disorders started to appear in public schools. The years in the 1900s had various modern theories and intervention approaches regarding emotional and behavior disorders. The educational models, along with biomedical and technological advancement in the past 40 years, created a variety of effective instructional and therapeutic strategies in the field of emotional and behavior disorders.

3. Although the precise causes of emotional and behavior disorders tend to be unidentified, the disabilities emotional and behavior disorders conditions may be related to the biological, environment or family, school, and society factors, prevention of some of the emotional and behavior disorders disabilities may be achieved by the removal of these factors.

4. Characteristics of children with emotional and behavior disorders may include: (a) learning characteristics (i.e., above- or below-average intelligence, lower academic performance, and deficits in social and adaptive skills; and (b) behavioral characteristics (i.e., externalizing or internalizing behavioral problems and low-incidence behavioral disorders).

5. Education of students with emotional and behavior disorders may be implemented using one or more of the behavioral, ecological, social cognitive, psychoeducational, psychoanalytic, humanistic, and biogenetic approaches.

6.   Instructional strategies may be different for students with emotional
      and behavior disorders at specific age and grade levels. General
      recommendations may include enhancement of communication, setting
      and following rules, encouraging cooperation and friendship, teaching
      problem-solving, conflict-resolution, and self-management skills, using
      peer support and cooperative learning strategies, creating a positive
      and caring learning environment, and utilizing school, family, and
      community resources.

ACTIVITIES

1.   Form small groups and discuss if students who are delinquents should
      receive special education services? Report your collective views to the
      class.
      {This issue remains difficult for many special educators. But the way
      in which the issue is resolved has grave consequences for children and
      youth with serious problems and their families and communities. What
      is the issue? Does every youngster with behavior problems have a
      disability? Are some delinquents simply naughty or bad and, therefore,
      the responsibility of regular education and their families? What about
      those who present difficult management problems for schools and their
      families? Should students be labeled as disordered or disturbed because
      schools have difficulty with them? Perhaps special education has
      nothing special to offer these students, and perhaps special education
      cannot be expected to succeed with them. Possibly, including these
      students broadens the role of special education too much. Special
      education is already serving over 9 percent of the school-age population.
      Should more children be included in special education? If so, how many
      more? What criteria should be used for these additional children? What
      about incarcerated youth and delinquents? Should they receive special
      education services? Certainly, some incarcerated children have
      behavioral disorders and emotional disturbance, but is the number high
      or low? Many children and youth in jails and juvenile correctional
      institutions are currently classified as socially maladjusted and therefore
      ineligible for special education services in those facilities in the US.
      Critics argue that these youngsters have a disability and are being
      unfairly denied special education services for which they are eligible.}
2.   Interview teachers of schools for social development who are likely to
      work with students with behavioral or emotional disorders to find out

behavioral and emotional characteristics of those children, the methods they use to help these children academically and behaviorally, the difficulties they encounter, and their recommendations of how situations can be improved. Write a short report and share data with your classmates to generate a profile of the educational intervention for children with emotional or behavioral disorders in Hong Kong.

3. Locate and interview parents with the help of schools for social development or the Education Department. Explore their experiences of having a child with emotional or behavioral disorders: (a) how the child's difficulty affects the family life, (b) how they work with the child at home, (c) what help they receive from the school, social service from government and non-governmental agencies, and (d) what help they think they need to further improve the situation. Write a short report and share data with your classmates to generate a profile of the experiences of family members of children with emotional or behavioral disorders in Hong Kong.

4. Many teachers use various behavioral games as part of their behavior management program. Some games use a kitchen timer. Some games divide the class into teams and have children compete against each other; others use the whole class as one team. The basic idea of behavior games is to motivate a group of students through an activity to behave better instructional settings. When teams are used, if any member of a team violates a classroom rule (e.g., being out of the seat, speaking out of turn, etc.), that team gets a mark. At the end of the period, the team with the fewest marks wins the game, which may or may not result in the team's earning a prize or special privilege. If all the teams have too many marks (possibly more than two), no team wins that day. Divide into groups of 4–5. Create a lesson plan for a behavior game it devises. When all groups have completed their plans, share game ideas with the class.

5. To learn more about the importance of pinpointing target behaviors for instructional purposes and collecting baseline data, identify a child (from any source such as your own students, students you encounter in your practicum, a child you know, or a child in your neighborhood) and a behavior of concern. Select an appropriate measurement system (e.g., frequency, duration, rate, event recording), one that matches the behavior of concern, and collect baseline data for a week. In small groups of 3–4, share your results and brainstorm interventions for the behavior.

6. Locate schools and ask for permission to observe classrooms for students with emotional or behavioral disorders. Then visit primary and secondary school classrooms for students without those disorders. Compare and contrast student characteristics, instructional methodology, technology, therapeutic approaches, professionals involved in the educational program, family services, and curriculum. Write a short report of your findings.

RESOURCES

Resources in Hong Kong

Autism-Hongkong (C) 2000
Web address: http://www.autism-hongkong.com

The Hong Kong Society of Child Neurology & Developmental Paediatrics
Web address: www.fmshk.com.hk/hksndp
Duke of Windsor Social Service Building
15 Hennessy Road, Hong Kong

Mental Health Association of Hong Kong
Web Address: http://www.mhahk.org.hk/
Jockey Club Building
2 Kung Lok Road, Kwun Tong, Kowloon., Hong Kong

Society for the Welfare of Autistic Persons
Web address: http://www.swap.org.hk/
Room 210-214, Block 19, Shek Kip Mei Estate, Kowloon, Hong Kong
Tel: 852-2788-3326   Fax: 852-2778-1414

Resources in Taiwan

中華民國自閉症基金會
台北市士林區111中山北路五段841號4樓之2
Tel: 886-02-2755-7589   Fax: 886-02-2755-7631
Web address: http://www.fact.org.tw

中華民國過動兒協會
台北市建國南路二段151巷30號3樓
Tel.: 886-02-8663-7393   Fax: 886-02-709-0062
Web address: http://www.taconet.com.tw/iceterry/

格瑞思心理工作室
台北市信義路四段265巷21弄26號1樓
Tel.: 886-02-2325-4648 or 2703-8492   Fax: 886-02-2701-5141
E-mail: grace@gracecc.com.tw
Web address: http://www.gracecc.com.tw/index.htm

International Resources

American Academy of Child and Adolescent Psychiatry
Web address: http://www.aacap.org
3615 Wisconsin Ave., N.W.
Washington, D.C. 20016-3007   U.S.A.
Tel.: 1-202-966-7300   Fax: 1-202-966-2891

Autism National Committee (ANC)
Web address: http://www.autcom.org

Checkmate Plus
Web address: http://www.checkmateplus.com/
P.O. Box 696, Department D
Stone Brook, NY 11790-0696 U.S.A.
Tel.: 1-800-779-4292   Fax: 1-631-360-3432

Council for Children with Behavioral Disorders (CCBD)
Web address: http://www.ccbd.net

Council for Exceptional Children (CEC)
Web address: http://www.cec.sped.org/

The Federation of Families for Children's Mental Health
Web address: http://www.ffcmh.org

Hidden Lake Academy
Web address: http://www.hiddenlakeacademy.com
Dahlonega, GA 30533 U.S.A.
Tel.: 1-800-394-0640   Fax: 1-706-864-9109

Oregon Social Learning Center (OSLC)
Web address: http://www.oslc.org

Research and Training Center on Family Support
and Children's Mental Health
Portland State University
Web address: http://www.rtc.pdx.edu
P.O. Box 751, Portland, OR 97207 U.S.A.

REFERENCES

Anderson, C.W. (1981). Parent-child relationships: A context for reciprocal developmental influence. *Counseling Psychologist, 4*, 35–44.

Ashem, B., & Janes, M.D. (1978). Deleterious effects of chronic undernutrition on cognitive abilities. *Journal of Child Psychology, 19*, 23–31.

Batshaw, M.L., & Perret, Y.M. (1986). *Children with handicaps: A medical primer* (2nd ed.). Baltimore: Brookes.

Berdine, W.H., & Blackhurst, A.E. (Eds.). (1985). *An introduction to special education*. Boston: Little, Brown.

Board of Education (1996). *Report of the Sub-committee on Special Education*. Hong Kong: The Government Printer.

Coleman, M.C. (1986). *Behavior disorders: Theory and practice*. Englewood Cliffs, NJ: Prentice Hall.

Council for Exceptional Children (1991). *Report of the CEC advocacy and governmental relations committee regarding the new proposed U.S. federal definition of serious emotional disturbance*. Reston, VA: CEC.

Fad, K.S. (1990). The fast track to success: Social-behavioral skills. *Intervention in School and Clinic, 26*, 39–43.

Forness, S.R., & Knitzer, J.K. (1990). *A new proposed definition and terminology to replace "serious emotional disturbance" in the Education of the Handicapped Act*. Alexandria, VA: National Mental Health Association.

Healy, W., & Bronner, A.F. (1926). *Delinquents and criminals: Their making and unmaking*. New York: Macmillan.

Hollinger, J.D. (1987). Social skills for behaviorally disordered children in preparation for mainstreaming: Theory, practice, and new directions. *Remedial and Special Education, 8*(4), 17–27.

Kauffman, J.M. (1996). *Characteristics of emotional and behavioral disorders of children and youth* (6th ed.). Upper Saddle River, NJ: Prentice-Hall.

Morse, W.C., Cutler, R.L., & Fink, A.H. (1964). *Public school classes for emotionally handicapped: A research analysis*. Washington, DC: Council for Exceptional Children.

Peschel, E., Peschel, R., Howe, C.W., & Howe, J.W. (Eds.). (1992). *Neurobiological disorders in children and adolescents*. San Francisco: Jossey-Bass.

Redl, F., & Wineman, D. (1957). *The aggressive child*. New York: Free Press.

Ross, D.M., & Ross, S.A. (1982). *Hyperactivity: Current issues, research, and theory* (2nd ed.). New York: Wiley.

Rubin, R.A., & Balow, B. (1978). Prevalence of teacher identified behavior problems: a longitudinal study. *Exceptional Children, 45*(2), 102–111.

Smith, D.D., & Rivera, D.M. (1993). *Effective discipline* (2nd ed.). Austin, TX: PRO-ED.

Walker, H.M., McConnell, S., Holmes, D., Todis, B., Walker, J., & Golden, N. (1988). *The Walker social skills curriculum: The ACCEPTS program*. Austin, TX: PRO-ED.

Williams, S.L., Walker, H.M., Holmes, D., Todis, B., & Fabre, T.R. (1989). Social validation of adolescent social skills by teachers and students. *Remedial and Special Education, 10*, 18–27, 37.

7

Communication Disorders

ADVANCED THINKING

Answer the following questions as you read:

1. What are the relationships between speech, language, and communication?
2. How are communication disorders defined?
3. What are the key events and efforts that contributed to the historical development of education for children with communication disorders?
4. What are the possible causes of communication disorders?
5. What are the strategies for preventing communication disorders?
6. What are the general and specific characteristics of children with communication disorders?
7. What are potential education-related arrangements and approaches for students with communication disorders?

KEY TERMS AND PHRASES

alternative/augmentative
  communication
articulation disorder
auditory discrimination
auxiliary communication
characteristics
central factor
cognitive development delay
cognitive processing phase
communication aid
communication code

communication disorder
communication symbols
communication system
decoding
emotional/behavior disorder
emotional factor
encoding
environmental factor
expressive language
fluency disorder
hearing impairments

hearing test	possible causes
history	prevention
language	receptive language
language development test	short-term memory
language sample test	speech
manual system	speech and language therapy
nonverbal condition	speech/language pathologist
nonvocal condition	speech impairment
peripheral factor	traumatic brain injury
phonological disorder	use of technology
physical health disabilities	voice disorder

INTRODUCTION

In our daily life, each individual needs to communicate with others. For example, a person may need to receive information from his or her friends, parents, or teachers and to respond to them verbally or nonverbally. As Rice (1988) described:

> In our society we place a high value on oral communication. We are surrounded daily by talking — people conversing, giving lectures, engaging in one-to-one interactions, radio dialogues, and television programs, and reporting play-by-play action in athletic events. We are highly aware of the manner of their speech, how appropriate it is to the occasion, and how effective. We want our children to be fluent, clever speakers, able to express their wants and needs in a winning manner. (p. 234)

Due to a number of disabling conditions, an individual may face the challenging situations of not being able to receive and understand spoken or written messages and express personal needs and feelings through various means of communication. These challenging situations can be caused by cognitive delays, sensory disabilities, physical and multiple impairments, and/or emotional disturbance/behavior disorders.

Lack of an effective channel of communication tends to cause limited exchange of ideas, frustration, and underachievement toward personal goals. Hsu (2000) pinpointed "segregation" and "sense of helplessness" in the life of persons with special needs as a result of not being able to communicate with others. She shared a woman's description of her feeling of isolation as "long staying in a silent corner" (p. 28) of a residential institution. This woman said, "When you cannot communicate with others, they'll think of you as mentally deficient; just like what they have done to persons with physical disabilities, it's hard to change other people's perception of you" (p. 38).

Other implications caused by *communication disorders* (CD) may include underachievement in academic work and, later, in independent and productive community living. As a result, there happens to be less expectations of higher standard of individual performance in schools, at work, and in the family and community environments, and lower quality of personal life. Nevertheless, persons with communication disorders deserve the opportunity to overcome communication barriers. Just like all others, they have potential to participate fully in our community.

Communication disorders probably have the highest incidence rate among the various types of classified disabilities, impairments, and disorders. It is estimated that communication disorders (including speech, language, and hearing disorders) affect one of every 10 people in the United States.

COMMUNICATION DISORDERS DEFINED

Before we try to define communication disorders, we first need to know the major concepts and related issues of speech, language, and communication. Let us try to answer the following questions: "Can speech be used for communication?" "Are all languages speech languages?" and "Is there nonspeech or nonlanguage communication?"

Figure 7.1 displays the relationships between speech, language and communication. Speech can be defined as the vocal production of a person. The following are further descriptions and concepts of speech: (1) verbal speech can be used for language communication; and (2) nonverbal speech can also be used for communication, e.g., making sounds to express emotions like feeling happy, excited, confused, or surprised.

Language is a structured system for communication. A group of people may use a specific language system they have developed to give meaning to sounded and/or printed symbols (e.g., voice, words) or others (e.g., gestures) for enabling communication (Heward, 1999). First, language can be oral or speech language (as "sounded language"). Language can also be nonspeech language ("silent language"), such as sign language, or language through symbols like icons, logos, as well as alphabets, words, and sentences. Speech language or nonspeech language can possibly be written

Figure 7.1   The Relationships Between Speech, Language and Communication

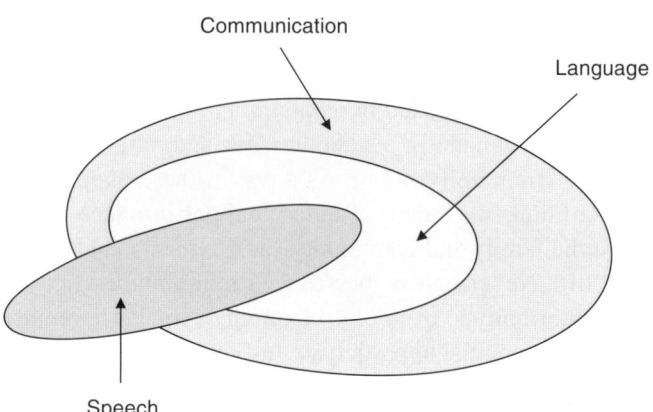

down and/or printed to become written language. In addition, a person may have "inner language." Its existence is especially critical to be recognized when he or she does not have appropriate skills to express such inner language.

Communication is for us to transmit messages from one person to another. It can be achieved by speaking, writing a note, showing body gestures, or signing. A person with special needs may be able to achieve nonverbal communication by eye contact, facial expression, hand movement, body movement, gesture/body position, pictures/objects, nonlanguage articulation, nonverbal speech, music/singing, use of pictures, and use of objects. In other words, communication can be through nonlanguage speech, such as sighing or yelling. It can also be through formal language (spoken, sign, or written). Besides, communication can be achieved without speech and language, such as gesture, facial expression, hand movement, pictures, objectives and body contact (e.g., shaking hands, a big hug, giving a "high five," etc.). We should know that most people combine multiple receptive and expressive efforts to communicate, such as to listen and to look at the speaker's facial expression, or to speak accompanied with hand movements.

Most types of communication generally include three phases: the input phase, the cognitive processing phase, and the output phase. During the first phase of communication, a person (e.g., a listener or an observer) receives a message from another person (e.g., a speaker or signer), while in phase two, the recipient of the message cognitively processes the message

— he/she may refer the message to his/her previous experience — and, then, determines the need and manner to respond to the message. Onto the third phase of communication, the message recipient becomes a message giver, by either verbal or nonverbal manner, to the original message giver or to a third person. Decoding is the cognitive ability to translate symbols into thoughts. Encoding is the cognitive ability to translate thoughts into symbols. A decoding effort is made when going from phase one to phase two, while an encoding effort is required when moving from phase two to phase three.

HISTORY OF THE FIELD

Communication disorders may have existed since the beginning of human history. Much of the currently available documentation of the incidences of speech or language impairments came from Europe and the United States. The majority of documentation is within the last century. Speech correction became available in the early 20th century. "Through the mid-1990s, the professional titles *speech teacher* and *speech correctionist* were popular, reflecting an emphasis on correcting articulation, fluency, and voice disorders" (Heward & Orlansky, 1992, p. 99).

According to Rice (1988) and Smith and Luckasson (1995), public schools in the United States employed speech clinicians to work with children who had speech problems during the 1920s, but services were limited. The military then played an important role in further development. During World War II, the military developed screening procedures to identify persons with speech and hearing difficulties and began their own clinical and research programs. The military's efforts demonstrated that speech therapy could be effective.

University programs to train speech and language pathologists increased in size and number after the war. Public school programs expanded in response to the availability of professional training. By 1935, 39 states in the U.S. provided funding and had laws permitting or mandating school districts to provide services for students with disabilities, including those with speech or language impairments.

Professionals of this field have gone through role changes over time and thus their titles have also changed from speech teachers, speech correctionists, speech therapists, speech clinicians, to speech/language pathologists. Because of the increased involvement of children with severe/profound and multiple disabilities in special needs education in the

1970s–1980s, whose communication abilities tend to be minimal, a more fundamental level of speech/language communication pathology and therapy services are needed. "Therefore, clinicians are shifting away from traditional services toward some alternative services, such as consultation with teachers and primary caregivers, in order to develop communicative activities that can be carried out repeatedly by these persons who are familiar to the child" (p. 235).

POSSIBLE CAUSES

As with several other disabilities, the nature of communication disorders can range from mild to severe levels. The disorders have different effects on adults than on children. However, there is no gender difference in that men and women are affected in similar ways. Table 7.1 shows that Nelson's (1993) four major categories of causes of communications.

Many adults acquire disorders of language as a result of stroke, head injury, dementia, or brain tumors. Some adults also failed to develop normal language because of childhood autism, hearing impairments, or other congenital or acquired disorders of brain development. For children who do not use language normally from birth, or for those who acquire the impairment in childhood, the disorder occurs in the context of a language system that is not fully developed or acquired.

Speech and language disorders can be associated with mental retardation, psychiatric disorders, and developmental disorders. In addition, when children have muscular disorders, hearing problems or developmental delays, their acquisition of speech, language and related skills are often affected (National Information Center for Children and Youth with Disabilities, 2000). The cause of many speech-language impairments,

Table 7.1 Four Categorical Factors Associated with Childhood Language Disorders

Central factors	Specific language disability; mental retardation; autism; attention-deficit hyperactivity disorder; acquired brain injury; others.
Peripheral factors	Hearing impairment; visual impairment; physical impairment.
Environmental and emotional factors	Neglect and abuse; behavioral and emotional development problems.
Mixed factors	

Source: Nelson, N.W. (1993). *Childhood language disorders in context: infancy through adolescence.* Needham Heights, MA: Allyn and Bacon.

however, is not known. Numerous experts believe that they are caused by conditions that affect brain development either before, during, or after birth. Subsequently, the individual's ability to interpret and interact with the world through speech and language is impaired.

Cognitive Developmental Delay

Children with cognitive developmental delay may also have communication disabilities. For example, children need to have object permanence or to pass Piaget's sensory-motor stage in order to develop a higher level of language skills (i.e., displacement and pragmatics). Delayed cognitive development, such as lack of short term memory (STM) and lack of understanding of signs and body gestures, may also influence a child's ability to use vocal and manual communication.

Hearing Impairments

Children with hearing impairments may use hearing aids to help receive sounded messages. However, their receptive communication may still be disadvantaged. For example, "the fewer sounds a person hears, the more difficult it is to produce intelligible speech" (Thompson & Beck, 1999, p. 3). As a result, they tend to have limited vocal communication (i.e., expressive speech language) and tend to rely on manual communication.

Traumatic Brain Injury (TBI)

Traumatic brain injury may cause specific communication disorders such as expressive or receptive aphasia. An injury in the following areas of the brain may lead to functional language/communication deficits:

1. Broca's area (speech production).
2. Wernicke's area (comprehension — perceptive).
3. Arcuate fasciculus (connecting above 2 areas).

Physical and Health Disabilities

Physical and health disabilities such as cleft palate, breathing through mouth, spastic oral area, tonic biting, jaw thrust, lip pursing/lip retraction, fluctuate arm move (i.e., athetosis) may cause vocal and manual communication difficulties. Children with these difficulties may develop adequate receptive language skills, but face the challenging situation of not being able to express their needs and ideas.

Environmental Factors

Environmental situations and events may influence a child's speech and language development. Children may be encouraged or discouraged to talk. They may be reinforced or punished to express their opinion. As a result, the appearance of teacher/parent as well as peers, or the appearance of specific social cues, may lead to specific psycho-pathological speech/ language communication patterns. For example, students who are victims of child abuse and neglect may develop withdrawal or aggressive communication behaviors.

Children who grow up in a different linguistic environment may be disadvantaged in attending mainstream language-medium schools. It is important to note that these children have a *communication difference*, not a communication disorder. As Heward & Orlansky (1992) indicated:

> Communication differences are of little concern as long as they do not impair our ability to express or receive speech and language. Social, cultural, educational, and geographic variables contribute to the communication differences all of us exhibit. When a communication difference is so pronounced, however, that it has an adverse effect on a child's achievement in school or interactions with his or her peers it may become a [disabling] communication disorder. (p. 95)

Emotional/Behavior Disorders

Children with emotional or behavior disabilities may have associated communication disorders. These children may display temper tantrum, verbal aggression, or withdrawal behaviors to respond to a teacher's commands or a peer's social invitation, or they may use similar responses to express their feelings and ideas.

Early detection of communication disorders is important to avoid further disabling conditions and to provide early intervention. Heward and Orlansky (1992) listed a series of tests which may be included in a comprehensive evaluation for identifying communication disorders among children (Table 7.2).

Prevention of Communication Disorders

According to American Speech-Language-Hearing Association (ASHA)

Table 7.2   Tests for Identifying Communication Disorders

Articulation Test	to assess speech errors; record defective sounds, mispronunciations, and number of errors.
Hearing Test	to see whether a hearing problem is the cause of the speech disorder.
Auditory Discrimination Test	to determine if child hears sounds correctly; if not, it will be hard for him to imitate language.
Language Development Test	to determine the amount of vocabulary acquired; vocabulary can be a good indicator of intelligence.
Overall Language Test	to determine child's understanding and production of language structure.
Language Sample Test	an accurate example of child's understanding and production of language structure.

Source: Heward, W.L., & Orlansky, M.D. (1992). *Exceptional children: An introductory survey of special education* (4th ed.). New York: Merrill.

(1982), some communication disorders can be prevented during three different phases:

> The *primary prevention* is the elimination and inhibition of the onset and development of a communicative disorder by altering susceptibility or reducing exposure for susceptible individuals. [For example], cigarette smoking is eliminated to prevent future laryngeal and breathing abnormalities ... *Secondary prevention* is the early detection and treatment of communicative disorders ... *Tertiary prevention* is the reduction of a disability by attempting to restore effective functioning. (pp. 425–431)

Marge (1984) provided 13 strategies for preventing communication disorders: "immunization, genetic counseling, prenatal care, mass screening and early identification, early intervention programs, family planning, medical care, public education, children and youth education, environmental quality control, quality of life programs (such as stress management), governmental action and elimination of poverty" (Rice, 1988, pp. 245–247).

CHARACTERISTICS

Speech Impairments

General communication disorders may include speech impairments, language disorders, and other communication disabilities. *Speech impairments* tend to interfere with a person's ability in speech sound production and control, resulting in articulation disorders, phonological disorders, voice disorders, and fluency disorders.

Articulation Disorder

An *articulation disorder,* for example, may cause a person to be unable to make certain sounds due to malfunctions of the central nervous system (CNS), and the muscles and organs (e.g., lips, tongue, larynx and pharynx) related to speech (Heward, 1999). As a result, an individual may skip the sound he/she finds difficult to pronounce. In this type of articulation disorder, the *omission,* the person may say "ea" for "eat," "cool" for "school," and "uk" for "book" or "look." He or she may also replace the sound by another sound, called *substitution.* The person may say "tat" for "cat," "doze" for "those," and "glight" for "flight." The third type of articulation disorder, the *distortion,* may cause a person to say "zleep" instead of "sleep," and "schwim" instead of "swim." In the fourth type of articulation disorder, the *addition*, the person may say "hamber" for 'hammer." Two or more of these four types of articulation disorders may occur simultaneously. They appear to be the most prevalent speech impairments in school-age children (Heward, 1999).

Phonological Disorder

The second type of speech impairment is the *phonological disorder*, in which a person may say "car" to refer to a number of things such as "Carol, " "milk carton," or "music record." He or she is not making the right sound due to mental, perceptual, or environmental/cultural disadvantages. The person has no articulation problem, but is still not making the sound of the phonemes right. Students in Hong Kong may face the challenging situation of learning to speak a new dialect (e.g., Mandarin Chinese, Cantonese) and language (e.g., English). We must be careful not to mix phonological disorders with difficulties related to learning a new dialect or language.

Voice Disorder

Voice disorder is the third type of speech impairments. Individuals with voice disorders may find it difficult to control the volume (too soft or too loud), pitch (too low, too high), vocal quality (hoarse, breathy, nasal, stridency) and duration of voice (Heward, 1999). Children with communication disorders may find it difficult to "coordinate the air flow in the lungs, the vibration of the vocal folds in the larynx, and the two resonance chambers in the oral (mouth) and nasal (nose) cavities" (Rice, 1988, p. 241).

Fluency Disorder

Fluency disorder causes interruption to the smooth flow of a person's speech. It may interfere with the rate and rhythm of speech. *Cluttering* is the condition with rapid and clipped speech to the point of unintelligibility, whereas *stuttering* is the condition of verbal blocks, resulting in repetitions of consonant or vowel sounds, and frequently occurs at the beginning of certain words (Heward, 1999). Another type of fluency disorder happens in persons who need many breaths to complete saying a sentence.

Language Disorders

Language disorders may lead to receptive and/or expressive inabilities to communicate. A person with *receptive language disorders* may have difficulty in understanding specific speech or spoken/written words (semantics) and sentences (syntax). As a result, he or she may not be able to follow a sequence of verbal commands or directions, for example, "Go to the kitchen, find a spoon and a fork, and bring to the dining table."). A person with an *expressive language disorder* may find it difficult to imitate and reproduce voice and say (or write/sign) specific words and sentences. He or she may also be unable to expand vocabulary, arrange correct order of sounds of words (e.g., hostipal," "aminal") and use correct plurals and tenses (e.g., "He goed to school and find three book and a pictures.") (Heward, 1999).

Students with learning disabilities may have *psycholinguistic disorders* as one type of receptive/expressive language disorders, in which deficits may exist in visual/auditory perception, association, sequential memory, and expression.

Other language disorders include the *morphological perspectives* (the appropriate use of morphemes, which are the meaningful units for language communication, e.g., "I eat." vs. "I ate." "baseball" vs. "basketball" and "The duck is about to bite." vs. "The duck is delicious to bite.") and the *pragmatics* (i.e., the social and functional aspects of language).

EDUCATION

Because all communication disorders carry the potential to isolate children from their social and educational surroundings, it is important to find appropriate and timely intervention. While many speech and language patterns can be called "baby talk" and are part of a young child's normal development, they can become problems if they are not outgrown as expected. As such, an initial delay in speech and language development or an initial speech pattern can become a disorder, which can cause difficulties in learning. Because of the way the brain develops, it is easier to learn language and communication skills before the age of five.

Promoting Children's Communication Skills

All children need to be encouraged and facilitated to develop efficient and effective communication skills. Heward and Orlansky (1992) suggested the following approaches for teachers:

1. Listen to students with interest.
2. Speak to students with feeling.
3. Use animation.
4. Rephrase children's errors.
5. Avoid punishing children's attempts to communicate.
6. Ask questions.
7. Create an environment with positive and encouraging opportunities for relaxed communication.

Team Effort

To help students overcome communication disorders is not a one-person job. It takes a team with teachers, speech/language pathologists or therapists, parents, and other professionals or supporting persons to work on assessment and intervention (Hallahan and Kauffman, 1994). As Heward and Orlansky (1992) explained:

> Communication is a social behavior ... the degree to which a communication disorder affects an individual's life is often related to the settings where communication takes place. Treating a communication disorder in isolation from the various places and situations where the child needs to communicate has little chance for success. Children must be able to practice and use the new skills they are learning. Parents, other family members, and the school community must coordinate their efforts so that the child has many opportunities to speak, many places to do so, and many people to talk to. (p. 96)

Speech and Language Therapy

Vocabulary and concept growth continues during the years children are in school. Reading and writing are taught and, as students get older, the understanding and use of language becomes more complex. Communication skills are at the heart of the education experience. Speech and/or language therapy may continue throughout a student's schooling either in the form of direct therapy or on a consultant basis. The speech-language pathologist may assist relevant professionals such as vocational teachers and counselors in establishing communication goals related to the work experiences of students and suggest strategies that are effective for the important transition from school to employment and adult life.

Speech and language pathologists or therapists assist children who have communication disorders in a number of ways: (a) providing individual therapy for the child; (b) consulting with the child's teacher about the most effective ways to facilitate the child's communication in the class setting; and (c) working closely with the family to develop goals and techniques for effective therapy in class and at home. Technology can help children whose physical conditions make communication difficult. The use of electronic communication systems allows non-speaking people and people with severe physical disabilities to engage in the sharing thoughts. Table 7.3 shows four common models for treating children with articulation disorders (Heward & Orlansky, 1992).

Heward and Orlansky (1992) also described remedial approaches for children with voice, fluency, and language disorders:

> Voice disorders can sometimes be treated medically or surgically, if there is an organic cause, but the most common remediation is direct vocal rehabilitation … [Treatments for] fluency disorders emphasize either symptom modification or fluency reinforcement … Language disorders are treated by either individual or group approaches. (p. 100)

Alternative and Augmentative Communication

According to the American Speech-Language-Hearing Association (1989), *alternative* and *augmentative* communication (AAC) is defined as "an area of clinical practice that attempts to compensate (either temporarily or permanently) for the impairment and disability patterns of individuals with severe expressive communication disorders" (ASHA, 1989, p. 107). AAC includes communication devices and techniques that are used to supplement

Table 7.3   Four Models for Treating Articulation Disorders

Discrimination Model	Emphasizes on developing child's ability to listen carefully and detect differences between similar sounds; child learns to match speech to standard model.
Phonologic Model	Identifies child's pattern of sound production and teaches her to produce gradually more acceptable sounds.
Sensorimotor Model	Emphasizes repetitive production of sounds in various contexts; special attention given to motor skills involved in articulation; frequent exercises to produce sounds with different stress patterns.
Operant Conditioning Model	Presents specific stimuli and shapes articulatory responses by providing reinforcing consequences.

Source: Heward, W.L., & Orlansky, M.D. (1992). *Exceptional children: An introductory survey of special education* (4th ed.). New York: Merrill.

naturally acquired and speech vocalization. As Franklin and Beukelman (1991) indicated:

> [Alternative and] augmentative communication refers to the variety of communication approaches that are used to assist persons who are limited in their ability to communicate messages through natural modes of communication. These approaches may be unaided, as is manual sigh and adapted gestures, or aided, with utilization of communication boards or electronic devices. Regardless of the communication mode employed, the goals of [alternative and] augmentative communicators are similar to those of natural speakers, that is, to express wants and needs, to share information, to engage in social closeness, and to manage social etiquette. (p. 321)

Manual Systems

Nietupski and Hamre-Nietupski (1979) suggested three options of auxiliary communication. The *manual systems* require a person to use his/her "arms, hands, and/or fingers to communicate" (pp. 110–111). Examples of manual systems are:

1.   Generally understood gestures, body movements.
2.   Sign systems — i.e., sign language.
3.   Finger spelling.

Communication Aids

The *communication aids* are "display devices which contain objects, pictures of objects or actions, symbols, or printed words" (Nietupski &

Hamre-Nietupski, 1979, p. 111). Considerations for using communication aids include the techniques and the symbol systems. There are two common types of techniques in using communication aids, the decoding and encoding systems.

Direct selection is one type of decoding techniques. Among a number of pictures or symbols, a person or this person's personal care attendant (PCA) can choose by pointing to the exact picture or symbol to communicate. A person who has too limited arm movement to do sign language and finger spelling may benefit in the use of:

1. a head pointer with pen light,
2. a mouth piece, or
3. foot/toes.

If direct selection cannot be achieved right away, the effort of selecting the right picture or symbol to communicate can still be accomplished via *manual scanning* (i.e., by a PCA) or by electronic *autoscanning*, which also fall under the category of the decoding systems.

The *encoding systems* include a set of pictures/icons, numbers, alphabets, etc., which can form various combinations and each combination can be pre-scheduled to mean a specific message. The following are examples of the combinations:

Numbers of 1, 7, 3 = "Hello! How are you today?"
Colors of pink + yellow = "Thank you!"
Icons of apple + boy + full cup of water = "Johnny is full; he can't eat any more."

Generally, younger children or persons at lower cognitive levels may use more concrete symbols such as real objects or pictures, and 2-digit combinations of numbers. More mature individuals or persons at higher cognitive functioning levels may be able to use more abstract symbols like alphabets, words, and sentences. It is also possible that different symbols are used together, e.g., blue + 2 + 2, or A114, to make it easier for the users to learn and memorize. In addition, a specific symbols can be used to mean a designated theme, e.g., the icon of apple = the "food and eat" topic; red color = warning; and blue color = emotional status.

The *communication symbols* for a communication aid may include:

1. Objects.
2. Pictures/icons.
3. Alphabets, words, sentences.

Communication Codes

The *communication codes* use the arrangement in which a person will ask yes/no questions for the individual with nonvocal/nonverbal conditions to answer by minimal efforts, such as:

1. Turning head: right = yes; left = no.
2. Knocking table or blinking eyes: once = yes; twice = no.
3. Smile = yes; frown = no.
4. Raising head (head extension) = yes; looking down = no.
5. Raising left arm = yes; rolling eyes = no.

Factors to be Considered

Table 7.4 lists factors to be considered when selecting an appropriate auxiliary communication system for a person with nonvocal or nonverbal conditions. These factors tend to be addressed by a teamwork to which members such as teachers, speech/language pathologists, physical and occupational/rehabilitation therapists, job coaches, leisure/recreational coordinators, and families/parents as well as the person himself/herself will contribute their expertise and concerns.

Table 7.4   Factors to be Considered

	Motor skill requirement	Portability	Training required by audience	Constant visual display	Allow students to initiate and respond to communicative attempts
Manual Systems	Extensive	No problem	Fairly extensive if standardized signs are used	For some signs or finger-spelling	Yes
Communication Aids	Minimal to extremely minimal	Problem for ambulatory students, especially if using crutches	Minimal	Yes or no	Yes
Communicative Codes	Extremely minimal	No problem	Minimal	Yes	No, only to respond

Source: Nietupski, J., & Hamre-Nietupski, S. (1979). Teaching auxiliary communication skills to severely handicapped students. *AAESPH Review, 4*(2), 107–124.

There are a number of factors to be considered when selecting an alternative or augmentative communication systems:

1. Communication needs: motivation, interest level, goals, emotional maturity, family/community perception.
2. Receptive and expressive language skills.
3. Motor abilities: range of motion of arms, wrists, and hands (or feet) including should, elbow and wrist joints' flexion and extension and crossing midline; upright standing or sitting position (by the use of a regular chair, wheelchair, crutches, or other adaptive equipment); muscle strength, endurance, and coordination (e.g., hold and release).
4. Perceptual skills: eye contact, visual tracking, matching, figure-ground spatial relationships, and other visual-auditory abilities to be able to recognize objects, pictures, and symbols.
5. Conceptual/intellectual skills: object permanence, causality, imitation, reading, spelling skills.
6. Academic, vocational, and leisure/recreational skills.

SUMMARY

1. Speech is the vocal sound production of a person. Language is a structured verbal, written, or sign system with phonological, semantic, syntactic, and morphological rules for communication. Communication is to transmit messages from one person to another.
2. Most types of communication include three phases: input (receptive), cognitive processing, and output (expressive). Decoding is the cognitive ability to translate symbols into thoughts; encoding is the cognitive ability to translate thoughts into symbols.
3. Speech correction became available in the early 1900s and was introduced to schools in the 1920s. At the time around World War II, the U.S. military services demonstrated effectiveness of speech therapy, which expanded the field of communication disorders. The involvement of children with severe/profound and multiple disabilities in the 1970s and 1980s shifted speech/language pathologists' role from traditional clinical services to consultation with teachers and primary caregivers.
4. Possible causes of communication disorders include cognitive developmental delay, sensory impairments, autism, attention deficit hyperactivity disorder, traumatic brain injury, physical and health

disabilities, emotional/behavior disabilities, and environmental factors. Prevention of some communication disorders can be implemented before, during, and after the appearance of potential causes.

5. Speech impairments include articulation disorder, phonological disorder, voice disorder, and fluency disorder. Language impairments consist of receptive language disorders and expressive language disorders.

6. Promoting children's communication skills and achieving speech/ language therapy goals need successful team effort. Team members may include teachers, speech and language pathologists/therapists, parents, and other school personnel and service/care providers.

7. Alternative and augmentative communication (AAC) may include the manual system, communication aids, and communication codes. Factors to be considered when selecting appropriate AAC systems include needs, receptive and expressive language skills, motor abilities, perceptual and conceptual skills, and academic, vocational, and leisure/ recreational skills.

ACTIVITIES

1. Keep a diary for several days. Describe ways messages are sent and received. Speculate about the cause of breakdowns and identify communication barriers.

2. Select and research a type of the speech and language impairments (voice, articulation, fluency, form, content, and use problems). Report your findings to the class.

3. Locate a teacher or speech therapist of children with speech or language impairments and ask him/her to record a lesson with a child with any of those disorders. Borrow the tape and listen to it. Try to identify the type(s) of impairment(s) and the age of the child. Write a short paper to report to class about how the language sample differs from the language of a typically developing child.

4. Locate a teacher or speech therapist of children with speech or language impairments and ask him/her to let you observe a teaching or therapy session or an assessment session. Record and discuss your observations about the lesson or the assessment instruments used, the intervention strategies applied, and the child's behavior.

5. Research the prevalence rate of speech and language impairments in Hong Kong and the types of services available for those children. Write a short report to share with the class.

6. Design an advertising campaign to heighten public awareness of the importance of preventive measures. Emphasize methods that prevent speech or language impairments and identify the target of the campaign, what might happen to make a prevention campaign successful, and the components of such a campaign.
7. Identify one area of curriculum (e.g., mathematics: division; reading: comprehension; science: photosynthesis), discuss the importance of language — teachers' language, students' language, language of the subject's content — for each curricular area. Brainstorm different words and language structures for each curricular area and ways for these items to be adjusted to match the language abilities of the child.
8. Work in small groups of four to five to devise guidelines for parents to follow when making decisions about specific equipment to purchase.
9. Work in small groups of four to five to devise guidelines for teachers to follow in making adaptations in the classroom.

RESOURCES

Resources in Hong Kong

言語治療部，博愛醫院
New Territories, 新界元朗凹
Tel.: 852-2486-8000   Fax: 852-2443-9593
Web address: http://www.poh.org.hk/speech.htm

香港基督教服務處 —— 培愛學校復康服務
E-Mail: cspos@hkstar.com
Web address: http://www.hkcs.org/rehab/pos/services.htm

John F. Kennedy Centre — Speech Therapy Division
15 Sandy Bay Road, Hong Kong
Tel.: 852-2817-0131   Fax: 852-2817-3730
Web Address: http://www.jfk.edu.hk

The Hong Kong Society for The Deaf
Room 903, Duke of Windsor Social Service Building
15 Hennessy Road, Wanchai, Hong Kong
Tel.: 852-2854-2676 or 852-2854-2713
Web address: http://www.deaf.org.hk

Princess Alexandra Red Cross Residential School —
Rehabilitation Services
Web address: http://pas.hkcampus.net/rehab.htm

The Spastic Association of Hong Kong —
B. M. Kotewall Memorial School Speech Therapy Division
22 Kwai Hop Street, Kwai Chung, New Territories, Hong Kong
Tel.: 852-2424-7766   Fax: 852-2422-8230
Web address: http://bmkms.spastic.org.hk

The University of Hong Kong, Department of Speech and Hearing Sciences
5th Floor, Prince Philip Dental Hospital
34 Hospital Road, Hong Kong
Tel.: 852-2859-0599 or 852-2859-0595
Fax: 852-2559-0060
Web address: http://www.hku.hk/speech

Resources in Taiwan

Tao-Yuan General Hospital, Department of Rehabilitation
桃園市中山路1492號
Web address: http://www.tygh.gov.tw

International Resources

AbleNet Inc.
1081 Tenth Street S.E.
Minneapolis, Minnesota 55414-1312 U.S.A.
Tel.: 1-800-322-0956 or 1-612-379-0956   Fax: 1-612-379-9143
Web address: http://www.ablenetinc.com/

Adaptive Consulting Services, Inc.
403-A Hawk Street, Rockledge, Florida 32955 U.S.A.
Tel.: 1-800-515-9169
Web address: http://www.augmentative.com/acs-dv2c.htm

American Speech-Language-Hearing Association (ASHA)
10801 Rockville Pike, Rockville, Maryland 20852 U.S.A.
Tel: 1-301-897-5700 or 1-800-638-8255
E-mail: actioncenter@asha.org
Web: www.asha.org

Canadian Association for People who Stutter (CAPS)
PO Box 444, Succ. N.D.G., Montreal, QC H4A 3P8 Canada
Tel: 1-888-STUTTER (1-888-788-8837)
Web address: http://www.webcon.net/~caps/

Center For Voice Disorders of Wake Forest University
Department of Otolaryngology, Wake Forest University School of Medicine
Wake Forest University Medical Center
Medical Center Boulevard, Winston-Salem, NC 27157-1034
Tel.: 1-336-716-4161   Fax 1-336-716-0385
Web address: http://www.bgsm.edu/voice/index.old.html

Closing The Gap, Inc.
P.O. Box 68, 526 Main Street, Henderson, Minnesota 56044, U.S.A.
Tel.: 1-507-248-3294   Fax: 1-507-248-3810
Email: info@closingthegap.com
Web address: www.closingthegap.com

Crestwood Company
6625 N. Sidney Place, Milwaukee, Wisconsin 53209-3259 U.S.A.
Tel.:1-414-352-5678   Fax: 1-414-352-5679
Web address: http://www.communicationaids.com

Council for Exceptional Children (CEC)
Division for Children's Communication Development
The Journal of Children's Communication Development
Web address: http://pegasus.cc.ucf.edu/~abrice/jccd.html

Don Johnston Incorporated
1000 N. Rand Road Bldg 115, Wauconda, IL 60084-0639 U.S.A.
Tel.: 1-800-999-4660 Fax: 1-847-526-4177
Web address: http://www.donjohnston.com/

Don Johnston Special Needs Ltd.
18 Clarendon Ct., Calver Road, Winwick Quay Warrington, England WA2
    8QP
Tel.: 44-01-925-241642 Fax: 44-01-925-241745
E-Mail: jmunro@djsn.u-net.com
DynaVox Systems Inc.
2100 Wharton Street Suite 400, Pittsburgh, PA 15203 U.S.A.
Tel.: 1-800-344-1778
Web address: http://www.sentient-sys.com

Indian Institute of Cerebral Palsy
(Formerly Spastics Society of Eastern India)
P 35/1 Taratalla Road, Calcutta 700 088 India
Tel.: 401-3488 or 401-0240   Fax: 91-33-401-4177
E-mail: ssei@vsnl.com
Web address: http://www.iicpindia.com/

IntelliTools, Inc.
55 Leveroni Court, Suite 9, Novato, Virginia 94949 U.S.A.
Tel.: 1-800-899-6687   Fax: 1-415-382-5963
Web address: http://www.intellitools.com/

International Stuttering Association
Mohrunger Str.17, 40599 Düsseldorf, Germany
Tel: 49-211-74 1585   Fax: 49- 211-7404428.
E-mail:100605.2720@compuserve.com
Web address: http://www.xs4all.nl/~edorlow/isa.html

Mayer-Johnson
P.O. Box 1579, Solana Beach, California 92075-1579 U.S.A.
Tel.: 1-800-841-8923   Fax: 1-609-921-0483
Web Address: http://www.mayer-johnson.com/

National Aphasia Association
Web address: http://www.aphasia.org/index.html
National Information Center for Children and Youth with Disabilities
P.O. Box 1492 , Washington, DC 20013
Tel.: 1-800-695-0285
E-Mail: nichcy@aed.org
Web address: http://www.nichcy.org

Prentke Romach Company
1022 Heyl Road, Wooster, OH 44691 U.S.A.
Tel.: 1-800-262-1984
Web address: http://www.prentrom.com/index.html

Sentient Systems Technology, Inc.
2100 Wharton Street, Pittsburgh, PA 15203 U.S.A.
Tel.: 1-800-344-1778 Fax: 1-412-381-5241
Web address: http://www.sentient-sys.com

Speech to Speech (STS)
Tel.: See website of http://www.stsnews.com/Pages/STSDial-UpTelnumbers.
  html

E-mail: publisher@stsnews.com
Web address: publisher@stsnews.com

Stuttering Foundation of America
3100 Walnut Grove Road, Suite 603
P.O. Box 11749, Memphis, TN 38111-0749
Tel: 1-800-992-9392, 1-901-452-7343; Fax: 1-901-452-3931
Web address: http://www.stuttersfa.org/

Technical Aids & Systems for the Handicapped, Inc. (TASH)
Unit 1 - 91 Station Street
Ajax, Ontario, Canada L1S 3H2
Tel.: 1-800-463-5685 or 1-800-841-8923 Fax: 1-905-686-6895

Words+, Inc.
40015 Sierra Highway, Building B-145, Palmdale, California 93550
U.S.A.
Tel.: 1-800-869-8521 Fax: 1-805-266-8969
Web address: http://www.words-plus.com/

REFERENCES

American Speech-Language-Hearing Association (1982). Definition of the word "prevention" as it relates to communication disorders. *ASHA, 24,* 425–431.

American Speech-Language-Hearing Association (1989). Competencies for speech language pathologists providing services in augmentative communication. *ASHA, 31,* 107–110.

Franklin, K., & Beukelman, D.R. (1991). Augmentative communication: Directions for future research. In J.F. Miller (Ed.), *Research on child language disorders: A decade of progress* (pp. 321–337). Austin, TX: PRO-ED.

Hallahan, D.P., & Kauffman, J.M. (1994). Exceptional Children: introduction to special education (6th ed.). Needham Heights, MA: Allyn and Bacon.

Heward, W. L. (1999). *Exceptional children: An introductory survey of special education.* Upper Saddle River, NJ: Prentice Hall.

Heward, W.L., & Orlansky, M.D. (1992). [Study guide to accompany] *Exceptional children: An introductory survey of special education* (4th ed.). New York: Merrill.

Hsu, Y. C. (2000, June). Assistive technologies for persons with communication disabilities: An introduction to alternative and augmentative communication. *Special Education Quarterly, 75,* 38–40.

Marge, M. (1984). The prevention of communication disorders. *ASHA, 26,* 29–37.

National Information Center for Children and Youth with Disabilities (2000, April).

Fact Sheet Number 11 (FS11). Website: http://www.nichcy.org/pubs/factshe/ fs11txt.htm

Nelson, N.W. (1993). *Childhood language disorders in context: Infancy through adolescence.* Needham Heights, MA: Allyn and Bacon.

Nietupski, J., & Hamre-Nietupski, S. (1979). Teaching auxiliary communication skills to severely handicapped students. *AAESPH Review, 4*(2), 107–124.

Rice, M.L. (1988). Speech and language impaired. In E.L. Meyer, & Skrtic, T.M. (Eds.), *Exceptional children and youth: An introduction* (3rd ed.) (pp. 233– 261). Denver, CO: Love Publishing Co.

Smith, D. D., & Luckasson, R. (1998). *Introduction to special education: Teaching in an age of challenge.* Boston: Allyn and Bacon.

Thompson, J. R., Beck, A. (1998). Technologies for Communication. In J. R. Thompson, M. E. Wall, & S. M. Winchip (Eds.), *Assistive technology: Competencies and skills for teachers* (Book 3). Normal, IL: University Communications, Illinois State University.

8

Visual Impairments

ADVANCED THINKING

Answer the following questions as you read:

1. How are visual impairments defined?
2. How did the field of visual impairments develop?
3. What are the possible causes of visual impairments?
4. What are the characteristics of children with visual impairments?
5. What are the areas of concern in the education of children with visual impairments?
6. What strategies will be helpful to the learning of children with visual impairments?
7. What is the significance of acquiring social skills for children with visual impairments?

KEY TERMS AND PHRASES

acquired visual impairment
adventitiously blind
albinism
amblyopia
anophthalmos
astigmatism
avocational development
blindness
cataract
characteristics
congenital visual impairment
cornea

educable blindness
educational achievement
field of vision
glaucoma
history
hyperopia
intelligence
listening skills
low vision
microphthalmus
mobility training
muscle disorder

myopia

nystagmus

optic atrophy

orientation and mobility

partially sighted

perceptual-motor development

peripheral vision

possible causes

prevention

reading and writing skill

receptive problem

refractive problem

retinal detachment

retinitis pigmentosa

retinopathy of prematurity

speech and language skills

social development

strabismus

visual acuity

visual aid

visual impairment

vocational development

INTRODUCTION

We use our sight during our waking moments but we seldom think about vision and how it functions. We may not think about the preciousness of having the sense of sight. Adults and children with visual impairments have limited or no use of their sight. They may encounter difficulties in a number of ways. Visual impairments can occur at any age. Those who are born with a severe impairment have a *congenital* visual impairment. Those who acquire a severe visual impairment sometime after birth (normally after the age of two) are called *adventitiously blind*. Visual impairments are in one of the low-incidence categories of disabilities.

VISUAL IMPAIRMENTS DEFINED

People's visual efficiency (i.e., how well a person can use sight) is affected by two factors, acuity and peripheral vision. *Visual acuity* refers to how well a person can see at various distances. *Peripheral vision* refers to the width and height of a person's field of vision. Visual specialists categorize individuals with visual impairments into two subgroups, low vision and blindness. *Low vision* (may be called *partially sighted*) refers to those who have a visual acuity greater than 20/200 but not greater than 20/70 in the best eye after correction. *Blindness* refers to the persons with visual acuity of 20/200 or worse, and field of vision no greater than 20°, in the best eye with best correction. *Educational blindness* can be defined as a student's inability to use vision as a primary channel of learning. The purpose of such a definition is to ensure that the child receives an appropriate instructional program and related accommodations.

In Hong Kong, visual impairments have also been defined into two broad categories: blindness and low vision. To match the global trend in classifying visual impairments, the government has adopted the following definitions to facilitate the provision of services:

(1) Total blindness: persons with no visual function, i.e., no light perception.
(2) Low vision:
   (a) The severe low vision group: persons with visual acuity from 6/120 to 6/1990, hand movement and light perception or persons with contracted visual field in which the widest field diameter subtends an angular subtense <20 irrespective of the central visual acuity.
   (b) The moderate low vision group: persons with visual acuity from 6/60 to 6/95.
   (c) The mild low vision group: persons with visual acuity from 8/18 to 6/48.

Central visual acuity listed above refers to that of the better eye with correcting glasses (Hong Kong 1990 Review of Rehabilitation Program Plan, Section 5.1).

HISTORY OF THE FIELD

In the West, there were indications of acceptance of people with visual impairments even in ancient times. There was, however, no record of a systematic attempt to educate persons who were blind and integrate them into society until the eighteenth century. In 1784, the Institution for Blind Youth, the first school for the blind, was founded in Paris. In the early 1800s, Louis Braille, a blind Frenchman, developed today's braille system, a tactile system for reading and writing that used an embossed six-dot code. In 1829, the New England Asylum for the Blind (now the Perkins School for the Blind), the first school for the blind, was established in the United States and Samuel Gridley served as the first director. The New York Institute for the Blind and the Pennsylvania Institution for the Instruction of the Blind were founded around 1832. Usually only children from wealthy families were able to afford to attend these private boarding schools.

In 1872, the Scottish Education Act, which required blind children to attend schools in their local communities with their sighted peers, fostered the beginning of day classes for children who were blind. In the United States, the first effort to integrate blind children into local public schools was found in Chicago. In 1897, Ms. Martha Postler, a German missionary from the Hildesheimer Blindenmission began to care for four blind girls and started the Ebenezer School and Home for the Visually Impaired in Hong Kong. In 1900, Frank Hall, the superintendent for the Illinois School for the Blind, convinced people to allow students who were blind to live at home. He then developed a plan to divide Chicago into several regions. One local school in each region served students with severe visual impairments. The students attended regular classes with support from a special education teacher who taught braille and encouraged students to participate fully in regular education.

In 1913, Edward Allen taught the first class for the partially sighted in Boston. Robert Irwin started a similar class in Cleveland later that year. Modeled after classes in England, reading and writing tasks were kept to a minimum in these classes. This method was popular for about 50 years (from 1915 to 1965). In 1964, Natalie Barraga, in her research on visual efficiency, proved that people do not have a limited amount of sight that can be used up but that vision can become more limited when it is not used.

The development of technology has also benefited people with visual impairments in different ways. In 1860, long canes were developed to help people with visual impairments to move about. In 1876, Alexander Graham Bell developed telephone. In 1877, Thomas Edison invented phonograph. Between 1918 and 1925, dogs were trained to help French and German veterans of World War I. Guide dogs were introduced in the United States in 1928. In 1944, Richard Hoover developed a mobility and orientation system. During the 1950s, parents began to call for mainstreaming their children. The Individuals with Disabilities Education Act, first passed in 1975, also provided an impetus for innovative ways of teaching and including children with visual impairments in regular classes. The use of computer as a tool of teaching and learning has brought the philosophy of integration much closer to its original intents.

POSSIBLE CAUSES

Visual impairments may be congenital or acquired. For *congenital visual impairments*, genetic conditions such as *albinism* (resulting in photophobia due to a lack of pigmentation in eyes, skin, and hair), *anophthalmos* (absence of the eyeball), *cataract*, *glaucoma* (abnormal widening and enlargement of the eyeball due to pressure), *severe myopia* associated with retinal detachment, lesions of the cornea, and *microphthalmos* (abnormally small eyeball) (Chapman & Stone, 1989).

Acquired visual disorders may occur before, during, or after birth. Radiation or the introduction of drugs into the fetal system before birth may result in vision loss. Infections during pregnancy as a result of rubella, syphilis, and measles, may cause blindness in the fetus. Accidents, inflammations, tumors, and infections after birth are related to vision loss as well. Injuries, diseases, and degeneration are associated with vision problems during adulthood while the majority of vision loss occurs before adulthood with approximately 60% occurs before the age of 1.

Prevention of Visual Impairments

Medical advancement has contributed to the reduction of the prevalence rate of severe visual impairments worldwide including Hong Kong. Medical treatments have also reduced the severity of the visual impairment. For progressive diseases such as dry eye, dietary treatment with vitamin A supplement may prevent or help reduce the damage. Regular visual screenings for children, particularly in early age, can help detect signs of impairments. Educating the public, parents, and teachers about the early signs of a disability (see Table 8.1) is crucial to the prevention of visual impairments.

For acquired visual impairments, public education on safety measures can help reduce disabilities caused by accidents. Many individuals suffer

Table 8.1 Signs of Possible Visual Impairments

The child cannot discriminate letters.
The child rubs eyes frequently.
The child tilts head frequently.
The child shuts or covers one eye when reading.
The child has difficulty in reading small print.
The child finds it difficult to see after sunset (night blindness).
The child has difficulty in seeing details in pictures.
The child's eyes water excessively.
The child's eyes are crusty in appearance.
The child's eyes look dull or cloudy.
The child's eyes are continually reddened or sore.
One or both pupils look gray or white.

from eye injuries that could have been avoided with some safety measures such as wearing goggles and protective devices. Continual public education will also help to reduce the practice of dangerous home remedies in certain cultures.

CHARACTERISTICS

The classifications of visual impairments are commonly based on the anatomical site of the problem. Such disorders may be grouped into the refractive structures of the eye, muscle anomalies in the visual system, and the receptive structures of the eye.

Refractive Problems

The most common type of visual impairments is in problems with refraction that occur when the refractive structures of the eye (cornea or lens) fail to focus light rays accurately on the retina. There are four types of refractive problems: hyperopia (farsightedness), myopia (nearsightedness), astigmatism (blurred vision), and cataract (lens becoming opaque).

Muscle Disorders

These disorders arise when one or more of the major eye muscles are weakened and destabilized, resulting in a loss of control and an ability to maintain tension. Individuals with muscle disorders generally have difficulty in maintaining their focus on a specific object for even short periods of time. There are three types of muscle disorders: nystagmus (uncontrolled rapid eye movement), strabismus (crossed eyes), amblyopia (an eye that appears normal but does not function properly).

Receptive Problems

These disorders result from the degeneration of or damage to the retina and the optic nerve. Disorders associated with receptive structures of the eye include optic atrophy, retinitis pigmentosa, retinal detachment, retinopathy of prematurity (ROP). Table 8.2 provides a brief description of these disorders.

The age of onset of vision loss significantly alters the degree and variation of effect on an individual's development. If sight is lost prior to

Table 8.2   Visual Disorders Associated with Receptive Structures of Eye

Optic Atrophy	A degenerative disease resulting from the deterioration of nerve fibers connecting the retina to the brain.
Retinitis Pigmentosa	Hereditary condition resulting in total blindness from the gradual degeneration of the retina.
Retinal Detachment	Separation of the retina from the choroid (the layer of tissue containing blood vessels that carry nutrients) and sclera (fibrous outside layer of tissue) due to glaucoma, retinal degeneration, or extreme myopia.
Retinopathy of Prematurity	An eye disorder in young children. It occurs when premature infants were administered an excessive amount of oxygen which causes the formation of scar tissue behind the lens of the eye and thus prevents light rays from reaching the retina.

the age of 5, useful visual imagery may disappear and negative influence on overall functioning tend to be the greatest. If sight is impaired or lost after the age of 5, some visual memories may be retained and may be helpful "in imagining and understanding many concepts" (Best, 1992, p. 3). Visual memories may be sustained for a number of years.

Intelligence

Existing literature on intellectual development indicate that children with vision loss are different from their sighted peers in some areas of intelligence, ranging from understanding spatial concepts to a general knowledge of the world (Parsons & Sabornie, 1987; Warren, 1989). However, the intellectual capabilities of children with vision loss can only be validly compared with sighted peers on tasks in which vision loss does not interfere with performance.

Speech and Language Skills

The development of speech and language for children with sight primarily occurs through the integration of visual experiences and the symbols of the spoken word. Children with vision loss are disadvantaged in developing speech and language skills because of their inability or lessened ability to use vision to associate words with objects. They must rely on hearing or touch for information input. Therefore, their speech may develop at a slower rate. Nevertheless, these children's speech is normally fluent once they have learned it.

Educational Achievement

The educational achievement of students with visual impairments may vary a great deal. Ranging from excessive school absences due to eye surgery or treatment to years of failure with instructions that did not meet individual students' unique needs, numerous variables influence educational achievements of students with visual impairments. Children with visual impairments are approximately 2 years behind sighted children in grade level on average. However, some of these individuals are equipped with extraordinary self-motivation, hard work, and talents in areas not affected by their vision loss and have achieved brilliantly by making full use of their abilities and talents.

Social Development

A number of hereditary and experiential factors affect one's ability to adapt to the social environment. Vision provides one of the common bonds for us to build perceptions of the world around us. Perceptions about ourselves and those around us would be drastically different without vision. People with a visual impairment do not develop body language because they are unable to imitate the physical mannerisms of others. The subtleties of nonverbal communication system can significantly change the intended meaning of spoken words; therefore, a person's inability to develop such a system through acquiring visual cues (e.g., facial expressions) seriously affects interpersonal interactions. Other social problems may include the exclusion of individuals with visual impairments from social activities that are completely related to the use of sight (e.g., movies). Often times excluding individuals with visual impairments from social experiences is due to negative public attitudes rather than the individual's lack of social adjustment skills.

Orientation and Mobility (O&M)

Individuals with a visual impairment have a common limitation of getting from place to place. They may not be able to orient themselves to other people or objects in the environment simply because they cannot see them. Consequently, they cannot understand their own relative position in space and move in the right direction. To protect themselves, they tend to restrict themselves going to places.

Perceptual-Motor Development

The lack of sight also affects fine motor coordination and one's ability to manipulate objects. Training programs for improving fine motor skills and eye-hand coordination must begin early and focus on experience to enhance opportunities for independent living (Best, 1992; Chapman & Stone, 1989).

Perceptual-motor development is not only essential in the development of locomotion skills, but also in the development of cognition, language, personality, and socialization. Those who had an early visual experience prior to the loss of sight or partial loss of sight may have an advantage in acquiring manipulatory and locomotor skills.

Vocational and Avocational Development

With modern advancement in training of skills, related accommodations, and technology, persons with visual impairments may greatly increase their vocational and avocational opportunities. As Tuttle (1988) described:

> A visual impairment does not restrict vocational and avocational possibilities as much as one might at first think. With a few exceptions, visually impaired persons have been successfully involved in almost every type of employment and recreation. Jobs that involve driving are, of course, not possible, but many blind persons have taken related jobs in the transportation industry. Visually impaired persons are at a disadvantage in team sports or in games such as badminton or tennis that involve following a moving object. With the 20th-century technology advances, and with the abundance of adaptive aids and devices, however, visually impaired persons can accomplish almost anything. (p. 137)

Today's children and youth with visual impairments, as well as their teachers and other related educational service provider, need to be aware of the existence of multiple potentials and possibilities and be encouraged to engage in training and development of necessary skills in order to actualize individualized life goals.

EDUCATION

Students with mild to moderate visual impairments generally learn alongside their sighted counterparts. Students with a severe visual impairment or total blindness in Hong Kong are generally educated in special schools for the blind. Heward and Orlansky (1992) indicated that "children with visual impairments can fully participate in the programs a school has to offer" (p. 134), and "[they] are educated increasingly in regular school programs" (p. 135). While it takes students with visual impairments more time to learn the skills because of their visual limitations, they perform adequately in academic work.

Common Strategies

Smith and Luckasson (1995) suggested the following general strategies which are very helpful for teachers of children with visual disabilities:

1. Free the classroom from dangerous obstacles; remove clutter and litter on the floor.
2. Open or close doors fully (a half-open door can be a dangerous obstacle).
3. Place the child's desk close to the teacher's desk, the blackboard, and the classroom door.
4. Arrange the child's desk in a well-lighted area but away from a light source to lessen distracting glare.
5. Eliminate noise from the learning environment as much as possible, including not to speak loudly because this may increase the volume level in a classroom.
6. Always place materials in the same places so that students know where certain items are located.
7. Encourage students with visual impairments to express their visual needs.
8. Encourage students to choose a partner for play and academics.
9. Explain the implicit and explicit rules of games and social situations.
10. Allow sighted students to assist in the social skill development of students with visual impairments.
11. Do not leave the room without telling the student with visual impairments.
12. Have high expectations toward students with visual impairments.

Visual Aids

The majority of students with mild to moderate visual impairments generally fare well with appropriate support and accommodation in the regular classroom. Aids such as glasses, large print, and machines that enlarge type can all be helpful. A sensitive teacher who gives instruction in elaborated description and provides appropriate seating arrangements and handouts in large print can be instrumental in helping a student with visual impairment to succeed.

Reading and Writing Skills

Students with very severe visual impairments may need to use different methods to learn to read and write. Braille is a key method for these children to learn to read. However, Braille provides a very cumbersome and slow way of reading. Other methods such as auditory readers (using personal readers or recorded materials) are gaining popularity. Gaining more understanding through research on visual efficiency, medical and education experts increasingly encourage individuals with visual impairments to make use of their residual vision to read and write. With advanced medical technology, other methods of reading and writing, such as the use of speech synthesizers to allow for immediate voice-to-print and print-to-voice translations of documents, may also become more commonly available and less expensive. The options are definitely expanding.

Listening Skills

The importance of listening skills for blind children cannot be over-emphasized. It becomes more crucial for a child to be a good listener if the child cannot rely on sight for gaining information from the environment. Making full use of the listening ability among those with visual impairments provides a valuable channel for communication and learning. Table 8.3 serves as a guide for teachers to pay attention to various listening skills that are essential for learning.

Social Skills

Visual information is important in acquisition of social skills. It helps one to interact appropriately with his/her peers. This learning process begins in infancy and continues throughout childhood. The infant learns to make eye contact, smile, and touch. The child learns to gain access to play groups, resolve conflicts, attract and direct attention of peers, and maintain friendships. While sighted children attain these skills through typical interactions and incidental learning, many children with severe visual impairments need to be directly taught.

Table 8.3   Listening Skills Hierarchy

Sound awareness	Does the child change behavior by the presence or absence of sound? (Startle reaction).
Auditory attending	Can the child interpret different sounds to have different meanings? (The sound of a dog barking, doorbell ringing).
Auditory attention span	Can the child attend to sounds for some length of time?
Sound localization	Can the child tell the location or direction of sound?
Auditory discrimination	Can the child recognize the similarities and differences between sounds?
Auditory memory	Can the child store and recall a series of sounds?
Auditory memory span	Can the child associate an event with a sound or remember verbal commands over some period of time?
Auditory sequencing	Can the child remember the order of items named in a sequence?
Auditory projection	Can the child attend to and interpret sounds at a distance?
Auditory figure-ground discrimination	Can the child attend to a particular sound even though there are competing sounds in the environment?
Auditory blending	Can the child put sounds together to make whole words?
Auditory closure	Can the child complete a word when only a part is presented?
Reauditorization	Can the child remember inflection patterns?

Source: Smith, D.D., & Luckasson, R. (1995). *Introduction to special education: Teaching in an age of challenge* (2nd ed.). Needham Heights, MA: Allyn & Bacon.

Many children with visual impairments are rejected by their sighted classmates, possibly because they have not learned what is expected in normal social interactions. For example, youngsters with severe visual impairments tend to lack play skills, ask too many irrelevant questions, and engage in inappropriate acts of affection (Kekelis, 1992). Many of these children also exhibit other inappropriate behaviors, such as body rocking, moving hands stereotypically in space, and eye poking. Due to their inappropriate or immature social behaviors, they tend to interact with and make friends with the least popular peers in their ordinary classes (MacCuspie, 1992).

Characteristics attributed to people with severe visual impairments such as being socially immature, self-conscious, isolated, passive, withdrawn, and dependent (Tuttle, 1988) may be a function of the disability, but some may be caused by the way people treat individuals with visual impairments. For example, people with visual impairments tend to be overprotected and are not encouraged to take risks or participate in sports or other physical activities. Overprotection often begins in early infancy and can result in patterns of behavior that reduce social integration. In addition, many sighted people seem uncomfortable when they are with those who have visual impairments (Jernigan, 1983). They do not know how to interact with a person who cannot see well and who may look different as well (Myers, 1994).

The lack of effective interpersonal social skills can have a lifelong impact in many aspects such as leisure-time activities, success on the job, and overall adjustment. Interpersonal skills can be taught and learned, and opportunities for using those skills can be increased (MacCuspie, 1992). Sighted peers should be informed about the visual status of their classmate with visual impairments and can take the role of helper for academic and social situations. They can also be taught to role-model proper behavior. Teachers can encourage students with visual impairments to participate fully in all school activities and to communicate their visual needs to others in a straightforward fashion. Teachers can also help these students understand the explicit and implicit rules of games and social interactions. Meanwhile, parents can organize small play groups at home and provide direct feedback about their child's interpersonal interactions as well as foster independence by allowing their child to take some risks.

Mobility Training

How well an individual can cope with a visual disability largely depends on how well he or she is able to move about. Whether a person withdraws from the social environment or becomes independent relies greatly on mobility skills. Four general methods are available to aid the mobility of people with visual impairments: (1) the long cane, (2) guide dogs, (3) human guides, and (4) electronic devices.

The Long Cane

Professionals most often recommend the long cane for those individuals with visual impairments in need of a mobility aid. It is called a long cane because it is longer than the canes typically used for support or balance.

Guide Dogs

The use of a guide dog is not frequently recommended for people with visual impairments. Extensive training is necessary to learn to use guide dogs correctly. It is questionable for children to use them as extended training is required and guide dogs are large, walk relatively fast, and need to be cared for. However, guide dogs have proven to be valuable aides and companions for some adults. The person must first know where he or she is going; the dog is primarily a safeguard against walking into obstacles or dangerous areas.

Human Guides

Human guides certainly enable individuals with visual impairments to have the greatest freedom in moving about safely, but this arrangement is not practical in most cases. Additionally, over-reliance on another person can cause a harmful dependency. For example, in order to converse with the companion, the person without sight can be distracted from paying attention to the cues he or she needs to travel efficiently and may have to rely on the sighted companion. The sighted person may then have the false impression that the blind person does not have good mobility skills.

If a person with a visual impairment looks as though he or she needs assistance, you should first ask if help is wanted. If physical guidance is required, allow the person to hold your arm above the elbow and to walk a half-step behind you.

Electronic Devices

Researchers constantly work on sophisticated electronic devices for sensing objects in the environment. Most are still experimental and expensive. Among them, the Laser cane and the Sonicguide are representative examples. These devices operate on the principle that human beings can learn to locate objects by means of echoes like bats.

The *laser cane* can be used as a long cane or as a sensing device that emits three beams of infrared light (one up, one down, and one straight ahead), which are converted into sound after they hit objects in the path of the traveler. The *sonicguide* can be used by individuals of all ages (Strelow & Boys, 1979). The device is worn on the head and emits ultrasound and converts reflections from objects into audible sound. The sonicguide wearer can learn about the distances, textures, and directions of objects based upon the characteristics of the sound, such as its pitch, clarity, and direction.

Using Advance Organizers to Structure Lessons

Accommodating students with visual impairments can sometimes be time-consuming and appear to benefit only the student who is being included in an ordinary class. Using the advance organizer does not take a lot of preparation time and can benefit all the students. Table 8.4 presents a classroom scenario for an American history class. Note how the teacher previews the material. The advance organizers are printed in italics.

Table 8.4   An Example of a Teacher Implementing Advance Organizers

Mrs. Sony has two students with visual impairments in his fifth-period American history class. Peter has low vision, and Angela is blind. Today's lecture concerns the American Revolutionary War. The subtopics include a discussion of why some colonists tried to convince England that changes in the relationship between England and the colonies were necessary. Mrs. Sony begins fifth period by welcoming the students to class and saying:

First, I am going to tell you what we will cover today to help you better understand my lecture. Today, we will talk some more about the conditions in America before the Revolutionary War. Last week, we learned about who lived in the American colonies and what they did for a living. For the next several days, we will be discussing control of the government, taxation, and the growing desire for independence among some colonists. Today, we will talk about the English government in London and the colonies' local governments.

Mrs. Sony *next puts an outline of the day's lecture on an overhead projector and gives an enlarged version of the text to Peter and a braille version to Angela.* Mrs. Sony *reminds the class to listen to his lecture, to take notes, and to participate in today's discussion.* As his next step, Mrs. Sony spends a few moments reviewing yesterday's lecture by asking the class the following questions.

. *Yesterday, we discussed the people who lived in Boston during the time of the Revolutionary War.* Where did these people come from originally? What were some of their complaints about the government in England? How did they feel about the government in England? Was England listening to their complaints?

Mrs. Sony goes on to explain that part of the day's discussion concerns people's need to feel involved in their own destiny — how they want to participate in decision making that is important to them. He then asks the class to *provide some examples of current affairs* that reflect a similar situation to the period before the American Revolution. Mrs. Sony has prepared several examples beforehand and uses a few to get the discussion started but is careful to allow the students to express their ideas. Mrs. Sony has selected Amy to be class recorder for this day's lecture and discussion. *Amy will take notes for the class and use them to summarize the day's class at the end of the session.*

Mrs. Sony then explains the importance of this information to the students. He reminds them that they are citizens of the United States and need to know the history of their country. He talks about mistakes of the past and how those mistakes are less likely to be repeated by an informed public. He then reviews three vocabulary words (parliamentary, participatory, representation) that he thinks might be difficult for the students. Finally, Mrs. Sony reminds the students that the content of this lecture will be included in the test he will give on the entire unit. This reminder is an important motivational tool for some students with exceptionalities.

Source: Adapted from Smith, D.D., & Luckasson, R. (1995). *Introduction to special education: Teaching in an age of challenge* (2nd ed.). Needham Heights, MA: Allyn & Bacon.

Lenz (1989) summarized the implementation of advance organizers into 10 steps (see Table 8.5).

SUMMARY

1. Blindness refers to persons with visual acuity of 20/200 or worse, and field of vision no greater than 20°, in the best eye with best correction.

Table 8.5　Steps for Using Advance Organizers

1. Inform students of advance organizers.
   * Announce advance organizer.
   * State benefits of advance organizer.
   * Suggest that student stake notes on the advance organizer.
2. Identify topics or tasks.
   * Identify major topics or activities.
   * Identify subtopics or components.
3. Provide an organizational framework.
   * Present an outline, list, or narrative of the lesson's content.
4. Clarify action to be taken.
   * State teacher's actions.
   * State student's actions.
5. Provide background information.
   * Relate topic to the course or previous lesson.
   * Relate topic to new information.
6. State the concepts to be learned.
   * State specific concepts or ideas from the lesson.
   * State general concepts or ideas broader than the lesson's content.
7. Clarify the concepts to be learned.
   * Clarify by examples.
   * Clarify by nonexample.
   * Caution students of possible misunderstandings.
8. Motivate students to learn.
   * Point out relevance to students.
   * Be specific, short-term, personalized, and believable.
9. Introduce vocabulary.
   * Identify new terms and define.
   * Repeat difficult terms and define.
10. State the general outcome desired.
    * State objectives of instruction/learning.
    * Relate outcomes to test performance.

Source: Lenz, B. K. (1989). Setting the stage for learning-use advance organizers, *Strategram, 1*, 3–4.

Low vision refers to those who have a visual acuity greater than 20/ 200 but less than 20/70 in the best eye after correction.

2. Educational blindness can be defined as a student's inability to use vision as a primary channel of learning; the condition requires special instructional programs and related accommodations.

3. Classification of visual impairments in Hong Kong includes mild low vision, moderate low vision, severe low vision, and total blindness.

4. There was no record of a systematic attempt to educate persons who were blind and to integrate them into society until the 18th century. The first school for the blind was founded in Paris in 1784. In the early 1800s, a number of similar schools as well as day classes for students who were blind or partially sighted were established in Europe and the United States. Louis Braille developed today's Braille system. A series of traditional technologies such as long canes, telephone, photography, and guide dogs were developed between 1860 and 1925.

5. In the late 1800s and early 1900s, there were efforts to educate students with visual impairments in regular classes of local schools with their nondisabled peers.

6. Visual impairments such as albinism and anophthalmos may be caused by congenital factors. Acquired visual disorders may be results of radiation, drugs, infection, and accidents.

7. Identification of early signs of visual impairments is key to prevention. Contemporary medical advancement may possibly prevent or reduce the severity of specific visual disabling conditions.

8. Visual impairments may be categorized into three groups: refractive problems, muscle disorders, and receptive problems.

9. Children with visual impairments may have various patterns of intelligence, speech and language skills, academic achievement, social development, orientation and mobility, and perceptual-motor development.

10. Education of students with visual impairments may aim at enhancement of reading and writing skills, listening skills, and orientation and mobility. Teachers may benefit in the use of advance organizers to structure lessons.

ACTIVITIES

1. Interview individuals with visual impairments to find out challenges they encounter in everyday life. Interview individuals with normal sight

to seek their perceptions about persons with visual impairments and difficulties they think those individuals encounter. Compare and contrast the interview data from the two groups of individuals and write a short paper to report your findings.

2. Document your use of vision by keeping a record for two days. The record should include information about how visual aids in your environment help with your daily living and about how visual aids help you avoid danger. Write a conclusion in your record with a personal observation about how life would be altered if you had a severe visual impairment.

3. Conduct library and online search to collect information about the most advanced types of technology and equipment that can assist students with visual impairments in learning environments and everyday life. Share your findings in a short presentation to your classmates.

4. Design a one-minute public service announcement advertising ways to prevent visual impairments.

5. Design a brochure for distributing to parents on causes of and ways to prevent visual impairments among children.

6. Visit the Ebenezer School & Home for the Visually Impaired in Hong Kong. Observe some of the classes and preferably classes with children of different ages and degrees of this disability so that you may learn firsthand about curriculum, mobility and orientation training, technology involved, and techniques and strategies used for teaching and learning. Write a report of what you have learned.

RESOURCES

Resources in Hong Kong

Canossa School for the Visually Disabled
44 St. Francis Street, Wanchai, Hong Kong

The Ebenezer School & Home for the Visually Impaired
131 Pokfulam Rd, Hong Kong
Tel.: 852-2817-0889/6076   Fax: 852-2817-4355
Web address: www.ebenezer.org.hk

Hong Kong Blind Union
Unit 13-20, G/F, Tsui Ying House, Tsui Ping Estate
Kwun Tong, Kowloon, Hong Kong

Tel.: 852-2339-0666   Fax: 852-2338-7850
Web address: http://www.hkbu.org.hk
E-Mail: info@hq.hkbu.org.hk

The Hong Kong Society for the Blind
[Headquarter] 248 Nam Cheong Street, Kowloon, Hong Kong
Tel.: 825-2778-8332   Fax: 852-2788-0040
Web address: www.hksb.org.hk/VH/hksb

[Service Departments]:
General Eye and Low Vision Clinic
Tel.: 852-2776-9993 or 852-2778-1772

Tuen Mun General Eye and Low Vision Clinic
Tel.: 852-2469-9333

Health Massage and Treatment Centre
Tel.: 852-2779-1888

Tuen Mun Health Massage and Treatment Centre
Tel.: 852-2469-9323

Factory for the Blind
Tel.: 852-2362-0451 or 852-2365-8698

Tun Mun Brand Factory
Tel.: 852-2462-7213

[Rehabilitation Division]:
Rehabilitation and Training Centre (Ext. 332)
Employment Service Unit (Ext. 334)
Centralized Braille Production Centre (Ext. 308)
Communication Department (Ext. 321)
Carolina Gutterres Technical and Advisory Services Centre (Ext. 360)
Deaf-Blind Rehabilitation Training Programme (Ext. 331 & 335)

[Residential Services Division]:
Kowloon Home for the Aged Blind (Ext. 371)
Morning Glory Day Activity Centre cum Hostel (Ext. 335) and Bradbury
   Home
Yuen Long Home for the Aged Blind
Jockey Club Tuen Mun Home for the Aged Blind
Bradbury Care and Attention Home for the Aged Blind

International Sources

AccessAbility, Inc. (AAI)
581 Altamont, Ashland, OR 97520 U.S.A.
Tel.: 1-888-664-1313 or 1-541-488-3324
Fax: 1-541-488-5280
Web address: http://www.4access.com/

American Council of the Blind (ACB)
1155 15th Street, NW, Suite 1004
Washington, DC 20005 U.S.A.
Tel.: 1-202-467-5081 or 1-800-424-8666
Fax: 1-202-467-5085
Web address: http://acb.org

The American Printing House for the Blind, Inc.
1839 Frankfort Avenue
Mailing Address: P.O. Box 6085
Louisville, Kentucky 40206-0085 U.S.A.
Tel.: 1-502-895-2405 or 1-800-223-1839 (U.S. and Canada)
Fax: 1-502-899-2274
Web address: http://www.aph.org

Blind Babies Foundation (BBF)
5016 Mission Street, San Francisco, CA 94112 U.S.A.
Tel.: 1-415-586-6140 Fax: 1-415-586-6279
Web address: http://www.blindbabies.org/

The Canadian Council on Rehabilitation and Work (CCRW)
500 University Avenue, Suite 302, Toronto, Ontario, Canada M5G 1V7
Tel.: 1-416-260-3060 TTY: 1-416-260-9223 Fax: 1-416-260-3093
Web address: http://www.ccrw.org/

Division on Visual Impairments (DVI)
Council for Exceptional Children (CEC)
Web address: http://www.ed.arizona.edu/dvi/welcome.htm

Hotbraille.com
Web address: http://www.hotbraille.com

International Council for Education of People with
Visual Impairment (ICEVI)
37 Jesselton Crescent, 10450 Penang, Malaysia
Tel: 60-4-229-0933   Fax: 60-4-228-9357

National Association for Visually Handicapped (NAVH)
Web address: http://www.navh.org

The Perkins School for the Blind
175 North Beacon Street
Watertown MA 02172 U.S.A.
Tel.: 1-617-924-3434   Fax: 1-617-926-2027
http://www.perkins.pvt.k12.ma.us

REFERENCES

Best, A.B. (1992). *Teaching children with visual impairments.* Philadelphia: Open University Press.

Chapman, E.K., & Stone, J.M. (1989). *The visually handicapped child in your classroom.* London: Cassell.

Heward, W.L., & Orlansky, M.D. (1992). [Study guide to accompany] *Exceptional Children* (4th ed.). New York: Merrill.

Jernigan, K. (1983). Blindness: Disabilities or nuisance? In R.L. Jones (Ed.), *Reflections on growing up disabled* (pp. 58–67). Reston, VA: Council for Exceptional Children.

Kekelis, L.S. (1992). Peer interactions in childhood: The impact of visual impairment. In S.Z. Sacks, L.S. Kekelis, & R.J. Gaylord-Ross (Eds.), *The development of social skills by blind and visually impaired students* (pp. 13–35). New York: American Foundation for the Blind.

Lenz, B. K. (1989). Setting the stage for learning-use advance organizers, *Strategram, 1*, 3–4.

MacCuspie, P.A. (1992). The social acceptance and interaction of visually impaired children in integrated settings. In S.Z. Sacks, L.S. Kekelis, & R.J. Gaylord-Ross (Eds.), *The development of social skills by blind and visually impaired students* (pp. 83–102). New York: American Foundation for the Blind.

Myers, K.A. (1994). *Preferences of communication styles and techniques of persons with disabilities: Implications for higher education.* Unpublished doctoral dissertation, Illinois State University, Normal, Il.

Parsons, A.S., & Sabornie, E.J. (1987). Language skills of young low-vision children: Performance on the preschool language scale. *Journal of the Division for Early Childhood, 11*(3), 217–225.

Smith, D.D., & Luckasson, R. (1995). *Introduction to special education: Teaching in an age of challenge* (2nd ed.). Needham Heights, MA: Allyn & Bacon.

Strelow, E.R., & Boys, J.T. (1979). The Canterbury child's aid: A binaural spatial sensor for research with blind children. *Journal of Visual Impairment and Blindness, 44*, 145–175.

Tuttle, D.W. (1988). Visually impaired. In E.L. Meyer, & Skrtic, T.M. (Eds.),

Exceptional children and youth: An introduction (3rd ed.) (pp. 351–385). Denver, CO: Love Publishing Co.

Warren, D.H. (1989). Implications of visual impairments for child development. In M.C. Wang, M.C. Reynolds, & H.J. Walberg (Eds.), *Handbook of special education: Research and practrice. Vol. 3. Low incidence conditions* (pp. 155–172). Oxford, England: Pergamon Press.

9

Hearing Impairments

ADVANCED THINKING

Answer the following questions as you read:

1. What is the definition of hearing impairments?
2. What are the causes of hearing impairments?
3. How can we prevent hearing impairments?
4. What are the characteristics of children with hearing impairments?
5. What is the framework of curriculum for children with hearing impairments in Hong Kong?
6. What are the general teaching strategies for working with children who have hearing impairments?

KEY TERMS AND PHRASES

amplification
auditory-oral option
computer assisted learning
conductive hearing loss
curriculum
cycle per second
deafness
decibel
educational achievement
hard of hearing
hearing aid
hearing impairment
hearing loss
heredity

history
intelligence
manual communication
maternal rubella
medical technology
meningitis
noise
otitis media
partially hearing
possible causes
postlingual deafness
prelingual deafness
prevention
sensorineural hearing loss

social development   teaching strategies
speech and language skills   total communication

INTRODUCTION

Being able to hear affects us in many ways. The sound of an old friend's voice warms us, the loud thunder astounds and frightens us, the cheers of a crowd may excite us, and the soothing sound of a symphony relaxes us. In addition to vision, we learn much about the world through our hearing. Often times we learn about others by listening to them telling us their experiences. In formal education, we learn a great deal by listening to lectures from primary schools to higher education. We use our speech and hearing abilities to expand our knowledge, understand concepts, share ideas, and express emotions.

Vision and hearing are the two primary channels of learning and communication. The learning and development of those without hearing could be significantly limited or delayed. As Hallahan and Kauffman (1994) indicated:

> Although it is impossible to predict the exact consequences of a disability on a person's functioning, in general, deafness poses more difficulties in adjustment than does blindness. This is largely due to the effects hearing loss can have on the ability to understand and speak oral language. (p. 303)

Nevertheless, many people with hearing impairments participate fully and independently in society. This chapter defines hearing impairments, discusses the causes and prevention of hearing impairments, and the major issues related to the education of children with hearing impairments.

HEARING IMPAIRMENTS DEFINED

Individuals with hearing impairments are normally divided into two groups: deaf and hard of hearing. Those who are included in the group of *deafness* have a hearing disability so severe that they have little residual hearing even with the use of hearing aids and cannot use hearing as their primary way to gain information. Those who have a *hard-of-hearing* condition can process information from sound with the use of a hearing aid. How much an individual can use sounded input to gain information depends on the degree of hearing loss.

According to the Rehabilitation Program Plan (1990) of Hong Kong, the following definitions of hearing impairments have been adopted for educational purposes:

1. *Deaf pupils* are those with impaired hearing and who require education by methods suitable for pupils with little or no naturally acquired speech or language.
2. *Partially hearing pupils* are those with impaired hearing whose development of speech and language, even if impaired, is following a normal pattern, and who require for their education special arrangement or facilities, though not necessarily all the educational methods used for deaf pupils.

A person's hearing can be measured by a pure tone audiometer. This hearing test device measures an individual's responses to the intensity of sound and the vibration of sound. *Decibel* (dB) is the common unit for measuring the intensity of sound, while *cycle per second* (c.p.s.) is the unit for measuring the vibration of sound. "Hearing sensitivity is measured at octave or half octave intervals through the range of frequencies that contribute to speech understanding (250–8,000 Hz)" (Lartz, 1998, p. 3). An individual with specific kinds of hearing loss may include high or low intensity of sounds at low or high pitch (vibration) levels.

Degree of Hearing Loss

There are different degrees of hearing loss, ranging from mild to profound levels (Lian, 1999):

1. Mild (class 1) hearing loss — not being able to hear below 40 dB.
2. Moderate (class 2) hearing loss — not being able to hear below 55 dB.
3. Moderate Severe (class 3) hearing loss — not being able to hear below 70 dB.
4. Severe (class 4) hearing loss — not being able to hear below 90 dB.
5. Profound (class 5) hearing loss — not being able to hear above 90 dB.

In addition to the degree of hearing loss, the age of onset is also important. *Prelingual deafness* refers to the loss of hearing before one learns to speak and understand language. Children who are prelingually deaf are seriously affected in their learning of language and academic subjects later taught in school. Approximately 10% of those who are prelingually deaf have at least one parent who is deaf (Smith & Luckasson, 1995). *Postlingual deafness* refers to the loss of hearing after one has learned to speak and understand language. Many of them are able to retain their ability to use speech and communicate with others verbally.

Types of Hearing Impairments

There are two general types of hearing impairments: conductive and sensorineural. *Conductive hearing* loss refers to loss of hearing resulting from blockage or damage to the outer or middle ear that prevents sound waves from traveling (being conducted) to the inner ear. In general, a conductive hearing loss causes a mild to moderate disability. Generally, we experience temporary conductive hearing loss from time to time. For instance, the temporary hearing loss resulting from the change of air pressure after flying in an airplane, riding in a car in the mountain, or having a head cold (especially among young children).

Sensorineural hearing loss refers to loss of hearing resulting from the damage to the inner ear or the auditory nerve. This type of hearing loss usually cannot be improved medically or surgically. Depending on the severity or the degree of damage, those with sensorineural hearing loss are able to hear different frequencies at different intensity levels.

HISTORY OF THE FIELD

The history of Western civilization reflected various attitudes toward deaf individuals. Some societies protected these individuals; others persecuted and even put them to death. Credited as the first teacher of deaf students, Pedro Ponce de Leon (1520–1548), a Spanish monk, had extraordinary success teaching his students to read, write, and speak. In the 1600s, William Holder and John Wallis began first educational programs in England for deaf individuals. They advocated the use of writing and manual communication (a two-handed alphabet signing system) to teach speech. In the 1700s, Henry Baker of England, Thomas Braidwood of Edinburgh, Abbe Charles Michel de l'Epee of France, and Samuel Heinicke of Germany established schools for the deaf in their own regions or countries.

In 1871, the first school in the United States for students who were deaf was established in Hartford, Connecticut. Thomas Hopkins Gallaudet founded the American Asylum for the Education of the Deaf and Dumb (now the American School for the Deaf). Having studied about deafness in England and France, Gallaudet was greatly influenced by methods of manual communication. He brought Laurent Clerc, a deaf Frenchman who was later credited as the father of education for the deaf in the U.S. Other Americans interested in deaf education also studied in Europe and were impressed by the oral approaches used in Germany.

The debate about whether the oral or the manual method of instruction and communication was initiated by Edward Gallaudet (Thomas Gallaudet's son) and Alexander Graham Bell. Each of these two men had a deaf mother and a highly successful father. Bell invented telephone, the audiometer, and worked on the phonograph. Gallaudet was the president of the nation's college for the deaf (Gallaudet University in Washington, DC) and a prominent legal scholar. Bell opposed to segregation of deaf individuals from the rest of the society. He proposed legislation that would prevent two deaf adults from marrying each other, abolish residential schools, prohibit the use of manual communication, and forbid deaf individuals from becoming teachers of deaf students. Gallaudet strongly opposed these positions and their debate was carried over into U.S. Congress and even influenced federal funding of teacher preparation programs. The Congress supported Gallaudet's position and he received funds to establish a teacher preparation program that stressed the use of both the oral and manual approach in educating the deaf students. In the late 1800s, Horace Mann, a leader in education and social reform, also advocated the oral approach which was popular throughout the late 19th century and for most of the 20th century. In the 1970s, "total communication", a combined approach was adopted. Total communication uses oral and manual communication systems for instructing deaf students.

In the 19th century, formal education for the deaf was primarily delivered in residential schools in the United States. Day schools began to be popular later in the 19th century. While day schools are popular, most states still have a residential school for deaf students. The invention of hearing aid made a significant impact on the lives of deaf and hard of hearing people. Battery-operated hearing aids were developed at the end of World War II. Following the development of the transistor in the 1950s, behind-the-ear hearing aids were constructed and continue in use today.

Today in Hong Kong, there are approximately 40,000 individuals who have different levels of hearing impairment (Mingpao, 2001). Two training centres have been provided for young children (2 to 6 years old) with severe to profound hearing loss by the Hong Kong Society for the Deaf and the Hong Kong Lions Club. For primary and secondary students, there are special schools for the deaf. A small number of students with hearing impairments have been attending mainstream schools. Deaf education teachers in Hong Kong tend to emphasize listening and oral language training and avoid students' relying on lip shape and movement and other manual inputs.

Possible Causes

Children may be born with hearing impairments, or they may have acquired deaf and hard-of-hearing conditions. Different age of onset may cause different level of educational implications. Hallahan and Kauffman (1994) defined *congenitally deaf* as "deafness that is present at birth; [it] can be caused by genetic factors, by injuries during fetal development, or by injury incurred at birth" and *adventitiously deaf* as "deafness that occurs through illness or accident in an individual who was born with normal hearing" (p. 304).

According to Hotchkiss (1989), the leading known causes of hearing impairments are heredity and meningitis. However, unknown causes still account for almost half of the incidence. Five major causes are discussed in this section.

Heredity

Most of the unknown causes are likely to be of genetic nature even though more than 150 different types of genetic deafness have been identified (Smith & Luckasson, 1995). Genetic counseling and prenatal testing may provide important information if a family has a history of congenital deafness.

Maternal Rubella

If a pregnant woman contracts rubella (German measles), the consequence for an unborn child is devastating. Depending on when the expectant mother contracts the disease, the infant may be born with a profound hearing impairment, a visual impairment, or other disabilities alone or in combinations. Vaccines are available to prevent women from contracting rubella and the incidence of hearing impairments caused by maternal rubella has greatly decreased.

Meningitis

This disease affects the central nervous system (specifically the meninges, the coverings of the brain and spinal cord, and its circulating fluid) and often results in a profound hearing loss and is often associated with other disabilities. meningitis is the most common cause of postnatal deafness in school-age children and is a major cause of sensorineural hearing losses that are not present at birth. The extent of influence on a person's ability to acquire speech and language depends on the age of onset and the amount of language skills the person has acquired prior to the hearing loss.

Otitis Media

Otitis media refers to the infection of the middle ear and accumulation of fluid behind the eardrum. Antibiotics and other medical procedures can be used to treat the condition. If the condition persists for long periods of time or is not detected in very young children, it may result in a language impairment that could affect future academic learning (Thake, 1988). Otitis media may damage the outer or middle ear and result in a mild to moderate conductive hearing loss.

Noise

In recent years, researchers are increasing their attention to the danger of noise as a cause of hearing impairments (Hess, 1991). The space shuttle Columbia has gathered information and shown that even sustained levels of noise at about 70 dB can cause some sensorineural hearing loss. The damage caused by the sound levels of a rock concert (which often reaches 125 dB), a car stereo, or a personal tape or CD player can be far greater. Table 9.1 shows what sounds are considered in the danger zone.

Other Causes

Another cause of hearing impairments was found more than a decade ago. The congenital cytomegalovirus (CMV) infection, a herpes virus, is found to affect 1% of all newborns (Pappas, 1985). Of these newborns, about 7.5% have a mild to profound sensorineural hearing loss and possibly other disabilities. Interestingly, some physical exercises such aerobics are now thought to contribute to hearing impairments. For example, high-impact aerobics is thought to cause damage to the delicate structures of the inner ear. Researchers believe that extended period of arduous jumping and twitching may displace otoliths, the tiny granules inside the inner ear. They float in a gel and transmit information to the hairlike stems linked to nerve fibers, a part of the system that turns sound impulses into nerve signals for transmission to the brain. The displacement of otoliths affects both hearing and balance.

Prevention of Hearing Impairments

Common measures to prevent hearing impairments can include early detection and public education. Early detection of hearing impairments that can be prevented is certainly a key approach. When the hearing problem is identified and diagnosed, medical treatment and educational services can be provided to prevent further deterioration and effect. Public education that can create a knowledgeable public as well as better prepared parents and teachers can play major roles in preventing hearing losses among children. Protecting children from developing severe hearing loss due to ear infections and noise are among the areas parents and teachers can be educated to do. Of these two common causes of hearing impairments, noise is a particular concern for citizens of Hong Kong. We will discuss with greater details in the following section.

Noise

Noise is a major problem in Hong Kong because of the density of population

Table 9.1   Range of Decibel Levels for Human Hearing

Hearing level in Decibels	Examples of Common Sounds
30	Soft whisper, quiet library.
40	Leaves rustling.
50	Rainfall, refrigerator.
60	Normal conversation, air conditioner.
70	City or freeway traffic, sewing machine.
80	Hair dryer, alarm clock.
90*	Lawn mower, motorcycle.
100	Garbage truck, snow mobile.
110	Shouting at close range, dance club, race car.
120	Jet plane taking off, car stereo turned all the way up.
130	Live rock music, jackhammer.
140	Firecracker, nearby gunshot blast, jet engine.

* Levels 85 decibels and above are considered hazardous.
Source: U.S. Congress Select Committee on Children, Youth, and Families

and the fast development in building construction. New gas and water pipes and electrical wiring seem to be installed all the time and old pipes and wiring seem to be constantly replaced or repaired. Not only do cars using diesel fuels cause pollution but they also frequently produce high levels of noise in busy and narrow streets surrounded by high-rise buildings in Hong Kong. Construction sites also frequently produce noise beyond the level of annoyance. Noise is one of the causes of hearing impairments. While statistics about the number of people developing hearing impairment because of the noise in this environment is not available, we will not be surprised that a good percentage of people in Hong Kong, particularly those who work in noisy environments such as construction sites and factories with noisy machines, have some degree of hearing loss. With the advancement of medical research and technology, many types of disabilities can be prevented. Preventive measures of hearing impairment related to noise can be as simple as wearing ear protectors when we are around loud noise, using a different type of fuel that is more environmentally friendly and quieter, or installing noise-limiting devices in equipment that can produce a high level of noise such as personal stereos. Public education on noise reduction and the effect of noise on hearing can certainly contribute to the prevention of hearing impairment related to noise. Preventive measures for other types of hearing impairments can be costly and may involve more complicated interventions such as medical technology.

Medical Technology

Medical research has increased our knowledge about the causes and treatment of hearing impairments. Medical technology that accompanies research efforts in turn provides measures to prevent and treat hearing difficulties. Most of the conductive hearing losses that involve the middle ear can be treated today. Surgical procedures can repair or replace poorly functioning small bones in the middle ear. Another medical advance applied today is the procedure of cochlear implants. While debates among professionals within the deaf community continue over whether this technology should be applied because cochlear implants bring only a basic awareness of sound to some people who are profoundly deaf, young children with profound deafness in Hong Kong are now routinely examined for suitability of receiving the implants. The use of cochlear implants in children still presents questions to be answered (Tye-Murray, 1992, p. vii):

1.   Who is a good candidate?

2. What is the optimal age to do the implant for a child?
3. How well will children hear?
4. What kind of learning curve will they demonstrate in developing auditory skills?

CHARACTERISTICS

Intelligence

Lowenbraun (1988) indicated that obtaining accurate measurement of intelligence of students with severe hearing impairments is difficult due to the design in traditional standardized testing instruments, i.e., oral directions and the norms established among hearing children. As a result, these students tend to score higher on the performance subtests than on the verbal subtests of an intelligence scale. Nevertheless, the existing literature suggested that the distribution of IQ scores for children with hearing impairments is similar to that of hearing children (Greenberg & Kusche, 1989; Meadow, 1980).

Speech & Language Skills

The most severely affected areas of development for individuals with a hearing impairment are speech and language skills. This is particularly true for those with congenital deafness. However, the degree of influence depends on the severity of hearing loss. For those with mild to moderate hearing loss, the effect on speech and language skills may be minimal, particularly with the help of hearing aids.

Educational Achievement

The educational achievement of students with hearing impairments varies. However, their average achievement is found to be 3 to 4 years behind their age-appropriate grade levels and low achievement is typical of deaf students (Greenberg & Kusche, 1989; Meadow, 1980). Of all the subjects, reading is the area most adversely affected for students with hearing impairments. Research studies (e.g., Cole, 1987; Gallaudet Research Institute, 1994; Greenberg & Kusche, 1989) show that detrimental effects on reading performance are found with these individuals whether their hearing impairments are mild or profound. Comparatively speaking, the written language of deaf students is simple and limited (Paul & Quigley,

1990) and their math achievement are deficient (Karchmer, 1985; Quigley & Paul, 1989).

Social Development

Reviews of literature have suggested that deaf children have deficiencies and differences in social and psychological development when compared to hearing peers (Greenberg & Kusche, 1989; Marschark, 1993). Delayed language acquisition may contribute to more limited opportunities for social interaction (Cole, 1987). However, some individuals with profound hearing impairments are still socially well adjusted.

EDUCATION

Options for Communication

Various options for communication have been chosen in educational programs for students with hearing impairments. *Manual communication* includes sign language (e.g., manually coded Chinese and English, or MCC/MCE) and fingerspelling. *American Sign Language* (ASL or Ameslan) is a special sign language developed by the deaf community in the United States. ASL has "its own vocabulary and complex syntactic, semantic, and pragmatic structures that are radically different from those of English or any other auditory-oral language" (Lowenbraun, 1988, p. 340).

The *auditory-oral option* for communication tends to avoid any manual communication efforts or cues of MCC/MCE, ASL, and fingerspelling. Enhancing "pure oral" communication in children with hearing impairments relies on auditory training, training for speechreading (lipreading), and speech training. Amplification devices (i.e., hearing aids) are used along with the training and, only if necessary, *cued-speech* is implemented to clarify confusing speech sounds.

Total communication is the option in which manual and auditory-oral methods are both utilized, including amplification, oral speech, and signs, along with facial expressions, gestures, body movements, and, if applicable, use of objects, pictures, and written words and sentences.

Framework of the Curriculum in Hong Kong

The framework of the curriculum for children with hearing impairments in

Hong Kong is developed with the notion that the process of cognitive development of these children is similar to that of ordinary children, only the development tends to be delayed due to various factors, particularly that of language deficit. Therefore, the learning experiences for these children should be similar to those for other children. The curriculum for them should basically follow the mainstream curriculum but with appropriate adaptations to the curriculum materials and teaching approaches to meet their specific learning needs. As language deficit is the root cause of their learning difficulties, special emphasis is placed on the development of language and communication skills in them with the help of appropriate teaching resources and equipment.

A large number of educators in Hong Kong have also adopted the oral communication approach in the education of children with profound deafness. Sign language is not taught or somewhat discouraged in a number of school settings. Children are encouraged to receive cochlear implants if deemed appropriate, to wear hearing aids, and to use their residual hearing.

General Teaching Strategies Recommended in Hong Kong

Based on the above principles, the Curriculum Development Council (1994) suggested the following general teaching strategies to be used for the general situation in the classroom:

1. Constant review with appropriate adjustments should be made to the teaching content and approaches according to the children's learning needs.
2. As language is best learned in meaningful situations, a motivating language environment should be provided to develop the children's communication competence.
3. Low achievers should be given more help to stimulate their interest in learning.
4. Rephrasing of sentences can be considered when children have difficulties in understanding them.
5. The teacher should discourage the children from using telegraphic speech by constantly setting examples of natural speech used in everyday lives.
6. Hearing impaired children may not be proficient in questioning techniques and may therefore hesitate to ask questions. It will help if a motivating environment is provided in which to encourage the children to form the habit of asking questions when they have difficulties.

7. Role-playing is a motivating and effective approach and is encouraged in teaching hearing impaired children.
8. Hearing impaired children, especially preschoolers, should be provided with opportunities to play and share with others and to take turns. This is a good basis for verbal interaction, apart from the development of social behavior.
9. Auditory learning should be provided to maximize the children's effective use of residual hearing. However, it should be noted that this could not be done without a good management of hearing aids.

Additionally, computer assisted learning (CAL) is encouraged to be used in assisting instruction as a tutor, a tool, and even as a tutee. Software programs are available on short-term loan from the Computer Education Center of the Hong Kong Education Department. Teachers are urged to note the following when selecting software for their children:

1. Software which are developed for English-speaking users usually display menus or instructions in English. This may be difficult for children with hearing impairment. Notes written in Chinese accompanying the software may be helpful.
2. At times children may have to use software made in other countries which can sometimes be culturally biased.

Smith and Luckasson (1995) also suggested general tips for teachers:

1. Place the child as close to the speaker as possible.
2. Make certain that the child's hearing aid is turned on and functioning properly by listening through it.
3. Reduce the background noise as much as possible.
4. Articulate clearly, but do not talk louder unless you have an unusually soft voice.
5. Make certain to have the student's attention before talking or starting a lesson.
6. Do not exaggerate your lip movements.
7. Do not chew gum or cover your mouth when talking.
8. Do not turn your back on the class.
9. Use an overhead projector instead of a blackboard, so that the student can see your mouth.
10. Avoid moving around the classroom while talking.
11. Speak slowly.
12. Repeat and restate information by paraphrasing.

13. Spend time talking to the child alone so that you become accustomed to each other's speech.
14. Avoid glare when talking or signing by not standing near a light source such as a window.
15. Do not bounce or move around while talking.
16. Bend down so that you are at students' eye level when you talk to individuals or small groups.
17. Consult with a certified teacher of the deaf.

Table 9.2 shows an example of using the puzzle technique to enhance writing skills of children with hearing impairments.

Table 9.2   The Puzzle Technique

Learning how to write is a very important skill that all students, including those with hearing impairments, need to become proficient at executing. By spending more time directly instructing students how to write more efficiently and accurately, teachers help students acquire these skills. The puzzle technique is well suited to group writing and language arts instruction.

Marcia Bassett teaches language arts at Jefferson Middle School. She has been worried about the writing skills of her seventh graders. Other teachers have told her that homework, in-class essays, and various assignments that require writing are unsatisfactory from this group of students. Ms. Bassett has 28 students in this section with varying writing abilities. Some students have moderately acceptable writing skills; other shave marginal skills, at best. Mark, a member of the class who has a moderate hearing impairment, needs special help in this area.

To tackle the problems, Ms. Bassett has devised a special teaching unit that she calls "Solve the Puzzle." First, she clusters her students into seven groups of four students each. Then she assigns each group at least one student who is more capable in writing. She assigns Mark to the group that includes the best writer of the class.

To prepare for the unit, Ms. Bassett wrote a number of short essays on different topics from the students' other courses: ecology, American explorers, food chains, disruption on the playground, and social issues like apartheid. She then rewrote each essay, deliberately incorporating a substantial number of errors in spelling, punctuation, grammar, and capitalization. She duplicated copies of each essay for each class member plus seven extras. These essays will serve as the materials the students use in their group activities.

Ms. Bassett begins each class session of this teaching unit by reminding the students of the importance of spelling, punctuation, grammar, and capitalization. She gives examples of each of these aspects of writing by showing the class errors they made in the previous day's class. The entire class works on the same essay during this period. In groups of four, they work to "solve the puzzle" of finding all the errors in one of the essays Ms. Bassett has prepared. Each student in a group has a different assignment: One student corrects all the spelling errors, another looks for all the punctuation errors, another the grammatical errors, and another the capitalization errors. After the four students have found errors of the types they were assigned, one student in the group then makes all the corrections on a clean copy of the essay. As each student reports the errors that he or she found, the others verify the corrections and look to see if others were missed.

Each day, the error-hunting assignments rotate. In this way, each student has a chance to look for different types of errors on different days.

Ms. Bassett finds that the students' writing abilities improve greatly over the course of several weeks; they all profit by helping one another proof read written material. Mark's progress has been remarkable: He has learned how to proofread written assignments and find all four types of writing errors. Perhaps more importantly, he has developed a nice relationship with the other students in his small group. Ms. Bassett has also observed comparable, supporting relationships develop among other students in other groups. This teaching tactic has had two results: the students' writing skills improved, and their interpersonal relationships developed and improved.

* The puzzle technique is similar to the cooperative learning approach to teaching.

(1) Work in small groups designing other activities that could be accomplished in small instructional groupings in the classroom.
(2) Identify how students with HI (and other disabilities as well) could benefit from the puzzle technique approach to instruction.

Source: Smith, D.D., & Luckasson, R. (1995). *Introduction to special education: Teaching in an age of challenge* (2nd ed.). Needham Heights, MA: Allyn & Bacon.

Summary

1. Two major categories of hearing impairments are deafness and hard-of-hearing conditions. The Hong Kong education system groups children with hearing impairments into (1) deaf pupils and (2) partially hearing pupils.

2. A pure tone audiometer is used to measure hearing loss according to intensity (dB) and vibration (c.p.s.) of sound. Hearing loss ranges from mild to severe/profound levels.

3. Based on the age of onset, there may be prelingual and postlingual deafness.

4. The two types of hearing impairments are conductive hearing loss and sensorineural hearing loss.

5. History cited teachers who taught deaf students in the 16th century. The pioneer schools for the deaf were established in Europe (i.e., England and Germany) during 1700s. The first school in the U.S. for deaf students was established in 1871. Pioneers such as Gallaudet, Clerc, Bell and Mann contributed to the field through dedicated teaching, successful communication, invention of telephone and audiometer, lobbying for legislation, and school or social reforms.

6. A child may be born with deafness (congenitally deaf) or he/she may acquire the condition after birth (adventitiously deaf). Possible causes included hereditary factors, maternal Rubella, meningitis, otitis media, noise, and other factors. Hearing impairments may be prevented through noise control and medical technology.

7. Children with hearing impairments have IQ scores similar to their hearing peers. Due to the deaf and hard-of-hearing conditions, they tend to have delayed speech and language development, reading or other academic areas' performance, and social adjustment.

8. School for children with hearing impairments may choose the option of manual, auditory-oral, or total communication.

9. The framework of the curriculum in Hong Kong asserts that the learning experiences of children with hearing impairments should be similar to those of other children.

10. Along with other instructional strategies and tips, computer-assisted learning (CAL) and the puzzle technique appear to be helpful for teachers of children with hearing impairments.

ACTIVITIES

1. Search for definitions of hearing impairments used in other countries and compare them with the Hong Kong definition. Discuss how similar or different they are.

2. Conduct research and trace the development of this field and document significant trends and issues, people, technology, and other related topics. Write a report about your findings.

3. Investigate the prevalence of children with hearing impairments in Hong Kong, their general learning environments, the instructional models used in special schools for these children, and their schooling experiences if they are in regular schools through the integration project initiated by the Education Department. Write a report on your findings and make recommendations for further improvement of their education.

4. Design a bulletin board or web page to display causes and prevention information.

5. Design posters that contain information on preventing hearing impairments for community display.

6. Form three groups for discussion. One group focuses on preschoolers with hearing impairments, one on children with hard-of-hearing conditions at school age, and one on deaf children at school age. Each

group should discuss the most appropriate educational program in the following areas: curriculum, instructional methods, extracurricular activities, technology, and language development.

RESOURCES

Resources in Hong Kong

Caritas Magdalene School
44st Francis Street, Wanchai, Hong Kong
Tel.: 852-2527-8287   Fax: 852-2527-0002
Web address: http://www.caritas.org.hk/list/list9.html

Bradbury Special Child Care Center
3/F Holy Trinity Church Bradbury Building
135 ma Tau Chung Road, Kowloon
E-mail: bsccc@enmpc.org.hk

Chinese Y.M.C.A. of Hong Kong — Y's Men's Centre For The Deaf
G/Floor, Unit No. 2 Sau On House, Sau Mau Ping Estate
Kowloon, Hong Kong
Tel.: 852-2717-1754   Fax: 852-2348-1612
Web address: http://www.ymca.org.hk

Hong Kong Host Lions Center for the Deaf &
Hong Kong Host Lions Special Child Care Center
Podium Floor, Hong Shing Court, Healthy Village
668 King's Road, North Point, Hong Kong
E-mail: hkcdeaf@enmpc.org.hk

Hong Kong School for the Deaf
171 Hammer Hill Road, Diamond Hill, Kowloon.
Tel.: 852-2326-5111   Fax: 852-2351-7244

Hong Kong Society for The Deaf
Room 903, Duke of Windsor Social Service Building
15 Hennessy Road, Wanchai, Hong Kong
Tel.: 852-2854-2676 or 852-2854-2713
Web address: http://www.deaf.org.hk

Hong Kong Sports Association of the Deaf
Sports House, 1 Stadium Path, So Kon Po, Causeway Bay, Hong Kong.
Tel.: 852-2504-8128 or 852-2504-8519   Fax: 852-2576-7952
Web address: http://www.geocities.com/Colosseum/Midfield/5984/

Hong Kong Sports Development Board
Sports House, 1 Stadium Path, So Kon Po, Causeway Bay, Hong Kong.
Lions Kowloon Centre for the Deaf & Speech Therapy Centre
509–516 Kar Man House,
Oi Man Estate, Homantin, Kowloon
E-mail: klncdeaf@enmpc.org.hk

Lions Nature Education Centre — Deaf Cafeteria
Tsiu Hang, Sai Kung, New Territories, Hong Kong

Lutheran School for the Deaf
89 Hing Shing Road, Kwai Chung, New Territories, Hong Kong
Tel.: 852-2489-8298   Fax: 852-2494-0197
E-mail: hlng@lsd.edu.hk
Web address: http://www.lsd.edu.hk

Resource Centre for Parents with Hearing Impaired Children
Podium Floor, Hong Shing Court, Healthy Village
No. 668 King's Road, North Point, Hong Kong

Suen Mei Speech & Hearing Centre for the Deaf
Unit 5 (South Portion), G/F, Lai Chi Kok Bay Garden
272 Lai King Hill Road, Kowloon.
Tel.: 852-2743-7377   Fax: 852-2370-3048

Victoria Park School for the Deaf
38 Hing Fat Street, Causeway Bay, Hong Kong
Tel.: 852-2571-2318   Fax: 852-2566-6442

Resources in China

Jinan Research Institute of Medical Sciences, Deaf Treatment Center
濟南市醫科所耳聾治療研究中心
Web address: http://www.deaf-treat-center.com/

Macau Deaf Association
E-mail: deafass@macau.ctm.net
Web address: http://home.macau.ctm.net/~eric1113/MDA/C_MDA_Main.
  html

Macau Social Service Centre for the Deaf
E-mail: deafass@macau.ctm.net

Resources in Taiwan

Chinese Deaf Association
錦西街4-1號3樓, Taipei, Taiwan
E-mail: ccda@TPTS8.seed.net.tw
Web address: http://www.deaf.org.tw/

The NWL Foundation for the Hearing Impaired, ROC
中正區長沙街一段27號, Taipei, Taiwan
Tel.: 886-02-2381-2811   Fax: 886-02-2389-2815
E-mail: nwlhif@tpts6.seed.net.tw
Web address: http://www.nwlhif.org.tw

中華民國聾啞資源協會
彰化縣田中鎮中州路二段93巷87號
Tel.: 886-04-875-7083   Fax: 886-04-874-3122
Web address: http://www.dra.org.tw/

中華民國愛加倍社會福利關懷協會
台北市重慶北路三段312巷6號2樓
Tel.: 886-02-2586-9329
Web address: http://aswa.wingnet.com.tw/

International Resources

Clarke School for the Deaf/Center for Oral Education
Round Hill Road, Northampton, MA 01060 U.S.A.
Tel.: 1-413-584-3450   Fax: 1-413-584-8273
Web address: http://www.clarkeschool.org

The Canadian Council on Rehabilitation and Work (CCRW)
500 University Avenue, Suite 302, Toronto, Ontario, Canada M5G 1V7
Tel.: 1-416-260-3060 TTY: 1-416-260-9223   Fax: 1-416-260-3093
Web address: http://www.ccrw.org/

Council for Exceptional Children (CEC)
Division for Children's Communication Development
The Journal of Children's Communication Development
Web address: http://pegasus.cc.ucf.edu/~abrice/jccd.html

Gallaudet University
800 Florida Ave., NE, Washington, DC 20002-3695 U.S.A.
Tel.: 1-202-651-5000
Web address: http://www.gallaudet.edu

REFERENCES

Cole, P.R. (1987). Recognizing language disorders. In F.N. Martin (Ed.), *Hearing disorders in children* (pp. 113–150). Austin, TX: PRO-ED.

Gallaudet Research Institute (1994). *Gallaudet Research Institute Working Papers 89-3*. Washington, DC: Author.

Greenberg, M.T., & Kusche, C.A. (1989). Cognitive, personal, social development of deaf children and adolescents. In M.C. Wang, M.C. Reynolds, & H.J. Walberg (Eds.), *Handbook of special education: Research and practice: Vol. 3. Low incidence conditions.* (pp. 95–129). Oxford, England: Pergamon Press.

Hallahan, D.P., & Kauffman, J.M. (1994). *Exceptional children: Introduction to special education* (6th ed.). Boston, Allyn and Bacon.

Hess, D. (1991, July 23). Say what? *Albuquerque Journal*, A1-A2.

Hotchkiss, D. (1989). *Aspects of hearing impairment: Questions and answers* (2nd ed.). Washington, DC: Center for Assessment and Demographic Studies, Gallaudet University.

Karchmer, M.A. (1985). Demographics and deaf adolescence. In G.B. Anderson & D. Watson (Eds.), *The habilitation and rehabilitation of deaf adolescents* (pp. 28–47). Washington, DC: Gallaudet College Press.

Lartz, M., & Prendergast, S. (1998). Technologies for people who are deaf and hard of hearing. In J.R. Thompson, M.E. Wall, & S.M. Winchip (Eds), *Assistive technology: Competencies and skills for teachers*. Normal, IL: University Communications, Illinois State University.

Lian, M-G.J. (1999). *Getting to know individuals with physical disabilities and health impairments*. Normal, IL: University Communications, Illinois State University.

Lowenbraun, S. (1988). Hearing impaired. In E.L. Meyen, Skrtic, T.M. (Eds), *Exceptional children and youth: An introduction* (3rd ed.) (pp. 321–350). Denver CO: Love Publishing Co.

Marschark, M. (1993). Origins and interactions in the social, cognitive, and language development of deaf children. In M. Marschark & M.D. Clark (Eds.), *Psychological perspectives on deafness* (pp. 7–26). Washington, DC: Gallaudet University Press.

Meadow, K.P. (1980). *Deafness and child development*. Berkeley: University of California Press.

Mingpao. (2001, May 21). *The emphasis on hearing and language training*. [Online] http://www.mingpaonews.com/

Pappas, D. (1985). *Diagnosis and treatment of hearing impairment in children*. San Diego: College-Hill.

Paul, P.V., & Quigley, S.P. (1990). *Education and deafness*. White Plains, NY: Longman.

Quigley, S.P., & Paul, P.V. (1989). English language development. In M.C. Wang,

M.C. Reynolds, & H.J. Walberg (Eds.), *Handbook of special education: Research and practice: Vol. 3. Low incidence conditions* (pp. 3–22). Oxford, UK: Pergamon..

Smith, D.D., & Luckasson, R. (1995). *Introduction to special education: Teaching in an age of challenge* (2nd ed.). Needham Heights, MA: Allyn & Bacon.

Thake, B. (1988). *The effects of otitis media on selected motor and vestibular functions of kindergarten children.* Unpublished master's thesis, Illinois State University, Normal, Il.

Tye-Murray, N. (Ed.). (1992). *Cochlear implants and children: A handbook for parents, teachers, and speech and hearing professionals.* Washington, DC: Alexander Graham Bell Association for the Deaf.

10

Physical and Health Disabilities

ADVANCED THINKING

Answer the following questions as you read:

1. How are physical and health disabilities defined?
2. What are the three major categories of physical and health disabilities?
3. What are the key events and efforts that contributed to the historical development of education for children with physical and health disabilities?
4. What are the possible causes of physical and health disabilities?
5. What are the strategies for preventing physical and health disabilities?
6. What are the general and specific characteristics of children with physical and health disabilities?
7. What are potential education-related arrangements and approaches for students with physical and health disabilities?

KEY TERMS AND PHRASES

adaptive equipment	cardiac disorder
adolescent pregnancy	cerebral palsy
AIDS	characteristics
amputation	child abuse and neglect
arthritis	convulsive disorder
arthrogryposis	cystic fribrosis
asthma	diabetes mellitus
ataxia	diplegia
athetosis	drug addiction
atonia	genetic disorder
cancer	health impairment

hemiplegia	prevention
hemophilia	progressive condition
hepatitis	pulmonary tuberculosis
hip dislocation	quadriplegia
history	range of motion
hypertonia	Rh incompatibility
hypotonia	rigidity
kidney disorder	scoliosis
legg-calve-perthes disease	seizures
lifting and transferring	severity
monoplegia	sickle cell anemia
muscle tone	spasticity
muscular dystrophy	specific health care need
orthopedic impairment	spina bifida
osteogenesis imperfecta	spinal cord injury
paraplegia	temporary condition
physical disability	traumatic brain injury
poliomyelitis	tremor
positioning	triplegia

INTRODUCTION

Physical disabilities and health impairments may affect an individual's ability to move about, to use arms and legs effectively, to breathe independently, and to swallow food. This individual's capacities to see, hear, think, or use language may also be affected. Lian (1998) listed the following educational and rehabilitation needs caused by physical and health disabilities:

1. Specific health care arrangements for seizures, heart defects, asthma or allergy; suction and ventilation; tube feeding and diet control; catheterization and personal hygiene; and tutoring for hospitalization or low school attendance.
2. Motor and mobility adaptations and training for individuals who are nonambulatory and those with scissored gait, infantile reflexes, lack of head control, or hyperextension.
3. Alternative or augmentative accommodations for speech and language communication deficits.

4. Remediation for learning deficits such as perceptual-conceptual disorders and perceptual-motor incoordination.
5. Accommodations for independent living, including self-feeding, dressing, grooming, traveling, vocational development, community living, and participating in leisure/recreational activities.
6. Coping with social/emotional problems, such as low self-concept, withdrawal, aggression, or negativism.

In the United States, the federal law of Individuals with Disabilities Education Act (IDEA) employs the terms *orthopedic impairments* to describe students with physical disabilities, *traumatic brain injury* (TBI) to describe students with an acquired injury caused by an external physical force to the head, and *other health impairments* (OHI) to describe students with health-related disabling conditions (20 USC 1401). The eligibility section in the Americans with Disabilities Act (ADA) of 1991 has a more specific and inclusive statement:

> ... any physiological disorder, or condition, cosmetic disfigurement, or anatomical loss affecting one or more of the following body systems: neurological, musculoskeletal, special sense organs, respiratory (including speech organs), cardiovascular, reproductive, digestive, genito-urinary, hemic and lymphatic, skin, and endocrine. (U.S. Equal Employment Opportunity Commission, 1992, p. II-2)

Legislation to support special needs education may need to specify that not only children with a permanent physical or health disability, but also those who have the similar but temporary conditions, would be provided with educational and related services, such as specific health care arrangements, physical and occupational therapy, accommodated transportation, and family support (Lian, 1999; Lowman, 1997).

In this chapter, we are going to discuss the definition of physical and health disabilities, history of the field of physical and health disabilities, possible causes and prevention, characteristics of children with physical and health disabilities, and curriculum and instruction for these children.

PHYSICAL AND HEALTH DISABILITIES DEFINED

Persons with physical and health disabilities are in a diverse group, which can generally be divided into three major categories:

1. *Neurological impairments*: damage to the central nervous system

(i.e., the brain and spinal cord) including cerebral palsy, traumatic brain injury, convulsive disorders, spina bifida, spinal cord injury, and poliomyelitis.

2. *Orthopedic impairments*: damage to the muscles, bones, and/or joints including muscular dystrophy, arthrogryposis, amputation, hip dislocation, legg-calve-perthes disease, osteogenesis imperfecta, arthritis, and scoliosis.

3. *Health impairments*: damage to specific body systems (e.g., pulmonary, circulatory, digestive, urological, and endocrine) including diabetes mellitus, asthma, cystic fibrosis, pulmonary tuberculosis, cardiac disorders, hemophilia, sickle cell anemia, cancer, kidney disorders, hepatitis, AIDS, child abuse and neglect, adolescent pregnancy, and drug addictions.

Neurological Impairments

Cerebral Palsy (CP)

Cerebral palsy is a nonprogressive condition resulting from damage to the motor areas of the brain before, during, or after birth (United Cerebral Palsy Association, 1992). The damage in cerebrum or cerebellum usually occurs prior to maturation of the central nervous system (CNS). We need to be reminded that, "cerebral palsy is a condition, not a disease and should never be referred to as a disease or illness" (Lian, 1999, p. 89). Children with *spastic, flaccid, athetoid,* or *ataxic* cerebral palsy may have motor control and postural difficulties, convulsive disorders, speech impairments, and other related disabling conditions. They tend to be considered multiply disabled because of its multifaceted nature. The extent of impact on an individual can range from mild to severe in many aspects.

Traumatic Brain Injury (TBI)

According to Lehr (1990), *traumatic brain injury* is caused by "rapid acceleration and deceleration of the brain, including shearing (tearing) of nerve fibers, contusion (bruising) of the brain tissue against the skull, brain stem injuries, and edema (swelling)" (p.15). A definition of TBI should exclude congenital or degenerative brain injuries, or the injuries caused by birth trauma (i.e., cerebral palsy). Students with TBI may have one or more of the following areas affected: cognition and memory, attention, reasoning, abstract thinking, judgment, problem-solving language, sensory, perceptual, and motor abilities. If the injuries do not involve penetration of the skull, they are called *closed-head injuries*. If the skull is penetrated, the conditions are referred to as *open-head injuries*, such as gunshot wounds. Students with traumatic injuries may need recovery, re-entry, and life curriculum, along with appropriate social and emotional rehabilitation.

Convulsive Disorders

Convulsive disorders, seizure disorders and *epilepsy* are used inter-changeably. These terms refer to body reactions caused by an abnormal neurochemical activity in the brain. Persons with convulsive disorders may have seizures and/or epileptic conditions. *Seizure* is an abnormal, unpredictable, yet temporary discharge of electrical impulses that alters the normal functioning of the individual. Anyone may have a seizure under certain conditions (e.g., severe head trauma, high fever during infancy, or low blood sugar). *Epilepsy* is a tendency toward recurrent seizures. It is a disorder of the central nervous system marked by transient periods of unconsciousness or psychic disturbance, twitching delirium or convulsive movements.

There are two types of seizures. Tonic-clonic seizures (formerly called *grand mal seizures*) affect the entire brain. The tonic phase comes before the *clonic phase*. Beginning with a loss of consciousness and falling to the ground, the *tonic phase* of these seizures then causes the stiffening of the body. The *clonic phase* follows with involuntary, repeated muscle contractions (violent shaking) and relaxation. Such seizures may last less than one minute or as long as more than 20 minutes. The best way to respond to this type of seizure is to ease the person to the floor, if possible, to avoid injuries from falling. Any dangerous objects from the immediate environment should be removed and placing a soft pad under the person's head to allow him/her to rest will be helpful. Tonic-clonic seizures are usually followed by a period of sleepiness and confusion. Other charac-teristics include saliva being forced from mouth and loss of bladder or bowel control. Teachers and caregivers are advised not to put any object between the person's teeth or pull out his/her tongue. Regarding treatment, medication usually can control tonic-clonic seizures well up to normal life.

Absence seizures (formerly called *petit mal seizures*) are less dangerous and last a shorter period of time. Symptoms may include brief periods (maybe seconds) of inattention that tends to be accompanied by rapid eye blinking and head twitching. The inattentive behaviors could mistakenly be viewed by teachers as daydreaming. Absence seizures may occur more than 100 times a day. Prescribed medication is usually effective in controlling absence seizures.

Spina Bifida (SB)

Spina bifida is a congenital malformation of the spine characterized by incomplete development of the vertebrae causing an opening in the spinal column. There are two types of spina bifida: spina bifida occulta and spina bifida cystica. *Spina bifida occulta (lipomenigecele)* is the condition in which the spinal cord does not protrude. There is no neurological damage, nor outward sign of a defect except occasionally a clump of hair growing from the area of the spine involved. It tends to be a rather mild condition in which only a small slit is present in one or more the vertebral structures. Most people who have spina bifida occulta do not realize they have the condition (March of Dimes, 1992). It has little impact on a developing infant.

Spina bifida cystica is a malformation of the spinal column with a sac protruding on the back. The two main types of spina bifida cystica are spina bifida-meningocele and spina bifida-myelomeningocele. *Meningocele* has a tumorlike sac along the backbone with cerebrospinal fluid but no nerve tissue. It tends not to cause significant neurological disability. *Myelomeningocele* (or *meningomyleocele*), on the other hand, is when the sac contains the spinal cord with neurological damage. It may cause more severe paraplegic or quadriplegic disabling conditions.

Hydrocephalus is a frequent complication of spina bifida-myelomeningocele because the open spine tends to cause the lower portion of the brain to slip through the opening into the spinal cord, which may stop the circulation of the cerebrospinal fluid. This leads to a fluid accumulation in the ventricles of the brain and enlargement of the head. A shunt, which is a plastic tube as a permanent drainage system, is commonly implanted in order to relieve the excessive fluid and pressure in the central nervous system.

Spinal Cord Injury (SCI)

Due traumatic causes such as birth injury, accidents at home, school, or other places (e.g., falling from a height, traffic accidents, gun shot wounds, sport injuries), and child abuse/neglect situations, *spinal cord injury* may include paralysis of the legs and lower parts of the body (*paraplegia*) or paralysis of all four limbs (*quadriplegia*). A student with spinal cord injury may face challenging conditions of nonambulation and difficulty in mobility.

If at young age, he/she may have insufficient cognitive learning through tactile-perceptual and kinesthetic stimulation. Specific health care needs may also exist, such as medical procedures for catheterization and enhancing breathing and ventilation. Teachers and other school personnel may need to remove architectural and classroom barriers, minimize social-emotional stress, and maximize encouragement and motivation in order to provide the student with better accessibility and more motivation for learning and social interaction with children.

Poliomyelitis

Poliomyelitis is a viral infection which destroys the anterior horn cells of the spinal cord and creates a gap between the central nervous system and the peripheral nerves. Paralysis occurs below the part that has been damaged by the infection. There are four forms of poliomyelitis. *Asymptomatic poliomyelitis* and *abortive poliomyelitis* have the least severe, flu-like symptoms which last about two to four days after infection with no paralytic result. *Nonparalytic poliomyelitis* causes viral meningitis which is associated with stiff neck, headache, and fever with no paralytic results. *Paralytic poliomyelitis* is the most severe form which causes permanent paralysis. Children with paralytic poliomyelitis generally need psychological and emotional support. In most cases, their intellectual abilities are not affected. They may need a wheelchair, crutches, and braces (*orthotics*) for postural support and mobility. Preparation is needed to cope with reoccurrence of progressive disabling conditions and to seek for medical and therapeutic support for in case of weakness, fatigue, and pain.

Orthopedic Impairments

Muscular Dystrophy (MD)

Muscular dystrophy refers to "a group of conditions that are inherited, progressive, and characterized by myodegeneration" (De Vivo & DiMauro, 1994, p. 2082). There are different forms of muscular dystrophy. The *Duchenne muscular dystrophy*, first delineated by Dr. Duchenne in 1968, is the most common form of MD. It occurs in early childhood (preschool age) with symptoms starting from lower extremities and, then, moves up to upper trunk and limbs. The diagnosis is rarely made prior to three years of age. A history of slow motor development with late onset of sitting, walking, and running, however, is usually obtained, indicating a much earlier onset.

The *limb-girdle muscular dystrophy* does not occur in childhood. Symptoms start, during late teenage, from shoulder and, then, move downward to lower limbs. The *facioscapulohumeral muscular dystrophy* (FSH) is a rare form of MD, which affects the facial and shoulder musculature and does not usually occur until the second decade of life. The *congenital myotublar myopathy* is another rare form of MD with underdeveloped muscles. The muscle development could be arrested in the gestational period and, while the muscle strength will not deteriorate, it will not improve, either (Frank, 1996).

Muscular dystrophy is a sex-linked, recessive disorder affecting mostly males. It causes a degeneration of muscle cells and their replacement by fatty and fibrous tissues, which weakens the muscles of the hips, legs, shoulders, and arms, leading to progressive loss of ability to walk and to use arms and hands effectively. Sometimes heart muscles may be affected to trigger symptoms of heart failure. The severity of muscular dystrophy is influenced by age of onset, the physical location and nature of onset, and the rate at which the condition progresses. It is recommended that teachers and other service providers give emotional assistance and motivation for life fulfillment for students with MD, give extra rest for common and frequent fatigue, and arrange continuous gross and fine motor training and the use of adaptive equipment for feeding, bathrooming, and other daily living requirements.

Arthrogryposis

Arthrogryposis is a nonprogressive congenital condition characterized by stiffness and deformity of the limbs and trunk. The term, arthrogryposis, refers to congenital contractures of joints in flexion. Persons with this condition may have little or no joint motion because the limb muscles tend to be absent or much smaller or weaker than normal. Arthrogryposis usually occurs alone, but may be associate with other malformations. Students with arthrogryposis need to use adaptive equipment for supporting independent walking, self-help, academic, and vocational development. Specific procedural adaptations may need to be arranged in the classroom, for example, the use of oral report, or computers with appropriate adaptations, in order to enable these students who may have handwriting problems.

Amputation

Amputation is the absence, failure of development, or removal of a limb or appendage which can be congenital or acquired (by surgery or accidents).

Amputation of a limb may occur when no normal structures are presented distal to the missing portion. It may also occur when a middle segment of the limb is absent, but the proximal and distal portions are intact. *Phocomelia* is the condition when hands or feet are attached proximally to the shoulders or hips. Children with amputation may need to go through a series of surgery and physical/occupational therapy. Appropriate artificial limbs (*prosthetics*) can be prescribed, followed with continuous adjustment, training and practice. Students with amputation tend to have possible emotional concerns in the school and among their nondisabled peers, including stares, withdrawal, embarrassment, curiosity, and teasing. Periodic evaluation of the situation and ongoing guidance and support are needed.

Hip Dislocation

Hip dislocation is a condition in which the head of femur (i.e., the thigh bone) is displaced in the hip socket (*acetabulum*). Correction of hip dislocation can be by gentle manipulation and brace or cast for 6–12 weeks. If the condition is not corrected for several months, the child may need to be placed in traction to first stretch tight muscles and ligaments before the replacement. If it is not discovered until the child begins to walk or reaches school age, the treatment will be much more complicated. Surgery is often necessary, in order to release adductor muscles and remove the nerve supplying these muscles (called *adductor tenotomy and obturator neurectomy*, or ATON) and remove soft tissues from the socket and body cast for about three months.

Children with hip dislocation need to avoid any standing or high kneeling on dislocated hip. Relaxation techniques can be applied to prevent scissoring, contractures, and abnormal posture. The physical therapist can suggest appropriate positioning and carrying to prevent pain or discomfort and further injury. Teachers may arrange modified activities after a child comes back from a surgery, e.g., less vigorous activities to avoid running, jumping, and twisting.

Legg-calve-perthes Disease

Legg-calve-perthes disease (or *legg-perthes disease*) is a temporary orthopedic disability, in which the *epiphysis* (growth center) of femur has been partially or completely destroyed. This condition may be caused by a loss of blood supply to the growth center due to blood disease, metabolic disorder, infection, injuries, or side-effects of drugs. Legg-calve-perthes disease requires operative treatment with surgical arrangements and transplant of live epiphysis tissues. The child may need to learn to use crutches or to get used to cast and braces, and take gentle physical activities (i.e., swimming) rather than active and rigorous sports. This orthopedic disability will exist only temporarily, generally, one to three years.

Osteogenesis Imperfecta (OI)

Osteogenesis imperfecta is a hereditary condition in which the bones do not grow normally and break easily. It has defective development of the quality and quantity of bones and may be diagnosed at birth or at later time after birth. *OI Congenital* has an onset at birth, while *OI Tarda* has a later onset. OI may also be called "*brittle bone disease*" or "*blue sclera*." The condition causes the white matter of the eye (*sclera*) to become thin and, as a result, the underlying layer of the eyeball shows through as a blue discoloration (Bleck & Nagel, 1982).

Infant who has osteogenesis imperfecta may suffer multiple fractures. Potentially, children with OI have physical deformities (e.g., small and bowed limbs, scoliosis, and barrel-shaped chest with forward protrusion of the breast bone), dental problems, hearing disabilities (due to defect of the inner-ear ossicles), and short statue. Students who have OI need to avoid situations which may cause bone fractures, have routine hearing tests to identify conductive auditory disorder, and utilize adaptive equipment for mobility, self-care, and independence.

Arthritis

Arthritis is the inflammation of the joint. The two most common types are osteoarthritis and rheumatoid arthritis. *Osteoarthritis* usually is associated with advanced age which limits the movements of joints. *Rheumatoid* arthritis can be the most disabling type of arthritis. It is not limited to joints; but it may also affect other organ systems such as lungs, muscles, skin, nervous system, and heart. Symptoms of arthritis may include swelling, redness, and pain, as well as difficulty in movement or bending. Medicine can be taken to reduce pain and inconvenience. Aspirin has been found to be one of the most effective drugs used in the treatment of arthritis. Appropriate exercise and rest can be used to strengthen joints and keep them moving smoothly.

Scoliosis

Scoliosis is a lateral or side-to-side curvature of the spine in the shape of an letter C or S. In *nonstructural scoliosis*, the curvature is secondary to a known cause and the curvature will resolve when the underlying cause is corrected or when the person bends. In *structural scoliosis* the curvature is secondary to a variety of known or unknown causes, which will not resolve with treatment of the underlying cause nor with simple bending. Children with scoliosis may need appropriate positioning (e.g., side lying with appropriate support), back brace, and physical/occupational therapy. Their health condition needs to be monitored to detect asymmetrical alignment, flattened and twisted ribcage, difficult or shallow breathing, muscle stiffness, contractures, and dislocated hip.

Health Impairments

Diabetes Mellitus

Diabetes mellitus is a hereditary or developmental disorder with which the pancreas does not produce adequate amount of insulin or utilize insulin adequately to process carbohydrates. Without insulin, glucose (a sugar used by the body for energy) accumulates in the blood, causing a condition known as *hyperglycemia*. This condition, if untreated, can lead to loss of consciousness or diabetic coma (Bianchi, 1994). Children with diabetes need balanced sugar intake, insulin level in the blood stream, and amount of activities and exercise. Specific times of a day may be critical for checking if potential *hyperglycemia* (too much sugar which may cause *diabetes coma*) or hypoglycemia (inadequate sugar or *insulin shock*) has been developed.

Asthma

Asthma is one of the most common chronic diseases among children. It is characterized by severe difficulty in breathing. *Wheezing* is usually accompanied by shortness of breath and a cough. Causes may include tightening of the muscles around the bronchial tubes; swelling of the tissues in these tubes; and increase of secretions in these tubes. It is believed that asthma is most frequently triggered by an allergic reaction to certain substances in those who have a physical predisposition to asthma. Possible substances may include dust mites, plants, foods, cigarette smoke, environmental pollutants, chemicals, or cockroaches. Students with asthma should not be totally excluded from physically exertive activities. Teachers need to avoid stimulating a child's allergic sensitivity and overly excited exercise. Instead, they can support his/her growth and functional daily skills toward independence.

Cystic Fribrosis (CF)

Cystic fribrosis (CF) is a hereditary, progressive condition of children and young adults involving defective production of *enzymes* in the pancreas with disturbances throughout the body and usually with pulmonary involvement. In children with cystic fribrosis, the mucus does not move effectively and the lungs are poorly cleared, even some areas totally collapse (*atelectasis*). Persistent coughing is one of the common characteristics, along with potential prolonged lung infections, frequent and large amount of stools, and great amount of salt loss through perspiration.

A child with CF has to avoid greasy food and, as a result, they tend to need vitamin A, D, E, K (all fat-soluble) supplement. He/she may be on multiple medication (for pancreas and lungs), including during class hours

Pulmonary Tuberculosis (TB)

Caused by the bacteria called *tubercle bacillus*, *pulmonary tuberculosis* (TB) is a chronic communicable subacute or acute disease which commonly affects the respiratory system but may involve parts of other systems. It is a significant debilitating infant and young adulthood disease. TB is generally a disease of poverty in which overcrowding, undernutrition, and poor body resistance to infection are typical.

Tuberculin test ("TB test") is the procedure to inject tuberculin under skin of forearm and check reactions in 24 to 36 hours. If the result is negative (–), no further examination is necessary. If it is positive (+), then chest X-ray examination is required. If the chest X-ray result is negative (–), usually no treatment is needed. However, if a person is found to become tuberculin test positive recently, preventive medicine may be required. If the chest X-ray result is positive (+), the person needs treatment. If he/she is an open case, specific procedures also need to be followed to prevent infection of others.

Students with open-case pulmonary tuberculosis may need to be arranged for hospital or homebound teaching. Those in recovery still need routine monitoring of nutrition and health conditions, as well as back-to-school efforts and support.

Cardiac Disorders

A number of children are born with defects of the heart. The defects may occur during the first 1–3 months of embryonic development at the time the heart is being formed. One of the most common congenital heart disorders is that, after birth, a child may still have open *foramen ovale* and *ductus arteriosus* in the blood circulation which cause insufficient oxygen in blood and symptoms of heart defects. During pregnancy, the foramen ovale and ductus arteriosus of the fetus are open because there is no need for blood to be sent to the lungs of the fetus for oxygen exchange. These foramen ovale and ductus arteriosus are usually closed shortly after birth, when the child picks up his/her own blood circulation to the lungs. If they are not closed, blood with insufficient oxygen exchange may be sent out to the whole body, causing cyanosis, heart murmur, and other symptoms.

Characteristics of a child with cardiac disorders include shortness of breath, weakness, and frequent fatigue. He/she may have *cyanosis* (blue appearance of the skin due to the poor oxygenation of the blood), chest deformity, and clubbing of fingers and toes. Modified school schedules may be needed due to weakness and frequent fatigue, along with counseling and guidance, support, and encouragement for participation in general activities together with nondisabled peers.

Hemophilia

Hemophilia is a sex-lined, recessive hereditary health impairment, in which one of the blood-clotting (*coagulation*) factors, the antihemophiliac factor (AHF), is missing. As a result, the most minor injury or accident can lead to uncontrolled bleeding. Permanent damage may occur if the bleeding is internal. Hemophilia is also called the "*bleeder's disease*." Specific arrangements may be needed to prevent a child from being too active; decisions about physical activities and sports will depend on the severity of the disease and the availability of prophylactic AHF program (i.e., blood transfusion). Because of frequent blood transfusion, children with hemophilia may be at risk to be infected with HIV. It is important to provide counseling and support services for stress and to prevent the child's excessive dependency. Therefore, he/she can be led to normal life.

Sickle Cell Anemia

Sickle cell anemia is an *autosomal, recessive* hereditary condition of shrunken, fragile red blood cells causing insufficient (in quantity and quality) hemoglobin and oxygen carrying in the blood stream. Symptoms include *sickling* (pain crisis), such as spleen (left-sided abdominal) pain, bone pain, or sickling in the brain, intestine, liver, lungs, or kidneys. The body size of a child with sickle cell anemia may be small for his/her age. The sickle-shape red blood cells may have a tendency to cause blockage of blood circulation, resulting in stroke or paralysis in other parts of the body. Multiple blood transfusions with supportive care are generally given to treat acute pain and other complications. The child can participate in most activities except for excessive physical exercise which may tire him/her. Teachers need to work with children who may be disturbed by uncertainty, frustration, and stress, and to increase their self-reliance and independence.

Cancer

Childhood cancer is a group of diseases which cause *neoplasia* (tumor formation), representing the unrestrained, abnormal and persistent proliferation of cells that results from a defect in the mechanisms that normally govern cell division and differentiation. The most common type of childhood cancer is *leukemia*, the so-called "blood cancer." It is characterized by a malignant proliferation of abnormal cells in the bone marrow and greatly increased number of white blood cell (*leukocytes*). Other malignant tumors may be developed in the brain, bone, skin, lung, stomach, pancreas, breast, or prostate areas. Children with cancer may need to receive surgical or radio treatment, along with chemotherapy, which tends to have side effects such as nausea, loss of hair, and change of personality. They need strong support for avoiding emotional disturbance and stress, and special guidance for coping with concerns of terminal illness. Modern medical sciences have greatly improved the prognosis of various types of childhood cancer.

Kidney Disorders

Kidney disorders are health impairments in one or both of the kidneys. There are a number of specific conditions relating to kidney disorders. The *end stage kidney disease* is the incapability of filtering water and waste products from the bloodstream. *Glomerolonephritis* is an inflammation of the filtering unit (*glomeruli*). *Nephrotic syndrome* is the glomerular damage, which allows excessive amounts of protein to leak into the urine and then be excreted from the body. *Hypertension* may be caused by kidney disorder-related high blood pressure. Children with kidney disorders may need special diet to control the amount of protein, fluid, and potassium; drug therapy to control blood pressure and abnormalities in blood chemistries; *peritoneal hemodialysis* through which a tube is inserted to fill the abdomen with premixed fluid in order to remove body wastes by diffusion of the substances from abdominal blood vessels; and, if necessary, kidney transplant. Schools need to plan appropriate accommodations and provide support accordingly, e.g., special diet for lunch, coping with child's emotional stress, and providing hospital or bedside teaching.

Hepatitis

Hepatitis is a viral infection of the liver with possible symptoms of loss of appetite, tenderness in the upper right abdomen, extreme fatigue, and often jaundice. Persons with abnormalities in their immune system and persons' lack of personal hygienic behaviors are more likely to become *carriers*. Students and school personnel may need to have hepatitis A and B screening tests to detect if they have antibodies. Vaccination is strongly recommended in epidemic areas, especially for those who work in food services and human services (e.g., education, therapy, and rehabilitation). Persons with hepatitis need medical treatment and support for better physical and emotional health and strength. Hospital or homebound teaching may need to be arranged.

Burns

Burns are one type of physical injuries affecting the different layers of skin and underneath organs. After burns occur, related health situations follow. There are three degrees of burn:

1. First degree burn: superficial burn, e.g., mild sunburn.
2. Second degree burn: partial thickness skin damage spares enough epidermis to allow healing without skin grafts.
3. Third degree burn: full thickness burn causing damage to the epidermis and dermis, loss of all dermis hair follicles and sweat glands; need of skin grafts to heal.

Children with burns may have the following physical and psychosocial implications:

1. Complications: loss of fluid, shock, heat loss, bacteria or fungus infections, function disturbance in organs (kidney, lungs, heart, liver, and brain), contractures and loss of movement of joints, damage to the sensory organs (loss of visual acuity, cataract, hearing loss, skin sensory deficit, etc.).
2. Physical limitations: protection to prevent infection, activity limitation due to insufficient sweat glands, formation of thick hard scar tissue and contracture causing decreased range of movement and related problems (i.e., difficulty of motor movement, speech problems, drooling, etc.), amputation, sensory damages.

3. Psychological implications: emotional disturbance of child and parent, feeling of guilt, pain and confinement (i.e., aggressiveness, learned helplessness, withdrawal, or over-protection), disfigurement (fears, withdrawal, feeling of rejection, overcompensation), morbidity and mortality (physician/nurse, parent, and other caregivers' strong emotions and continuous stress causing child's uncertainty and anxiety).

Treatment of burns generally needs a multidisciplinary team approach for both acute and chronic stages:

1. The acute stage (during initial wound coverage): wounds cleaned as necessary, fluid administration, monitoring of cardiovascular status, antibiotics to prevent or control infections.
2. Chronic: grafting when patient is stable, multiple reconstructive surgeries, use of splints to maintain positions of limbs, physical/ occupational therapy and rehabilitation services, feeding and nutritional program, and family care.

Lian (1999) listed the following educational considerations and arrangements:

1. A child with burns may need hospital or home tutoring.
2. There may be residual effects of burns, which are more likely to have other health problems and emotional disturbance.
3. The mental capacity of the person who suffers burns is rarely affected.
4. Evaluation of home environment is necessary if burns are a result of child abuse/neglect.
5. There may be feeding and/or speech problems and need for specific nutrition or diet programs.
6. There may be contractures in specific joints and difficulty of motor movement.
7. There may be other affected body functions.
8. There may be emotional instability, disturbance and depression.
9. There may be needs for adapted leisure/recreational and physical education goals and activities.
10. There may be need to avoid temperature extremes and prolonged or strenuous exercise.
11. The child in school may have short attention span and need frequent rest periods.
12. Team efforts are essential for full recovery.

Acquired Immune Deficiency Syndrome (AIDS)

Acquired immune deficiency syndrome is caused by the human immuno-deficiency virus (HIV) which attacks the white blood cells to break down an individual's immune system and causes fatality through the acquisition of other infections and diseases. The virus is primarily transmitted through exchange of body fluids in sexual activities or by contaminated needles. It was also transmitted in blood transfusions before the institution of blood-screening procedures. Infants may be infected through an infected mother. In many countries, the right to school education for children with AIDS is protected by law and schools need to develop appropriate handling and supporting procedures for these children.

Child Abuse and Neglect

Child abuse is found in every society and all walks of life across social, religious, and professional boundaries. The scope of child abuse ranges from intentional inflicted injury to any act that impairs the developmental potential of a child (Monteleone & Brodeur, 1994). Child abuse includes physical, psychological, and sexual injuries. It can be perceived as parents' or caretakers' maladaptive behaviors in coping with personal and family problems that affect their responses to children. *Child neglect* happens when parents or caretakers fail to care for children in healthy and safe ways or when they abandon their children. Neglected children are often times left without suitable supervision, infrequently bathed, and malnourished. Child abuse and neglect can result in severe emotional and physical trauma that may be difficult to reconstruct. Teachers and other school personnel are responsible for reporting existing child abuse and neglect cases that they discover. They need to work closely with social workers and other family crisis specialists to protect the child, provide psychological and emotional support, and facilitate physical, mental, and academic development.

Adolescent Pregnancy

Adolescent pregnancy refers to pregnancy in girls 19 years or younger. According to Testa (1992a), at least 75% of the adolescent pregnancies are unwanted. Approximately 40% of these unwanted pregnancies are terminated by abortion. A large number of adolescent mothers remain unmarried, drop out of school, and frequently rely on welfare assistance (Rosenheim, 1992), while some of them do successfully overcome the challenges related to adolescent pregnancy in that they complete their schooling and enter the work force without depending on welfare assistance (Testa, 1992b). The special needs education system can offer guidance and support for continuing the students' education.

Drug Addiction

Drugs such as cocaine or heroine used by expectant mothers can place not only themselves but also their babies at risk for a number of serious and sometimes life-threatening problems. For the pregnant women, problems may include lung damage, seizures, cardiac failure, high blood pressure, shortness of breath, and premature labor (Smith, 1988). For the infants (e.g., "crack babies"), negative effects may include diarrhea, gastrointestinal problems, neurological damage, elevated respiratory rate and heart rate, increased distractibility, shorter attention span, and increased irritability. Problems that are suspected but not established yet include a higher risk for sudden infant death syndrome (SIDS), eye defects, cerebral artery injury, and acute hypertension (Hardman, Drew, & Egan, 1996).

HISTORY OF THE FIELD

Historical development relating to persons with physical and health disabilities can be divided into five major stages: the early years, the stage of initiation, the stage of rapid development, the stage of enlightenment, and the stage of information networking and collaboration.

The Early Years

In ancient time, the majority of persons with physical and health disabilities tended to be neglected, rejected, segregated, isolated, and even punished or abandoned because of their difference and superstition, fear, prejudice, and misunderstanding. Many rights of individuals with physical and health disabilities were denied. In the 1919 *Beatti vs. Board of Education of City of Antigo* court case of the United States, for example, it was ruled that the right of a school-age child to attend public school should not be insisted if his appearance was harmful to the best interests of the school.

However, there were pioneers in the field who devoted their time and efforts to improve life of persons with physical and health disabilities. In Chicago, the first class for students with physical disabilities was established in the public school system in 1900 by two physicians: Dr. Winthrops Phelps, who demonstrated that children could be helped through physical therapy and the effective use of braces; and Dr. While Carlson, who himself had cerebral palsy, was a strong advocate for enhancing intellectual potential of children with physical disabilities through appropriate education.

The Stage of Initiation

In the years between 1920 and 1943, there was an increasing number of people with physical disabilities due to World War I and the rapid development of manufacturing industry. The society also started to pay attention to the welfare of children, with and without physical and health disabilities. In the United States, the first Whitehouse Conference on Childhood was held in 1909, with the 2nd and 3rd conferences held in 1920 and 1930, respectively, and more once every ten years thereafter. The National Society for Cripple Children was established in 1921 to enhance care and welfare for children with physical disabilities.

The stage of initiation also found governmental involvement. In 1920, the Congress of the United States passed the Vocational Rehabilitation Act (VRA) for persons with physical disabilities. However, children with physical and health disabilities were still denied for public education. In the court action of *State vs. Christ* in 1936, a polio victim was ruled to stay in special school because of his inability to meet the standard of the grade school.

The Stage of Rapid Development

From 1943 to 1969, there were increasing awareness and concerns regarding persons with physical and health disabilities. During this stage, an infectious disease attacking the spinal cord, poliomyelitis, caused a great number of children paralyzed with lower body muscle atrophy. A group of women in Hong Kong found urgent post-operative needs of children who were recovering from this epidemic crisis. They started taking these children out for recreational activities. In 1963, these female volunteers established the Heep Hong Society. This nonprofit organization provided special child care centres (SCCCs) which, later when episodes of poliomyelitis became almost obsolete in the 1970s, began to provide services for children with broader range of physical, mental, behavioral and development disabilities (Heep Hong Society, 2001). Similarly, at about the same time when epidemic poliomyelitis was controlled by vaccines in the United States, the attention was switched to children with cerebral palsy. The United Cerebral Palsy Association (UCPA) became active.

One of the special schools providing educational and rehabilitation programs for students with orthopedic disabilities in Hong Kong, the John F. Kennedy (JFK) Centre, was established in 1967. A branch of the Hong Kong Red Cross, the mission of JFK Centre is to prepare healthy, happy, knowledgeable, confident, responsible, and independent individuals with potential to be integrated into, and to contribute to, the community (John F. Kennedy Centre, 2001).

In the United States, there were many wounded soldiers who came back from World War II and, then, the Korean conflict. This increased public awareness and it became urgent that the federal government had to provide appropriate educational and rehabilitation services. The 14th Amendment of the U.S. Constitution further encouraged the disadvantaged to advocate for equal rights and opportunities. As a result, the Urban Mass Transit Act was passed by the U.S. Congress in 1964 for persons with disabilities to have the right to use mass transportation. In 1966, the Bureau of Education for the Handicapped (BEH) was established in the U.S. Office of Education for training, research, and service. The Elimination of Architectural Barriers to the Physically Handicapped in Certain Federal Financed Buildings Act of 1968 enhanced the effort for accessibility.

Segregated education was still the main service delivery model during the stage of rapid development. In the U.S. court case of *State Board of Education vs. Petty* in 1950, a deaf child was ruled to attend special school instead of public school because this child had a "physical defect" and "necessarily must" receive a different type of instruction than one who was not handicapped. In another U.S. litigation case, *Department of Public Welfare vs. Haas* of 1958, there was an implied "capacity to learn" attached to the right to an education; public schools were not responsible to provide education to handicapped children. However, the historical train has moved toward inclusion of students with physical and health disabilities. There were increased amount of programs and procedures especially developed and provided for minorities and persons with physical and health disabilities.

The Stage of Enlightenment

The 1970s continued the spirit of equal rights and equal opportunity. Highly developed science and technology coexisted with the concepts of normalization, individualized educational programming (IEP), and desegregation (i.e., deinstitutionalization, mainstreaming, zero rejection, and education in the least restrictive environment, or LRE).

The Federal Highway Act of 1973 mandates that curbs of streets must be cut to permit wheelchair accessibility. The American National Standards Institute (ANSI) Act of 1973 required accommodations for persons with disabilities, such as ramps, elevators, wide doorways, and accessible bathrooms for persons who were physically disabled. Also passed in 1973, the Amendments to the Vocational Rehabilitation Act (VRA) included the following milestone sections:

Sec. 501   For enhancement of employment of persons with disabilities.
Sec. 502   For establishment of the Architectural and Transportation Barriers Compliance Board.
Sec. 503   For affirmative action-private business may receive $2,500 or more in federal fund if searched out and employed persons with disabilities.
Sec. 504   For persons with disabilities not to be excluded from any program or activity receiving federal funds.

The Housing and Community Development Act of 1974 provided federal dollars for suitable housing for persons with physical disabilities and the elderly. The Direct Loan Program Act of 1974 provided loans for builders to make accessible housing, including architectural modifications, which promoted more community living and opposed institutionalization.

The Sahk B. M. Kotewall Memorial School in Kowloon was established in 1974 by the Hong Kong Spastic Association. This school has provided educational and rehabilitation opportunities for students with physical disabilities to achieve holistic growth and development, and their ability and intent to be a contributing member in the community (Sahk B. M. Kotewall Memorial School, 2000).

In 1975, the Education for All Handicapped Children Act (CEAHCA or Public Law 94–142) was passed in United States to guarantee free, appropriate, public education for children with disabilities aged 3 to 21, with priorities for those with most severe disabilities and those who had never had special education services before.

The Public Buildings Cooperative Use Act of 1976 mandated that buildings, which were preserved for historical or for architectural significance by the U.S. federal government, must be accessible for persons with disabilities.

In this stage of enlightenment, detailed and technical programs and procedures were developed and protected by the government for persons with physical and health disabilities.

The Stage of Information Networking and Collaboration

The years of 1980s and 1990s reflected the fast development of personal computers and assistive technology; biological, genetic, and other medical sciences; and Internet and world wide web. Passed in1988, the Technology-Related Assistance for Persons with Disabilities Act in the United States was to enhance statewide assistive technology (AT) programs for persons with disabilities, including need assessment, resources, demonstration, public awareness, and group support.

The Americans with Disabilities Act (ADA) of 1990 defined a person with disabilities as a person who had a physical or mental impairment that substantially limited a major life activity, including persons who were addicted to drugs or alcohol and persons who had AIDS. The U.S. Congress estimated that there were 43 million Americans with disabilities, and 12 million adults with disabilities were employable but were not working. ADA included sanctions for those who discriminated in hiring. This law allowed victims of employment discrimination to seek backpay, reinstatement, and attorneys' fees. It mandated that companies made reasonable accommodations: 25 or more workers had 2 years to comply; 15 to 25 workers had 4 years to comply; and 15 or less workers were exempted. ADA meant a declaration of independence for millions of persons with disabilities. For example, public transportation systems must buy only buses or rail cars that were readily accessible to persons with disabilities. In 5 years, all inter-city and commuter rail services must have at least one passenger car per train for persons with disabilities. In 20 years, all train stations must be accessible to persons with disabilities. In 18 months, all restaurants, theaters, grocery stores, golf courses, etc., had to be accessible to persons with disabilities.

The Individuals with Disabilities Education Act (IDEA) of 1990 amended Public Law 94–142, changed the title of the legislation from the "Education for All Handicapped Children Act" to "IDEA," included autism and traumatic brain injury (TBI) as two new categories of disabling conditions, and added rehabilitation counseling and social work services to the list of related services.

Major trends in the 1980s and 1990s included:

1. High tech in education, therapy, and rehabilitation.
2. Information network.
3. Outcome-based assessment (OBA)
4. Excellence/best practices and quality of life.
5. Increase of community resources.
6. Full inclusion in school and community.
7. Emphasis of families.
8 Emphasis of friendship and relations.
9. Multicultural/crosscultural approaches.
10. Collaborative services.

In conclusion, the historical development relating to persons with physical and health disabilities has demonstrated evolutional and progressive inclusion, and community acceptance and integration for all individuals.

POSSIBLE CAUSES

A variety of prenatal, perinatal, and postnatal factors may cause a physical or health disability. The following are potential *prenatal causes*:

1. Genetic disorders, including chromosomal abnormalities due to nondisjunction, translocation, and mosaicism, as well as autosomal dominant, autosomal recessive, and sex-linked disorders.
2. Drugs, including alcohol (which is the number 1 cause by drug), cigarette, cocaine, barbiturates, antibiotics, hormones (cortisone, steroid), aspirin, and Thalidomide. Smoking cigarettes during pregnancy, for example, may lead to decrease of fetus' body weight, prematurity, increased possibility of stillbirth, increased possibility of bronchitis after birth, and possible intellectual and social delay during infancy. Alcohol consumption during pregnancy may cause delay of fetus' physical growth and development of the nervous system, delay of physical, mental, and social development after birth, and possible behavior disorders during childhood. Thalidomide was prescribed in the 1960s to 1970s by medical doctors for pregnant women who had morning sickness. This drug's side effects happened to be the worst when taken during 34th through 50th days of pregnancy, causing amputation deformity, especially upper extremities and ear, blood vessel tumor, and heart defects.

3. Radiation, such as X-ray and radioisotope, and toxic substances, including lead, carbon monoxide (CO), and insecticides.
4. Maternal infections, such as Rubella, sexually transmitted diseases (e.g., syphilis, AIDS), and virus infections (e.g., cytomegalovirus, or CMV).
5. Prenatal care and maternal health conditions, for example, malnutrition, multiple-fetus pregnancy, fainting, diabetes, lack of oxygen, and premature labor.
6. Traumatic injuries caused by accidents and family crisis.

The following are potential *perinatal causes*:

1. *Rh incompatibility*, which is the combination of the mother's Rh⁻ blood type and the baby's Rh+ blood type, which came from the father, leading to a massive breakdown of the baby's red blood cells. Batshaw and Perret (1981) explained the mechanism and its implications:

   > While the fetal and maternal circulatory systems are separate, an occasional fetal blood cell gets into the maternal circulation. When a birth or miscarriage takes place, a larger number of fetal cells cross over to the maternal circulatory system. If the baby is Rh+ and the mother is Rh⁻, the mother's immune system recognizes the baby's red blood cells as being foreign and begins to develop antibodies to destroy them. Although Rh incompatibility is not a problem for the first child, since the infant will be born before the mother's immune system is set off, subsequent babies may be affected. If the mother becomes pregnant again, and the second child is Rh+, the few fetal red blood cells that cross over to the mother will trigger a massive response from the maternal immune system. The antibodies that are produced by the mother can cross the placenta and destroy the fetus's red blood cells. This results in severe anemia and a buildup of bilirubin in the fetus. In the past, many infants died *in utero* and those who survived suffered brain damage. These children had cerebral palsy, a high-frequency hearing loss, paralysis of the upward gaze, and discoloration of the teeth. (p. 78)

2. Injuries caused by prolonged labor, difficult or precipitant birth, excessive birth weight, obstetrical procedures (e.g., forceps delivery), umbilical cord wrapped around the baby's neck, and lack of oxygen.
3. Infections, such as sexually transmitted diseases (i.e., gonorrhea, AIDS).

The following are potential *postnatal causes*:

1. Body function complications, such as *jaundice*. Newborn babies may have the immaturity of an enzyme system in the liver which causes the delay of metabolizing and neutralizing the brokendown red blood cells (a process called *conjugation*). As a result, one of the components in the hemoglobin, the *bilirubin*, is accumulated in the blood stream which causes the yellow discoloration of the skin and eyes (the *jaundice*) of the baby. New born babies with marked increase of bilirubin, i.e., above 20 mg per 100 ml of blood (called *hyperbilirubinemia*), may need to be put under florescent lights for phototherapy to help metabolize and neutralize the bilirubin if it continues to increase in the blood circulation (Batshaw, 1997).
2. Infections, for example, meningitis and encephalitis.
3. Accidents, including traffic accidents (which is number 1 cause of accidents), falling, sports accidents, violence, and other trauma. Over 50,000 children per year in the U.S. were permanently disabled by accidents; half of these children were under the age of five years.
4. Environmental factors, such as malnutrition, pollution and poison, and child abuse and neglect, which may cause severe burns, bone fractures, brain damage, allergy, breathing problems, and social/ emotional trauma.
5. Progressive health conditions and neurological disorders, such as tumor, hardening of the spinal cord, high blood pressure, arthritis, and kidney failure.

Prevention of Physical and Health Disabilities

A number of causes of physical and health disabilities may possibly be prevented through strategies targeting women before and during pregnancy, babies, children, and society.

For Women Before and During Pregnancy

*   Avoid drugs, including cigarettes, alcohol, and cocaine.
*   Avoid exposure to radiation or other toxic substances.
*   Avoid infections, including HIV and other sexually transmitted diseases (STD).
*   Control diabetes or other illness.

- Prevent malnutrition.
- Avoid domestic battery.
- Have routine physical examinations and maternal care.
- Provide genetic counseling.
- Test for Rh factor.

If the mother's blood is Rh⁻, she can be immunized by injecting gamma globin, such as the RhoGAM, within 72 hours after the pregnancy terminates (i.e., after each delivery or miscarriage of an infant) and prevent adverse consequences of blood incompatibility in a subsequent pregnancy. The RhoGAM is one type of antibody which may block the formation of certain antibodies in the mother's blood circulation (Batshaw, 1997). If the mother is not immunized, the consequences of blood incompatibility in the new-born can be prevented by blood exchange transfusion in the baby (UCPA, 1992).

For Infants

- Have neonatal checkup.
- Provide intensive care of high-risk infants, e.g., premature babies.
- Provide phototherapy for newborn jaundice.
- Provide immunization.
- Prevent traumatic injuries.
- Prevent obstruction of airway.
- Prevent malnutrition.
- Prevent infections.
- Avoid toxic substances
- Eliminate child abuse and neglect.

For Children

- Prevent traumatic injuries.
- Prevent obstruction of airway.
- Prevent malnutrition.
- Provide immunizations.
- Prevent infections.
- Avoid toxic substances.
- Eliminate child abuse and neglect.
- Have routine physical examinations.

For Society

- Enhance proper maternal and child health programs.

- Assure the proper vision of nutrition for pregnant women and young children.
- Provide continuing education for parents.
- Improve sanitation and safety.
- Control harmful and toxic substances.
- Eliminate child poverty.
- Increase disability awareness of the general public.

CHARACTERISTICS

Persons with physical and health disabilities are in a diverse group. We will explore the general characteristics of this special group based on the severity, implications, duration, progressiveness of the disabling conditions and the learning and behavioral perspective.

Severity of Physical and Health Disabilities

Physical and health disabilities may be at mild, moderate and severe levels (Heward & Orlansky, 1992, p. 379). Individuals with *mild* physical and health disabilities may have:

1. independence in meeting physical needs,
2. potential to improve motor and/or perceptual skills with therapy intervention, and
3. potential for regression in quality of motor and perceptual skills without intervention.

Individuals with *moderate* physical and health disabilities may have:

1. some independence in meeting physical needs,
2. functional head control,
3. deformities, present or potential, that limit independent function or produce pain, and
4. perceptual and/or sensory-integrative deficits that interfere with achievement of academic and age-appropriate motor skills.

Individuals with *severe* physical and health disabilities may have:

1. total dependence in meeting physical needs,
2. poor head control,
3. deformities, present or potential, that limit function or produce pain, and

4. perceptual and/or sensory-integrative deficits that prevent achievement of academic and age-appropriate motor skills.

Implications Caused by the Condition

Physical and health disabilities may cause specific implications in motor movement and coordination. The following are implications in different body parts (the *topographical aspect*):

Monoplegia	one limb (arm or leg) is involved.
Diplegia	two limbs of the same kind (both arms or both legs) are involved (more often the legs are involved as paraplegia).
Hemiplegia	one side of the body is involved (left or right hemiplegia).
Triplegia	three limbs (one arm and two legs or two arms and one leg) are involved.
Quadriplegia	all four limbs are involved (one side may be more affected as "*double hemiplegia*").

The following are potential implications caused by physical and health disabilities on movement (the physiological aspect):

Atonia	hypotonia or low muscle tone (flaccis).
Spasticity	hypertonia or high muscle tone (stiffness).
Athetosis	involuntary fluctuate muscle tone (dystonia).
Rigidity	extremely high muscle tone causing severe spasticity.
Ataxia	lack of balance and position sense or spatial orientation.
Tremor	repetitive rhythmic shaking.
Mixed	more than one movement disorder.

Duration of the Condition

The condition of a physical or health disability may be permanent, indefinite, or temporary:

Permanent	a condition that will continue.
Indefinite	a condition that may terminate at a later date, such as asthma, arthritis.
Temporary	a condition that may terminate or may be corrected within a comparatively short period of time, such as knee injury, legg-calve-perthes disease.

Progressiveness of the Condition

A physical or health disability may be progress or nonprogressive. A *progressive disability* is a condition that tends to become worse, such as cancer, muscular dystrophy, and cystic fibrosis. A *nonprogressive disability* is a condition that will not become worse by itself, such as cerebral palsy and amputation.

Learning and Behavioral Characteristics

Two of the potential misconceptions about persons with physical and health disabilities are: "the more severe a person's physical disability, the lower his or her intelligence," and "the greatest educational problem involving children with physical disabilities is highly specialized instruction" (Hallahan & Kauffman, 1994, p. 387). Field practitioners may find that students with physical and health disabilities range from severe cognitive/intellectual performance level to gifted/talented level. In addition, teachers of most students with physical and health disabilities provide instructional materials and approaches which are not different from the teaching of nondisabled children. Nevertheless, certain individuals with physical and health disabilities may have one or more of the following general learning and behavioral characteristics (Lian, 1999):

1. Potential associated disabling conditions, such as mental retardation, sensory impairments, and communication disorders,
2. Repeated absence from school activities due to the need for medication, therapy, hospitalization, and bed rest at home,
3. Underachievement in academics and vocational development,
4. Low self-esteem/self-confidence and feeling of uncertainty,
5. Excessive isolation or involvement,
6. Aggression or hostility, and
7. Efforts to compensate.

With the above learning and behavioral characteristics, teachers of students with physical and health disabilities, as well as other related service providers of the transdisciplinary team (i.e., school nurse, psychologists, counselors, speech pathologists, physical and occupational/rehabilitation therapists) may work on the following:

1. Accepting the students as they are,
2. Fulfilling individualized needs and life-centered educational goals,

3. Providing motivation, encouragement, and guidance,
4. Setting expectations at the students' ability level for accomplishment,
5. Engaging appropriate therapies (i.e., physical, occupational, music, recreational, and rehabilitation).
6. Implementing effective positioning, lifting, carrying, and other physical handling techniques,
7. Utilizing adaptive equipment for enhancing motor movement and coordination, such as bolster, wedge, side lier, cornerchair, pronestander, braces (*orthotics*), and *prosthetics*.
8. Providing appropriate self-help devices, such as adaptive switches, utensils with handles, food guard for dishes, and reacher.
9. Utilizing assistive technology (AT).
10. Changing general public's attitudes and behaviors.

In summary, each child with a physical or health disability has individualized needs. Educators must be aware of a wide variety of other potential obstacles to a student's education. Teachers need to learn how to assist a child with health care needs, how to deal with frequent absences, how to assist a child who is having a seizure, how to make scheduling accommodations, how to address special issues relating to paralysis, how to adapt the class activities, how to adapt teaching techniques, and how to promote social integration.

EDUCATION

Sirvis (1988) suggested the following areas of assessment for students with physical and health disabilities: activities of daily living, mobility, physical abilities and limitations, psychosocial development, communication, academic potential, adaptations for learning, and transition skills. With the gathered assessment data, she further invited the transdisciplinary teams in schools to develop educational goals in five developmental areas for these students: "(a) physical independence, including mastering of daily living skills; (b) self-awareness and social maturation; (c) communication; (d) academic growth; and (e) life skills training" (p. 400). In an attempt for students with physical and health disabilities to achieve these educational goals, specific instructional and therapeutic strategies need to be implemented, including normalizing muscle tone, positioning to facilitate functional posture and motor movement/control, lifting and transferring, utilizing adaptations, responding to seizures, and mealtime arrangements.

Normalizing Muscle Tone

For a student with *spasticity*, the following approaches can be implemented to reduce his/her muscle tone:

1. Use warm and soft surface for environment and equipment, such as padding, cushion, forms, and blanket.
2. Give gentle touch and gentle pressure.
3. Engage in slow and rhythmic movement.
4. Let him/her know before movement.
5. Help trunk and hip rotation to increase range of motion.
6. Help joint extension, flexion, and rotation of extremities.
7. Gently rub on flexors or extensors to encourage relaxation.
8. Use deep bone pressure on tight palms and joints.
9. Use proximal key points in facilitating normal movement.
10. Use appropriate positioning, such as supine lying, side lying, corner chair sitting, or standing over a prone stander.
11. Keep hip, trunk, and shoulder flexion for hyperextended students.
12. Use swimming pool or water therapy with warm water for relaxation exercise.
13. Joint compression to be equal to or less than the child's body weight.

For a student with *flaccid* conditions, the following approaches can be implemented to increase his/her muscle tone:

1. Use cold and hard surface for environment and equipment, such as wood, hard plastic cushion, metal, wet towel, etc.
2. Give firm touch, e.g., firm pressure over muscle belly.
3. Engage in quick and irregular movement, e.g., quick stretch.
4. Engage in sudden movement.
5. Push head, trunk and extremities for counter movement.
6. Use appropriate positioning and stimulation for extension, such as prone lying over wedge and bolster, side sitting, standing box, rubbing extensors, and catching the child's attention for him or her to sit up or look up.
7. Use proximal fixation — push both sides of a joint toward the joint; joint compression to be more than the child's body weight.
8. Work on weight bearing and weight shifting.
9. Work on protective reactions and balance.
10. Work on resistance exercise, such as lifting legs with sand bags.

11. Use physical education, recreational, and game activities for maintaining head control and upright sitting response.

For a student with *athetosis*, the following approaches can be implemented to stabilize his/her muscle tone:

1. Use postural control.
2. Use proximal fixation — push body parts, such as head, arms, hands, legs, etc., toward center of body.
3. Keep symmetrical alignment.
4. Use distal key points in facilitating normal movement.
5. Tell the student to slow down and "hold" the movement.

Positioning

Appropriate positioning of a child with physical and health disabilities may successfully facilitate his/her positive posture and functional motor movement and coordination. The following are potential advantages of supine lying, prone lying, side lying, four-point position, sitting, side sitting, and standing:

Supine Lying

- Increase eye contact.
- Increase head staying in midline.
- Increase relaxation.

Prone Lying

- Increase head control.
- Increase visual alertness.
- Increase trunk extension.
- Encourage weight bearing on arms.
- Enhance respiration.
- Decrease flexor contracture in hips and knees.
- Increase shoulder motion.

Side Lying

- Decrease spasticity.
- Increase relaxation.
- Increase hand-to-mouth/midline movement.
- Decrease scoliosis.

- Shape ribcage; enhance breathing.
- Encourage shoulders to move forward (for relaxation).
- Decrease asymmetrical posturing.

Side Sitting

- Increase head control.
- Increase trunk extension and rotation.
- Increase weight bearing.
- Increase effort to maintain balance.

Four-Point Position (i.e., on hands and knees)

- Increase of head control.
- Strengthen muscles.
- Increase weight bearing.
- Increase weight shifting for maintaining balance.
- Increase potential for crawling and other reciprocal movements.

Sitting

- Increase head control.
- Increase trunk control.
- Increase visual alertness.
- Free hands for manipulation of objects.
- Increase hip and knee flexion.

Standing

- Increase visual exploration.
- Increase development of hip socket
- Increase hip stability.
- Increase circulation.
- Stimulate bone growth.
- Decrease probability of fractures.
- Tighten hips, knees, ankles.
- Increase free hands.

Lifting and Transferring

Special training is required for teachers to work with children who are paralyzed with spinal cord defects as well as paraplegic cerebral palsy. Some children may need the teacher to lift and physically move them from one place to another. The physical therapist can provide the teacher with suggestions on the safest and most appropriate manner to lift and carry a particular child, such as:

1. Use good body mechanics.
2. Relax the child with high muscle tone before proceeding with lifting or carrying.
3. Rotate the child up to sitting position whenever possible before lifting (i.e., supine — side lying — side sitting — sitting).
4. Support only where necessary; let the child do as much work as possible.
5. Make the child feel secure with your handling.
6. Tell the child what you are about to do.
7. Do not lift the child under the arms, especially if the child has muscular dystrophy.
8. Carry prone if the child lacks head control.
9. Place your arms between child's legs if the child has tight adductors or scissored legs.
10. Prevent abnormal patterns of movement.

Lian (2000) suggested the following steps for teachers and other service providers to follow when transferring a child to a wheelchair:

1. Stabilize the wheelchair.
2. Get as close to the student as possible.
3. Bend legs and keep back straight; use large muscles of the legs, not the back.
4. Encourage the student to bear weight if possible.
5. Have one foot pointing to the student and another pointing to the wheelchair.
6. Do not hesitate to get help.
7. Use adaptive device such as gait belt and walker.

Adaptive Equipment

Teachers need to be sensitive to each child's needs in the physical environment. A child may require specially fitted chairs, desks, and workstations and need extra space for maneuvering bulky leg braces, crutches, or his/her wheelchair. Table 10.1 list specific adaptive equipment for enhancing appropriate positioning and motor movement. Many children also require

Table 10.1 Adaptive Equipment for Enhancing Positioning and Motor Movement

Adapted Tricycle
- enhances independent mobility.
- develops lower extremity strength.
- encourages reciprocal movement of legs.
- increases head and trunk control.
- increases eye-hand, eye-leg coordination.
- promotes balance.
- increases protective reactions.

Balance Ball/Vestibular Ball
- provides prone and supine positioning.
- reduces or increases muscle tone.
- increases protective reactions.
- encourages trunk and hips extension/flexion.
- encourages arms to reach for the floor or objects.
- helps digestive system (pass gas, bowel movement, etc.).
- encourages raising head.
- enhances weight shifting and balance.

Balance Beam
- enhances walking.
- enhances balancing.
- encourages alternating arms and leg movement.
- encourages trunk and hip rotation.

Balloon/Ball
- increasing hand reaching.
- improves eye-hand coordination.
- encourages hitting, banging, and pushing.
- encourages throwing and catching.
- encourages trunk rotation.
- increases head control.
- encourages arms and legs movement.

Bolster
- aids in prone lying position to enhance raising head, trunk extension, and weight bearing on elbows.
- increases relaxation when placed under knee joints in supine position; increases knee joint/leg flexion.
- aids in side sitting position to encourage head and trunk control, sitting balance, and trunk rotation.
- aids in pony chair sitting (riding) position to develop head and trunk control, sitting balance, and increase abduction in lower extremities.

Corner Chair
- gets shoulder flexed and forward.
- straightens the spine; prevents scoliosis.
- provides good support for symmetrical sitting.

Table 10.1   (Cont'd)

- supports for students with spastic quadriplegia.
- increases head and trunk control.
- reduces muscle tone; increases relaxation.
- allows arm movement.

Feeder's Chair
- increases flexed pattern.
- provides functional sitting position for feeding.
- helps with support sitting.

Parallel Bars
- enhances walking with support.
- promotes balance and equilibrium.
- encourages early ambulation and balance training.
- develops reciprocal movements.
- promotes movement of hands.
- encourages trunk and hip extension and rotation.

Pony Chair
- enhances pony chair sitting.
- increases trunk control and rotation.
- frees arm movement.
- prevents scissoring of legs.
- increases sitting balancing.

Prone Stander
- provides standing position.
- improves head and trunk control.
- helps achieve proper body alignment.
- encourages weight bearing.
- frees arms and hands for movement.
- prevents contractures.
- serves as an alternative to wheelchair.

Scooter Boards
- encourages mobility
- provides prone positioning.
- promotes reciprocal movement.
- increases extension of hands, head and trunk; improves head control.
- prevents contractures.
- allows the use of hands (for movement).
- improves upper extremity function (use of hands).
- increases strength in upper and lower extremities.
- works on midline.
- increases muscle tone in hypotonics.
- reduces muscle tone in spastics.

Sidelyer
- shapes ribcage (makes the rib cage round).
- prevents scoliosis.

Table 10.1 (Cont'd)

- allows arm movement.
- gets hands together at midline.
- reduces asymmetry.
- keeps shoulders, trunks and hips flexed.
- reduces extensor pattern and muscle tone; decreases spasticity.

Stairs
- encourages stepping up and down.
- enhances balancing.
- increases weight bearing.
- increases strengthening of legs and ankles.
- increases defensive reactions.

Standing Box
- provides standing position.
- encourages weight bearing.
- increases trunk and hips rotation.
- increases arm movement.

Standing Table
- frees arms and hands for movement.
- develops head and trunk control.
- provides standing position.
- maximizes positional control at hips and knees.
- encourages weight bearing.

Tilt Board
- promotes weight shifting.
- promotes protective reactions.
- promotes balance.
- provides lying and sitting positioning.

Tilt Table
- provides supine position.
- develops support.
- encourages weight bearing.
- frees arms and hands for movement.
- allows for supine lying to standing position.
- promotes head and trunk control.

Trampoline
- provides sitting, kneeling and standing position.
- increases bouncing activities
- strengthens legs, arms, ankles.
- increases efforts for balance
- increases defensive reactions.

Walker
- encourages mobility.
- increases balancing.
- promotes normal gait.

Table 10.1   (Cont'd)

- encourages functional movement.
- encourages weight bearing.
- strengthens arm muscles.
- supports lower limbs and trunk if hips are weak.

Wedge
- increases head and trunk control in prone position.
- promotes weight bearing on elbows or hands.
- promotes controlled extension of neck, back and trunk.

Source: Lian, M-G.J. (2000). *Teaching students with physical and multiple disabilities.* Normal, IL: University Communications, Illinois State University, pp. 218–221.

specially designed tools to perform tasks for themselves. For example, children with athetoid cerebral palsy may use pointers strapped to their heads, because they may have better control with their head movement than with their hand movement. Other children may need mouthpieces and mouthsticks that allow them to hold and use pencils or crayons for their schoolwork. The physical therapist and occupational therapist can assist the teacher in developing these accommodations. Many students with severe physical disabilities require language boards or an augmentative communication device for communication. Teachers must thus learn to interact with the child using whatever communication accommodations are required.

Responding to Seizures

Children with epilepsy fall within all ranges of intelligence, but have a higher risk of learning disabilities, mental retardation, or other related disabling conditions than their peers without epilepsy. Even children whose IQs are normal may experience some problems caused by epilepsy or its treatment. These problems include lack of concentration, restlessness, fidgeting, or the possible side effects of medication. Table 10.2 shows a list of anti-seizure drugs and potential side effects.

Since teachers spend a great amount of time with a child, they can help the child and the child's physician by monitoring the effects and dosage of anti-seizure medication. Teachers should also be prepared to respond effectively to a child's seizure and to show other students and school personnel how to help a child experiencing a seizure. Table 10.3 provides general guidelines for managing seizures in school settings. When implementing these guidelines, a teacher may remind other students that epilepsy is just a disordered condition; it is not a disease and is not contagious.

Table 10.2   Anti-seizure Drugs and Potential Side-effects

ACTH	Cataracts, pathological fractures, risk of infection, weight gain, and high blood pressure.
Artane	Drowsiness, dizziness, headache, loss of appetite, stomach upset, vision changes, sleeplessness, trembling of hands, and dry mouth.
Ativane	Drowsiness, dizziness, lack of coordination, grogginess, headache, nausea, dry mouth, and blurred vision.
Clonopin	Low white blood cell count, and drowsiness.
Depakene	Mild stomach pain, loss of appetite, nausea, liver damage, changes in menstruation, diarrhea, mild hair loss, unsteadiness, drowsiness/dizziness, rash or headache.
Dilantin	Constipation, dizziness, drowsiness, gum enlargement, vomiting, sensitivity to light, excess hair growth, and impaired concentration.
Gabitril	Dizziness, weakness, shakiness, trouble sleeping, nausea, diarrhea, or vomiting.
Klonopin	Indigestion, change in appetite, nausea, seizures, drowsiness, dizziness, headaches, tiredness, weakness, mood changes, sleeplessness, excessive hair growth or loss of hair, blurred vision, dry mouth, sore gums, increased sex drive, muscle pain, and weight changes.
Mysoline	Drowsiness, sleepiness, stomach upset, nausea, loss of appetite, clumsiness, and fatigue.
Neurontin	Drowsiness, dizziness, unsteadiness, fatigue, and nausea.
Phenobarbitol	Drowsiness or dizziness, stomach upset, headache, weakness, grogginess, and dreaming.
Tegretol	Drowsiness, dizziness, blurred vision, upset stomach, nausea, loss of appetite, dry mouth, mood changes, muscle aches, restlessness, hyperactivity, low white blood cell count, liver toxicity, and impaired concentration.
Topamax	Weakness, tiredness, drowsiness, dizziness, tingling sensations, loss of appetite and weight loss.
Zarontin	Drowsiness, dizziness, blurred vision, stomach upset, loss of appetite, headache, or hiccups.

Note: Consumption of alcohol together with some of the above anticonvulsant medicine may greatly increase the side effects. In addition, Tegretol combined with erythromycin was reported as number one cause of drug interaction death in the U.S.

Source: Lian, M-G.J. (1999). *Getting to know individuals with physical disabilities and/or health impairments*. Normal, IL: University Communications, Illinois State University, pp. 103–104.

Table 10.3   Convulsive or Generalized Tonic-Clonic

According to the Epilepsy Foundation of America, the following steps are appropriate to assist a person experiencing a convulsive seizure or a generalized *tonic-clonic seizure*:

- Prevent the person from hurting himself or herself. Place something soft under the head, loosen tight clothing, and clear the area of any sharp or hard objects.
- Do not force any objects into the person's mouth.
- Do not restrain the person's movements.
- Turn the person on his or her side to allow saliva to drain from the mouth.
- Stay with the person until the seizure ends naturally.
- Do not pour any liquids into the person's mouth or offer any food, drink, or medication until the person is fully awake.
- Give artificial respiration if the person does not resume breathing after the seizure.
- Provide an area for the person to rest until fully awakened, accompanied by a responsible adult.
- Be reassuring and supportive when consciousness returns.
- While a convulsive seizure is not a medical emergency, occasionally a seizure may last longer than ten minutes or a second seizure may occur. This requires prompt medical attention in a properly equipped medical facility.

The following are recommended steps in assisting a person with *nonconvulsive/complex partial seizure*:

- Do not restrain the person.
- Remove harmful objects from the person's path.
- Calmly try to encourage the person to sit down or encourage him or her to be away from dangerous situations. (If the person does not respond to these measures, force should not be used.)
- Observe but do not approach the person who appears angry or combative.
- Remain with the person until he or she is fully alert.

Source: Smith, D.D., & Luckasson, R. (1995). *Introduction to special education: Teaching in an age of challenge* (2nd ed.). Needham Heights, MA: Allyn & Bacon.

Other Specific Health Care

In addition to seizures and convulsive disorders, persons with physical and health disabilities may have other needs for specific health care. In previous literature, these persons might have been identified as "*medically complex and technology dependent*" or "*medically fragile.*" Lehr (1996) adopts the definition of the California Board of Registered Nurses to differentiate between (a) those who are medically fragile, i.e., those who "are in an acute phase of an illness, or are in an unstable state," and (b) those "whose health is stable but have ongoing needs for health care services" (p. 8).

On a daily basis, school personnel may need to monitor specific health conditions such as diabetes, heart defects, high blood pressure, allergies, asthma, cancer, shunt, diet, and pressure sores. The school nurse and/or other service providers tend to have a routine schedule to do one or more of the following:

Medications

- Assist the person to take own medication.
- Give oral medication.
- Give medications via gastrotomy nasogastric tube.
- Give intravenous (IV) medication.
- Give intramuscular (IM) medication.

Respiration Assistance

- Suction.
- Monitoring and assisting respiration/oxygen ventilation.
- Respiratory therapy

Assisting Circulation

- Monitoring skin color, body temperature, and heartbeat.
- Using a respiratory/circulatory monitor.

Feeding/Foods and Nutrition

- Spoon feeding.
- Gastrotomy tube (G-tube) or nasogastric tube feeding.
- Foods and liquid preparation.
- Preventing dehydration.
- Preventing malnutrition.

Bowel and Urinary Care

- Use of bed pan and urinal.
- Stoma care.
- Diapering.
- Administering enema.
- Prescribed bowel and bladder training.
- External catheterization.
- Endwelling catheter.

Mealtime Arrangements

Mealtime is one of the important considerations when professionals plan an educational program for a child with physical or health disabilities. Some children are vulnerable to anemia, cannot chew or swallow, require tube feeding, or lose their appetite because of medication. Some children need special utensils such as a large-handled spoon or a plate held firmly to the table by suction cups or nonskid mat. Children who have difficulty eating may be self-conscious about the problem, and their classmates may feel uncomfortable initially. The teacher should try to create a comfortable, accepting atmosphere for eating. An example in Table 10.4 is adapted from Smith and Luckasson (1995).

Table 10.4 Independence at Mealtime

Mr. Jones works with children with physical disabilities and orthopedic impairments and with their teachers. One of his students, Mike, is 9 years old and has cerebral palsy. Mike has been struggling to feed himself, but trying to grasp the silverware and scoop food from the lunch tray is frustrating for him.

Mr. Jones decided to teach Mike how to hold a spoon independently. Mr. Jones first observed Mike attempting to grasp a spoon. Mike was clearly motivated but his cerebral palsy made it difficult for him to make the tight fist necessary to hold the spoon. Even when Mike managed to get hold of the spoon, the tray scooted along the table as soon as Mike attempted to scoop the food and food spilled over the sides whenever he got a scoop. This was obviously very frustrating for Mike. Meanwhile, at home and at school, someone fed Mike.

Mr. Jones then observed Mike during other activities. Mike could hold some items such as grasping and lifting the small juice can when they made juice in class. Mr. Jones decided to try to adapt a handle as fat as the juice can on Mike's spoon. Mr. Jones taped some rubber onto the handle of the spoon.

Mike was able to grasp this built-up spoon, and soon was trying to feed himself but the problems of the scooting tray and spilling food remained. Mr. Jones then found some small suction cups and glued them to the bottom of the tray so that it would stick to the table. He also used some heavy aluminum foil to build up the sides of the tray so that the food would not spill over when Mike scooped his food.

Soon, Mike's ability to eat independently improved. Mr. Jones later discussed these adaptations with the occupational therapist. After evaluating Mike and the adapted eating utensils, the therapist was able to provide eating utensils that looked more normal and did not need replacing and repairing as often. The occupational therapist also provided side head guards and a chin guard so that Mike could hold his head steadier when he was eating.

Mealtimes now take longer, with Mike feeding himself rather than being fed by someone else. Mike's parents have managed to schedule longer mealtimes to accommodate Mike's new skill.

All the members of the IEP team in this example had contributions to make as Mike took an important step toward increased independence at mealtimes. The team is now working together to adapt his pencils, markers, and crayons so that he can do his homework independently.

Source: Smith, D.D., & Luckasson, R. (1995). *Introduction to special education: Teaching in an age of challenge* (2nd ed.). Needham Heights, MA: Allyn & Bacon.

SUMMARY

1. Persons with physical and health disabilities are in a special group with unique educational and rehabilitation needs such as specific health care arrangements, motor and mobility adaptations, alternative or augmentative communication accommodations, remediation for learning deficits, accommodations for independent living, and coping with social and emotional problems.

2. Legislation relating to physical and health disabilities in the United States includes temporary and permanent neurological/orthopedic impairments, traumatic brain injury, and other health impairments.

3. Neurological impairments may include cerebral palsy, traumatic brain injury, convulsive disorders, spina bifida, spinal cord injury, and poliomyelitis. Orthopedic impairments may include muscular dystrophy, arthrogryposis, amputation, hip dislocation, legg-calve-perthes disease, osteogenesis imperfecta, arthritis, and scoliosis. Health impairments may include diabetes mellitus, asthma, cystic fibrosis, pulmonary tuberculosis, cardiac disorders, hemophilia, sickle cell anemia, cancer, kidney disorders, hepatitis, AIDS, child abuse and neglect, adolescent pregnancy, and drug addictions.

4. Historical development relating to physical and health disabilities can be divided into five major stages: the early years, the stage of initiation, the stage of rapid development, the stage of enlightenment, and the stage of information networking and collaboration. The history has witnessed evolutional and progressive inclusion as well as increase of community acceptance and integration for all individuals.

5. Prenatal causes of physical and health disabilities include genetic disorders, drugs, radiation, maternal infections, prenatal care and maternal health conditions, and traumatic injuries during pregnancy. Perinatal causes may include Rh incompatibility, injuries, and infection. Postnatal causes may include body function complications, infections, accidents, environmental factors, and progressive degeneration of the CNS or other health systems. Strategies to prevent physical and health disabilities can be implemented through women before and during pregnancy, babies, children, and society.

6. General characteristics of children with physical and health disabilities can be identified based on severity, implications, duration, and progressiveness of the condition. Specific characteristics may include a wide range of cognitive abilities, similarities as compared to

nondisabled peers, potential associated disabling conditions, repeated absence from school for treatment, underachievement in academic and vocational development, low self-esteem and self-confidence, excessive isolation or lack of involvement, aggression or hostility, and/or efforts to compensate.

7. Field practitioners need to accept individuals with physical and health disabilities as they are, fulfill their needs and educational goals, provide motivation, setting appropriate expectations, engage therapies, utilize adaptive equipment, self-help devices, and assistive technology and devote time and efforts to change general public's attitudes and behaviors.

8. For successful education of students with physical disabilities, teachers and related service providers may need to work on normalizing muscle tone, positioning, lifting and transferring, utilizing adaptations, responding to seizures, and mealtime arrangements.

ACTIVITIES

1. Persons with physical and health disabilities used to be labeled as "crippled" or "handicapped." Review related literature (including the mass media) and investigate the evolution of the definition of physical and health disabilities and share the findings in class.

2. Find where students with physical and health disabilities are placed in Hong Kong. Are they in specially designed orthopedic schools or in local ordinary schools?

3. Contact the Hong Kong Spasticity Association, the Hospital Authority, and/or appropriate branches of the Hong Kong Government to obtain information on vocational rehabilitation and supported independent living. Interview related policy makers or service providers. If possible, schedule a visit to the above organizations or agencies. Write a report based on the information you gathered and give comments and recommendations.

4. Investigate general wheelchair accessibility to buildings, transportation, parks, and public restrooms in Hong Kong.

5. Investigate how individuals with physical and health disabilities are treated in other countries.

6. Design a one-minute public service announcement advertising ways to prevent physical and health disabilities.

7. Work in small groups to design brochures to present to a primary school

health class documenting causes of, and ways to prevent, physical and health disabilities.

8. Hold a prevention debate on the following issues: (a) Why has our society not taken more aggressive steps to prevent physical and health disabilities? (b) Are prevention strategies too expensive? (c) Is the connection between a prevention strategy and the birth of a healthy baby too obscure? (d) Would the imposition of strategies put a clamp on many cherished freedoms of our society? (e) What strategies has the government implemented to prevent physical and health disabilities?

9. Investigate social trends and how these trends have influenced treatment for and attitudes toward persons with physical and health disabilities. How did living conditions evolve? How did involvement in public education evolve? How did attitudes change? Write a short paper on what you have found.

10. Form small groups of 4–5. Design a task analysis for the following: (a) moving from supine position into standing position, (b) putting on and taking off a coat, (c) tying shoelace, (d) sending an email message, and (e) preparing for a job interview.

RESOURCES

Resources in Hong Kong

Apleichau Pre-school Centre
1–16, G/F., Lei Yee House, Apleichau Estate West, Hong Kong

B.M. Kotewall Memorial School
22 Kwai Hop Street, Kwai Chung, New Territories, Hong Kong
Tel.: 852-2424-7766 Fax: 852-2422-8230
Web address: http://bmkms.spastic.org.hk

Bradbury Shek Wai Kok Parents' Resource Centre
Tel: 852-2492-4200

Bradbury Tak Tin Workshop
G/F., Tak Shing House, Tak Tin Estate, Lam Tin, Kowloon

Bradbury Wong Tai Sin Hostel
G/F., Lung Fung House, Lower Wong Tai Sin Estate, Kowloon

Chaiwan Hostel
201–210, Lok Hing House, Hing Wah Estate, Chaiwan, Hong Kong

Chaiwan Workshop
511–516, On Hing House, Hing Wah Estate, Chaiwan, Hong Kong

Chan Tseng Hsi Early Education and Training Centre
101–104, G/F., Wang Hing House, Wang Tau Hom Estate, Kowloon

Direction Association for the Handicapped
Rm 111–112, G/F, Kai Fai House, Choi Wan Estate, Kowloon
Tel.: 852-2330-6308   Fax: 852-2774-4216
Web address: http://www.healthbasic.com/direction/

Domiciliary Occupational Therapy Unit
1–2A, G/F., Wang Fu House, Wang Tau Hom Estate, Kowloon

Fu Tung Hostel
1/F., Tung Po House, Fu Tung Estate, Tung Chung, Lantau, New Territories

Fu Tung Training Centre
G/F., Wing B & C, Tung Po House, Fu Tung Estate,
Tung Chung, Lantau, New Territories

Heep Hong Society 協康會
G1-11, Tung Yu House, Tai Hang Yung Estate, Kowloon
Tel.: 852-2776-3111   Fax: 852-2776-1837
E-mail: info@heephong.org
Web address: Http://www.heephong.org

Independent Home Scheme (Leung King)
412, Leung Yin House, Leung King Estate, Tuen Mun, New Territories

Jockey Club Bradbury Wah Sum Care Centre
G/F. & 1/F., Wah Min House, Wah Sum Estate, Fanling, New Territories

Jockey Club Conductive Learning Centre (Pre-school Unit)
6–17, G/F., Wang Leung House, Wang Tau Hom Estate, Kowloon

Jockey Club Conductive Learning Centre (Teaching Unit)
6–17, G/F., Wang Leung House, Wang Tau Hom Estate, Kowloon

Jockey Club Elaine Field School
1 Fu Chung Lane, Tung Leung Road, Area 9, Tai Po, New Territories

John F. Kennedy Centre
15 Sandy Bay Road, Hong Kong
Tel.: 852-2817-0131   Fax: 852-2817-3730
Web Address: http://www.jfk.edu.hk

Ko Fook Iu Memorial School
2 Fung Wo Lane, Woche Estate, Shatin, New Territories

Lok Wah Hostel
G/F., Man Wah House, Lok Wah South Estate, Ngau Tau Kok, Kowloon

Lung Hang Pre-school Centre
118–125, G/F., Sin Sam House, Lung Hang Estate, Shatin, New Territories

Lung Tai Hostel
1–9, Wing C, G/F., Lung Tai House, Lower Wong Tai Sin Estate, Kowloon

On Ting Hostel
G/F., Ting Tai House, On Ting Estate, Tuen Mun, New Territories

On Ting Workshop
G/F., Ting Tai House, On Ting Estate, Tuen Mun, New Territories

Rehabilitation Alliance Hong Kong
香港九龍橫頭磡邨宏孝樓地下12-13及16-17號
Tel.:852-2337-0826   Fax: 852-2337-1549
Web Address: http://www.rehaballiance.org.hk/cht/home/

Sahk B. M. Kotewall Memorial School
22 Kwai Hop Street, Kwai Shing, New Territories

Shek Kip Mei Pre-school Centre
116–126, G/F., Block 23, Shek Kip Mei Estate, Kowloon

Shek Wai Kok Pre-school Centre
105–119, G/F., Shek Ho House, Shek Wai Kok Estate, New Territories

The Spastic Association of Hong Kong
Web Address: http://www.spastic.org.hk

Supported Employment — Laundry Team
G/F., Tak Shing House, Tak Tin Estate, Lam Tin, Kowloon

Tak Tin Early Education and Training Centre
Unit 1, Podium,, Tak Hong House, Tak Tin Estate, Lam Tin, Kowloon.

Tang Siu King Memorial Workshop
(Wheelchair Repair/Adaptive Seating & Appliance Work/Computer &
   Electronic Equipment Repair)
118–123, G/F., Man Wo House, Woche Estate, Shatin, New Territories

Tin Yiu Hostel
G/F., Yiu Foo House, Tin Yiu Estate, Tin Shui Wai, Yuen Long, New Territories

Tin Yiu Workshop
G/F., Yiu Man House, Tin Yiu Estate, Tin Shui Wai, Yuen Long, New
Territories

Wang Tau Hom Pre-school Centre
8-14, G/F., Wang Fu House, Wang Tau Hom Estate, Kowloon

Woche Hostel/Recreation Centre
G/F., Hip Wo House, Woche Estate, Shatin, New Territories

Woche Workshop
G/F., Man Wo House, Woche Estate, Shatin, New Territories

Resources in Taiwan

長庚醫院神經外科二科
Web address: http://www.cgmh.com.tw/intr/intr2/c323b/NS2home.htm

Jen-Ai School
Ho-mei, Changhua, Taiwan

R.O.C. Disability-Free Environment Promotional Association
Web Address: http://www.depa.org.tw/

Taiwan Muscular Dystrophy Association
高雄市鼓山區明華路9號
Tel.: 886-07-5526082   Fax: 886-07-5526107
Web Address: http://www3.nsysu.edu.tw/tmdawww/index.htm

International resources

Adapted Physical Education National Standards (APENS)
Web Address: http://www.twu.edu/apens/

American Occupational Therapy Association (AOTA)
Web Address: http://www.aota.org/
American Physical Therapy Association (APTA)
Web Address: https://www.apta.org/

Assistance Dogs International Inc.
Web Address: http://www.assistance-dogs-intl.org/index.html

The Canadian Council on Rehabilitation and Work (CCRW)
500 University Avenue, Suite 302, Toronto, Ontario, Canada M5G 1V7
Tel.: 1-416-260-3060 TTY: 1-416-260-9223   Fax: 1-416-260-3093
Web address: http://www.ccrw.org/

Canadian Paraplegic Association
Web Address: http://www.canparaplegic.org/national/index.html

Commission on Mental and Physical Disability Law
740 15th St., NW, Washington, DC 20005 U.S.A.
Tel.: 1-202-662-1570 TTY: 1-202-662-1012   Fax: 1-202-662-1032
Web Address: http://www.abanet.org/disability/

Community Playthings/Rifton Equipment
P.O. Box 901, Route 213, Rifton, New York 12471 U.S.A.
Tel.: 1-800-777-4244   Fax: 1-845-658-8065
Robertsbridge, East Sussex, England TN32 5DR
Tel.: 0800 387 457   Fax: 0800 387 531
Web address: http://www.communityplaythings.com/

Consortium for Citizens with Disabilities (CCD)
1730 K Street, NW, Suite 1212, Washington, DC 20006 U.S.A.
Phone: 1-202-785-3388 / Fax: 1-202-467-4179
Web Address: http://www.c-c-d.org/

Council for Exceptional Children — Division for Physical and Health
   Disabilities
Web Address: http://www.cec.sped.org/dv-menu.htm#10

Disabled Persons Community Resources
1525 Carling Avenue, Lower Level, Ottawa, Ontario K1Z 8R9 Canada
Tel/TTY: 1-613-724-5886   Fax: 1-613-724-5889
Web Address: http://www.ncf.carleton.ca/disability/

Flaghouse for Special Populations
601 Flaghouse Drive, Hasbrouck Heights, NJ 07604-3116 U.S.A.
Tel.: 1-201-288-7600   Fax: 1-201-288-7887
Web address: http://www.flaghouse.com/

Indian Institute of Cerebral Palsy
(Formerly Spastics Society of Eastern India)
P 35/1 Taratalla Road, Calcutta 700 088 India
Tel.: 401-3488 or 401-0240   Fax: 91-33-401-4177
E-mail: ssei@vsnl.com
Web address: http://www.iicpindia.com/

International Association of Assistance Dog Partners (IAADP)
Editor/Information and Advocacy Center
38691 Filly Drive, Sterling Heights, MI 48310 U.S.A.

Tel.: 1-810-826-3938
Web Address: http://www.ismi.net/iaadp/

J. A. Preston Corporation
60 Page Road, Clifton, New Jersey 07012 U.S.A.
Tel.: 1-800-631-7277

National Center on Physical Activity and Disability (NCPAD)
Tel.: 1-800-900-8086   Fax: 1-312-355-4058
Web Address: http://www.uic.edu/orgs/ncpad/

National Institute on Disability and Rehabilitation Research (NIDRR)
400 Maryland Avenue, SW, Washington, DC 20202-2572 U.S.A.
Tel.: 1-202-205-8134 TTY: 1-202-205-9433 1-202-205-8189
Web Address: http://www.ed.gov/offices/OSERS/NIDRR/

Thai Rheumatism Association, Thailand
Web address: http://www.thairheumatology.org

TherAdapt
17Wa63 Oak Lane, Bensenville, Illinois 60106 U.S.A.
Tel.: 1-630-834-2461   Fax: 1-630-2478
E-mail: mail@theradapt.com
Web address: http://www.theradapt.com/

UCP National/United Cerebral Palsy Association (UCPA)
1020 Mary Street, Utica, New York 13501 U.S.A.
Tel.: 1-315-724-6907
Web Address: http://www.ucp-utica.org

REFERENCES

20 USC 1401
Batshaw, M.L. (1997). *Children with Disabilities*. Baltimore, MD: Paul H. Brookes.
Batshaw, M.L., & Perret, Y.M. (1981). *Children with handicaps: A medical primer*.
    Baltimore, MD: Paul H. Brookes.
Bianchi, D.W. (1994). Endocrinology. In M.E. Avery & L.R. First (Eds.), *Pediatric
    Medicine* (2nd ed.) (pp. 887–1012). Baltimore, MD: Williams & Wilkins.
Bleck, E.E., & Nagel, D.A. (Eds.). (1982). *Physically handicapped children: A
    medical atlas for teachers*. New York: Grune & Stratton.
De Vivo, D.C., & DiMauro, S. (1994). Hereditary and acquired types of myopathy.
    In F.A.Oski, C.D. DeAngelis, R.D. Feigin, J.A. McMillan, & J.B. Warshaw
    (Eds.), *Principles and practices of pediatrics* (2nd ed.) (pp. 2082–2096).
    Philadelphia, PA: J.B. Lippincott.

Frank, A. (1966, December 13). 7-year-old's wish list is short, despite illness. Patagraph, A6.

Hardman, M.L., Drew, C.J., & Egan, M.W. (1996). *Human exceptionality: Society, school, and family* (5th ed.). Needham Heights, MA: Allyn & Bacon.

Hallahan, D.P., & Kauffman, J.M. (1994). *Exceptional children: Introduction to special education* (6th ed.). Needham Heights, MA: Allyn and Bacon.

Heep Hong Society. (2001, February 8). *Heep Hong brings hope and joy.* [online] http://heephong.org.

Heward, W.L., & Orlansky, M.D. (1992). [Study guide to accompany] *Exceptional children: An introductory survey of special education* (4th ed.). New York: Merrill.

John F. Kennedy Centre (2001, February 15). [online] http://www.jfk.edu.hk.

Lehr, E. (1990). *Psychological management of traumatic brain injuries in children and adolescents.* Rockville, MD: Aspen.

Lian, M-G.J. (1998). *Technologies for persons with physical disabilities.* Normal, IL: University Communications, Illinois State University.

Lian, M-G.J. (1999). *Getting to know individuals with physical disabilities and/or health impairments.* Normal, IL: University Communications, Illinois State University.

Lian, M-G.J. (2000). *Teaching students with physical and multiple disabilities.* Normal, IL: University Communications, Illinois State University.

Lowman, D.K. (1997). Planning for students with complex health care needs. *Physical Disabilities: Education and Related Services, 16*(1), 7–24.

March of Dimes (1992). *Spina bifida: Public health education information sheet.* White Plains, NY: Author.

Monteleone, J.A., & Brodeur, A.E. (1994). *Child maltreatment: A clinical perspective.* St. Louis, MO: G.W. Medical Publishing.

Rosenheim, M.K. (1992). Teenage parenthood: Policies and perspectives. In M.K. Rosenheim & M.F. Testa (Eds.), *Early parenthood and coming of age in the 1990s* (pp. 200–266). New Brunswick, NJ: Rutgers University Press.

Sahk B. M. Kotewall Memorial School (2000, March). [online] http://bmkms. spastic.org.hk.

Sirvis, B. (1988). Physical disabilities. In E.L. Meyen & T.M. Skirtic (Eds), *Exceptional children and youth: An introduction* (pp. 387–411). Denver, CO: Love Publishing Co.

Smith, J. (1988). The dangers of prenatal cocaine use. *American Journal of Maternal Child Nursing, 13*(3), 174–179.

Smith, D.D., & Luckasson, R. (1995). *Introduction to special education: Teaching in an age of challenge* (2nd ed.). Needham Heights, MA: Allyn and Bacon.

Testa, M.F. (1992a). Introduction. In M.K. Rosenheim & M.F. Testa (Eds.), *Early parenthood and coming of age in the 1990s* (pp. 1–16). New Brunswick, NJ: Rutgers University Press.

Testa, M.F. (1992b). Racial and ethnic variation in the early life course of adolescent welfare mothers. In M.K. Rosenheim & M.F. Testa (Eds.), *Early parenthood and coming of age in the 1990s* (pp. 88–112). New Brunswick, NJ: Rutgers University Press.

United Cerebral Palsy Association (1992). *What is cerebral palsy?* New York: UCPA.

U.S. Equal Employment Opportunity Commission (1992). *A technical assistance manual on the employment provisions (Title I) of the Americans with Disabilities Act.* Washington, DC: U.S. Government Printing Office.

11

Parents and Families

ADVANCED THINKING

Answer the following questions as you read:

1. Why involving parents and families in school programs for children with exceptionalities is important?
2. How were parents and other family members treated in the history of special needs education? What did they do to make a change?
3. How did parents and families get involved in Hong Kong for their children with special needs?
4. What are general responses of parents and families when having a child with exceptionalities?
5. What are the common needs of parents and families with a child with special needs?
6. How to establish a productive home-school relationship?
7. What are the suggested approaches for enhancing positive parental and family attitudes?
8. What are recommended approaches to provide parents and families appropriate information?
9. What are potential strategies for encouraging parental and family participation in school programs?
10. What can parents and other family members do when participating in the programs of their children with special needs?

KEY TERMS AND PHRASES

confidentiality	extended family
consent	general services
due process procedure	history

home-school relationship   parent/family response
IEP   parent/family responsibility
legislation   parent/family right
litigation   parent/family role
MDC   parent/family support group
nondiscrimination   prejudice
parent organization   PTA
parent resource center   sibling
parent/family attitude   stress
parent/family involvement   zero rejection
parent/family need

INTRODUCTION

Parents and other members in an *extended family* (e.g., brothers and sisters, grandparents, aunts and uncles, cousins) play a very important role in the life of children with special needs. Leo Buscaglia (1975) emphasized that "no matter how many professionals work with a child during his or her life, none will have a more influential, lasting, and significant effect than that of his or her parents" (cited in Lian & Aloia, 1994, p. 52). The family, which is the most fundamental unit in our society, is usually where children obtain not only custodial care (e.g., feeding, bathing, dressing) but also beliefs, concepts of value, and tradition. Education of a child first takes place in family. A main portion of children's behavior and response patterns tend to be influenced by their familial environments and experiences, in which parents and other family members may serve as role models, guide, and feedback providers. In other words, parents and family may be the main reasons of what a child is and does.

Professionals in special needs education are increasing awareness of the importance of involving parents and families in the school programs. The rationale for parental and family involvement may include (Lian, 1984):

1. Parents spend the most time each day with their children. Also, the time spent to provide parents' care, teaching, and discipline in their children's life time is much more than any educator or other service providers who may work with these children for only less than a few years.

2. Before children with special needs reach school age, most of the critical development and learning take place in the family.

3. Children with special needs tend to recognize, trust, and rely on their parents and other family members.
4. Parents tend to know their children's strengths, weaknesses, likes, and dislikes more than other professionals and caregivers.
5. After each day's school work, parents and other family members can continue or extend/expand their children's school learning, and provide them with opportunities to apply what they have learned.

In this chapter, we will review historical development relating to parental and family involvement in special needs education, and the generally recommended approaches relating to parental and family involvement in school programs for children with special needs.

HISTORICAL DEVELOPMENT

The study of historical development regarding special needs education cannot omit the extensive contributions made by parents and families of children with exceptionalities. Numerous times these parents and families worked together as an influencing group to share their feelings and concerns, exchange ideas and experiences, establish network, support each other, lobby for legislation, request funding, protect children's right, enhance education and related services, help personnel preparation, and educate the general public.

In the United States, the first parent organization, the National Society for Cripple Children, was established in 1921. During 1940s and 1950s, many other parent groups were organized, including the National Association for Retarded Children (NARC) and the United Cerebral Palsy Association (UCPA). A great number of state and local chapters followed. These organizations actively recruited parents and supportive community residents as new members. They held routine meetings, invited professionals to speak and demonstrate effective educational and therapeutic strategies, as well as engaged in fund raising activities in order to sponsor special needs education and related services, assisted professional training, supported legislation and litigation, and protect children's right.

The efforts of these parents and families led to a number of major accomplishments. In their court action of *Pennsylvania Association for Retarded Children (PARC) vs. the Commonwealth of Pennsylvania*, for example, the judge ruled that children with mental retardation had a right to attend public school. The pass of the Education for All Handicapped Children Act in 1975, which was the forerunner of the Individuals with

Disabilities Education Act (IDEA) of 1990, was another victory of parents and families of children with special needs. This legislation guaranteed zero rejection, that is, a free, appropriate, public education for all children with disabilities. It also mandated socially and culturally nondiscriminatory assessment, individualized education program (IEP), placement of children with disabilities in least restrictive environment, periodic evaluation, and procedural due process. Due process is a legal procedure which can be used to protect rights of parents and families with a child with disabilities (see Table 11.1).

In Hong Kong, professionals in most schools for children with special needs have realized the significance of involving parents and families. *Parent Teacher Association* (PTA) and *parent resource centers* were generally established in these schools over the past 20 to 30 years. In addition, there have been a number of *parent support groups* for children with specific exceptionalities. The Society for the Welfare of the Autistic Persons (SWAP), for example, was organized by a group of parents of autistic children. Registered in 1982, the SWAP's missions included: (1) increasing understanding of the general public regarding autism; (2) seeking welfare for persons with autism; (3) enhancing government-supported

Table 11.1 Due Process Procedure

The due process procedure includes:

1. Written notification before evaluation of the child.
2. Written notification before change in educational placement.
3. Periodic review of educational placement.
4. Opportunity for an impartial hearing including the right to:
   - receive timely and specific notice of such hearing,
   - review records,
   - obtain an independent evaluation,
   - be represented by a counsel,
   - cross-examine,
   - bring witness,
   - present evidence,
   - receive a complete and accurate record of proceedings, and
   - appeal the decision.
5. Assignment of a surrogate parent for children when:
   - the child's parent or guardian is not known,
   - the child's parents are unavailable, or
   - the child is a word of the state.
6. Access to educational records.

education for autistic children; and (4) promoting rehabilitation of persons with autism. Services provided by this parent organization include children's training, library for loaned play materials, preservice training, workshops, parent counseling, community education, and other social/leisure activities.

The Parents' Association for Preschool Handicapped Children was organized in 1986 and registered in 1987. Missions of this parent group included: (1) enhancing opportunities of education, training, vocational development, and quality assurance for children with disabilities; (2) supporting families of children with early developmental disabilities; (3) enhancing self-reliance, interaction, and teamwork among individuals with disabilities; and (4) increasing understanding and acceptance of the general public. The organization has had ten local districts to serve the greater Hong Kong area (i.e., Hong Kong, Kowloon, and New Territories). Recent focus includes:

1. Monitoring and supporting inclusive education for children with disabilities,
2. Conducting workshops and conferences, exhibits, and related activities to increase community awareness,
3. Providing parents with appropriate training curriculum in order to achieve children's full potential,
4. Publishing periodicals, and
5. Raising funds for sponsoring programs.

One of the most recently organized parent groups is the Hong Kong Association for Specific Learning Disabilities, which covers four districts: Tuen Mun, Kwai Chung South, Kowloon Central, and Sha Tin. Organized by parents in 1998, this association aims at (1) increasing understanding of the general public regarding specific learning disabilities; (2) supporting each other in an attempt to provide children with appropriate education; and (3) enhancing family welfare and eliminating discrimination. The website of this organization provides a variety of helpful information; it shares parents' and children's concerns and personal experiences, gives successful examples and products, lists resources and links, and makes announcement of activities.

Because of parents' and other family members' effort, discrimination and segregation were rejected, minimum standards in special needs education were assured, and the quality of services for children with exceptionalities was enhanced. A study of the historical development indicated that we as the school professionals and field practitioners need to be aware of the long lasting contributing roles parents and families have played, and be encouraged to implement appropriate and effective approaches to involve them for better educational programs and related services to be available for their children with exceptionalities.

UNDERSTANDING PARENTS AND FAMILIES

Lian (1988) suggested a five-stage approach to involve parents and families in school programs for their children with special needs: (1) understanding parents and families; (2) enhancing home-school relationships; (3) changing attitudes; (4) providing information; and (5) encouraging participation. In order to have a better understanding of parents and families of children with special needs, school professionals need to increase awareness of parental and family responses and needs.

Parental and Family Responses

Most parents are not ever prepared to be parents of a child with an exceptionality. "Although there are similarities in the ways parents react to the birth of a child with a disabling condition, there are also many other factors that mitigate a wide range of parental responses" (Lian & Aloia, 1994, p. 55). The following are possible feelings and thoughts of parents when having a child with disabilities (Featherstone, 1980; Gorham, 1975; Hollingsworth & Pasnau, 1977; Lian, 1999; Massie & Massie, 1975; Menolascino, 1974; Murray, 1980; Peterson, 1987; Turnbull, 1985):

1. Shock — "Why me?"
2. Anxiety and confusion.
3. Anger and resentment.
4. Denial and defense mechanism — "Not us!"
5. Child is rejected — disappointed and bewildered.
6. Ambivalence.
7. Guilt.
8. Stress and depression.
9. Other emotional overtones at this point: helplessness, self-punishment, hopelessness.
10. Other problems with feeling: frustrated, injured, agitated, miserable.
11. Overprotection and overindulgence.
12. Parent seeks genuine help.

An Emmy Award-winning writer of the Sesame Street and the Dick

Cavett Show, Emily Kingsley (1989) wrote "Welcome to Holland" to describe her experiences of having a child with Down syndrome (see Table 11.2).

Lian and Aloia (1994) indicated that teachers and other school professionals should be reminded that:

> … identifying parental feelings and responses when having a child with disabilities is not to produce an uncaring chronology of parents' movement from one stage of feelings and reactions to another. Rather, it is [for us] to provide appropriate assistance. Professionals are encouraged to determine exactly what services parents need and prefer at each specific stage" (Lian & Aloia, 1994, p. 61).

Table 11.2   Welcome to Holland

I am often asked to describe the experience of raising a child with a disability — to try to help people who have not shared that unique experience to understand it, to imagine how it would feel. It is like this …

When you are going to have a baby, it's like planning a fabulous vacation trip — to Italy. You buy a bunch of guidebooks and make your wonderful plans. The Coliseum. The Michelangelo David. The gondolas in Venice. You may learn some handy phrases in Italian. It's all very exciting.

After months of eager anticipation, the day finally arrives. You pack your bags and off you go. Several hours later, the plane lands. The stewardess comes in and says, "Welcome to Holland."

"Holland ?!?" you say. "What do you mean, Holland?" I signed up for Italy!

I'm supposed to be in Italy. All my life I've dreamed of going to Italy."

"But there's been a change in the flight plan. They've landed in Holland and you must stay."

The important thing is that they haven't taken you to a horrible, disgusting, filthy place, full of pestilence, famine and disease. It's just a different place.

So you must go out and buy new guidebooks. And you must learn a whole new language. And you will meet a whole new group of people you would never have met. It's just a different place. It's slower-paced than Italy, less flashy than Italy. But after you've been there for a while and you catch your breath, you look around, and you begin to notice that Holland has windmills, Holland has tulips. Holland even has Rembrandts.

But everyone you know is busy coming and going from Italy, and they're all bragging about what a wonderful time they had there. And for the rest of your life, you will say, "Yes, that's where I was supposed to go. That's what I had planned."

And the pain of that will never, ever go away, because the loss of that dream is a very significant loss.

But if you spend your life mourning the fact that you didn't get to Italy, you may never be free to enjoy the very special, the very lovely things about Holland."

Source: Kingsley, E. (1989, November 5). Welcome to Holland. [In the Dear Abby Column] *The Pantagraph*, p. C5.

Researchers and field practitioners often recommend that school professionals should (1) keep positive attitudes, (2) try not to blame or complain against parents and family, and (3) be willing to share and work together as a team. Lian (2000) gave the following suggestions:

1. Parents should be considered as full participating members of the educational team.
2. Professionals should try to accept parents where they are and learn to listen and to encourage full disclosure.
3. Professionals should share all relevant information with parents.
4. Professionals should have the major responsibility for methodology and technology; parents should have the principal responsibility for selecting goals and objectives.
5. Since clear communication is vital, professional jargons should be minimized.
6. Parents often need support and encouragement as they struggle to cope with the problems and frustration of raising a child with disabilities. (pp. 39–40)

Hallahan and Kauffman (1994) indicated that, like their parents, *siblings* (brothers and sisters) of a child with special needs may experience similar reactions such as fear, anger, and guilt; "in some ways [they] may have an even more difficult time than their parents in coping with some of these feelings" (p. 499). Powell and Olge (1985) gave the following suggestions for parents to respond to siblings:

1. Be open and honest.
2. Value each child individually.
3. Limit caregiving responsibilities.
4. Use respite care and other supportive services.
5. Be fair.
6. Accept disability.
7. Put together a library of children's books on disabilities.
8. Schedule special time with each sibling.
9. Let siblings settle their own differences.
10. Welcome other children and friends into the home.
11. Praise siblings.
12. Recognize that parents are the most important and most powerful teachers of their children.
13. Recognize the uniqueness of each family.

14. Listen to siblings.
15. Involve the siblings.
16. Require the child with a disability to do as much for himself or herself as possible.
17. Recognize each child's unique qualities and family contribution.
18. Encourage the development of special sibling programs.
19. Help establish a sibling support group.
20. Recognize special stress times for siblings and plan to minimize negative effect.

After certain stages of feelings and responses, parents and families may start to become more positive viewing the situation. They begin to take the challenge and accept the role and responsibility for their children with special needs. They:

1. learn to accept and understand the child,
2. give real love,
3. provide necessary ingredients for growth, development and maturity,
4. make realistic plans for the future of the child as well as for the entire family, and
5. follow-through their responsibilities and roles.

Parental and Family Needs

Garshelis and McConnell (1993) list a number of needs of parents and families of persons with disabilities:

1. I need more information about my child's condition or disability.
2. I need more information on the services that are presently available for my child.
3. I need more information on the services that my child might receive in the future.
4. I need more information about how children grow and develop (normal developmental stages).
5. I need more reading materials about how other parents cope (who have a child similar to mine).
6. I need to have someone in my family that I can talk to about problems.
7. I need to have more friends that I can talk to.

8. I need more opportunities to meet and talk with other parents of children with special needs.
9. I would like to meet with a counselor (psychologist, social worker) to talk about problems.
10. I need to have more time for myself.
11. I need help locating babysitters (or respite care providers) who are willing and able to care for my child.
12. I need help locating a day care center or preschool for my child.
13. I need help with providing transportation for my child.
14. I need information on support groups for parents with a child with special needs.
15. I need to have more time just to talk with my child's teacher.
16. I need more time just to talk with my child's physical therapist, occupational therapist, or visiting nurse.
17. I need help locating a doctor who understands my child's needs.
18. I need help locating a dentist who will see my child.
19. Our family needs help discussing problems and reaching solutions.
20. I need more help paying for expenses such as food, housing, or clothing.
21. I need help finding insurance coverage for my child to pay for medical care, medicine, therapy, or other services my child needs.
22. I need more help in getting special equipment for my child's needs.
23. I or my spouse need job counseling or help getting a job.
24. I need help explaining my child's condition to others (people inside or outside my family).
25. Someone in my family needs help in accepting the child's condition. (pp. 41–42)

In our education career, we as school professionals and field practitioners need to be aware of:

1. parents' and family's feelings when having children with a disability,
2. parents' and family's needs for psychological, emotional, and social help,
3. parents' and family's needs for educational information and skills,
4. parents' and family's needs for getting to know and obtaining available community resources,
5. parents' and family's rights to information and participation in child's educational assessment activities,

6. parents' and family's right to information and participation in child's individualized educational planning (IEP),
7. parents' and family's right to information and participation in evaluation of child's progress, and
8. if applicable, parents' and family's right to translator's or interpreter's services to be provided for those who are from culturally and linguistically diverse backgrounds.

Table 11.3 shows an example of a checklist developed by Sexton, Burrell, and Thompson (1992) for getting to learn about family needs.

Table 11.3 Family Needs Survey

_____ I need more information about my child's disability.

_____ I need more information about how to handle my child's behavior.

_____ I need more information about how to teach my child.

_____ I need more information on how to play with or talk to my child.

_____ I need more information on the services that are presently available for my child.

_____ I need more information about the services that my child might receive in the future.

_____ I need more information about how children grow and develop.

_____ I need to have someone in my family that I can talk to.

_____ I need to have more friends that I can talk to.

_____ I need to have more opportunities to meet and talk with other parents of children with disabilities.

_____ I need to have more time just to talk with my child's teacher or therapist.

_____ I would like to meet more regularly with a counselor (psychologist, social worker, psychiatrist) to talk about problems.

_____ I need to talk more to a minister who could help me deal with problems.

_____ I need reading material about other parents who have a child similar to mine.

_____ I need to have more time for myself.

_____ I need more help in how to explain my child's condition to his/her siblings.

_____ I need more help in explaining my child's condition to either my parents or my spouse's parents.

_____ My spouse needs help in understanding and accepting this child's condition.

_____ I need help in knowing how to respond when friends, neighbors, or strangers ask questions about my child's condition.

_____ I need help in explaining my child's condition to other children.

_____ I need help locating a doctor who understands me and my child's needs.

_____ I need help locating a dentist who will see my child.

Table 11.3   (Cont'd)

_____	I need help locating baby-sitters or respite care providers who are willing and able to care for my child.
_____	I need help locating a day care center or preschool for my child.
_____	I need help in getting appropriate care for my child in our church or synagogue nursery during church services.
_____	I need more help in paying for expenses such as food, housing, medical care.
_____	I need more help in getting special equipment for my child's needs.
_____	I need more help in paying for therapy, day care, or other services my child needs.
_____	I or my spouse need more counseling or help in getting a job.
_____	I need more help paying for babysitting or respite care.
_____	I need more help paying for toys that my child needs.
_____	Our family needs help in discussing problems and reaching solutions.
_____	Our family needs help in learning how to support each other during difficult times.
_____	Our family needs help in deciding who will do household chores, child care, and other family tasks.
_____	Our family needs help in deciding on and doing recreational activities.

Source: Sexton, D., Burrell, B., & Thompson, B. (1992). Measurement integrity of the family needs survey. *Journal of Early Intervention, 16* (4), 343–352.

With data from a survey in Taiwan, Yeh, Morreau, and Lian (1993) listed general services needed by parents and families of children with disabilities:

1. Somebody to take care of my child so that we can go on a weekend or holiday trip without him/her.
2. Day care services so that we can work during the day.
3. somebody to help us deal with our emotional problems.
4. Somebody to help my child deal with his/her emotional problems.
5. Medical services to deal with my child's unique health problems.
6. A place to get needed information about my child's disabilities.
7. A governmental agency to get financial support or a loan to help my child.
8. A place to get needed therapy.
9. A place to get needed technological devices.
10. A place for my child to go for recreation.
11. Transportation for my child.
12. Convenient handicapped parking provided at places where I go often (i.e., shopping center, post office, park, hospital, bank, etc.).

13. Convenient access to places where I go often.
14. Legal services to assist us when I have legal problems related to my child.
15. Training for my child on daily living skills.
16. Training for my child on physical development.
17. Training for my child on social skills.
18. Training for my child on emotional development.
19. Training for my child on language and communication development.
20. Training for my child to improve his/her movement from place to place.
21. Training for my child to develop problem-solving skills.
22. Training for my child on transitional skills.
23. Training for my child to enjoy his/her leisure time.
24. Training for my child in vocational skills.
25. Employment services to help my child find a job when he/she is ready.

Levine (1985) developed the *Parent Questionnaire for Developmental, Behavioral, and Health Assessment of Elementary School Children*. Major contents of this questionnaire include: child's basic information, person providing information, current problems needing help, previous evaluation, and previous treatment. There is a rating scale in this questionnaire which consists of the following categories for specific information:

1. Possible pregnancy problems and medications.
2. Newborn infant problems.
3. Health problems.
4. Functional problems.
5. Early development.
6. Family history.
7. Specific skills and abilities.
8. Special interests.
9. Selective attention — activity.
10. Associated behaviors.
11. Associated strengths.

ENHANCING HOME-SCHOOL RELATIONSHIPS

When working with parents and families, teachers and other school professionals are encouraged to:

1. maintain positive attitudes, help rather than blame parents,
2. remain nonjudgemental,
3. show that you care and have shared concerns,
4. establish positive communication,
5. be an active listener
   - maintain eye contact and pay attention,
   - grasp key points,
   - rephrase to confirm,
   - use open-ended question and encourage parents to elaborate,
   - give positive feedback (e.g., show appreciation, summarize key points, and work together to plan for actions,
6. use appropriate verbal language (e.g., without jargons and inappropriate tones),
7. use appropriate nonverbal language (e.g., facial expression and body gesture),
8. avoid professional authority,
9. perceive parents as equal partners,
10. change communication format or environment, in case parents hesitate or become upset or withdrawn,
11. try not to take notes, tape or video record,
12. encourage experienced and enthusiastic parents to help,
13. answer parents' and family's questions, accept their suggestions, and report results to them,
14. prepare well before the conference to get right to the point instead of wasting parents' time, and
15. utilize available resources, e.g., parent organizations, therapists, social workers.

CHANGING ATTITUDES

A teacher may utilize the following approaches to enhance positive parental and family's attitudes:

1. Planning meaningful/functional teaching activities for parents' consent and support.
2. Providing parents and family with information.
3. Inviting parents and family to be resources and home observers
4. Inviting parents and family to participate in special education policy and objective decision making.

5. Inviting parents and family to participate in assessment and placement of child and explain procedures and results.
6. Inviting parents and family to join in school and classroom activities.
7. Giving parents and family more than one option whenever possible.
8. Letting parents and family see inclusion of disabled children in regular education with positive results.
9. Arranging schedule for parents and family to get together.
10. Inviting parents and family members to do objective evaluation of program and child's progress.

PROVIDING INFORMATION

Teachers and other school professionals can provide parents and families with useful information by preparing parent handbooks, sending routine or occasional notes to parents, sending assessment, test, and progress reports to parents, arranging individual or group conference, and opening the library and the learning resource center for families. Mapes, Mapes, and Lian (1988) gave detailed suggestions in Table 11.4.

In the U.S., most state educational agencies have convenient handbooks which contain detailed rights of parents and families of a student with disabilities (see Table 11.5).

Along with school services, a number of parent organizations are active in providing information to families of a child with special needs. The Association for Retarded Citizens (ARC) in the U.S., for example, offers a legal and financial planning workshop (see Table 11.6).

Mapes et al. (1988) contented that it is a two-way street when providing parents and families with information:

> Sometimes parents, even before involvement in a [school] program, acquire a wealth of information regarding a specific disability. Through discussing with medical specialists, reading pamphlets, magazines, journal articles and books, and talking with other parents who are facing similar challenges, parents may become "experts." By sharing this information with [educational] staff, a real framework for communication is established. (pp. 60–61).

ENCOURAGING PARTICIPATION

Teachers are encouraged to invite parents and families for them to be

Table 11.4   Ways to Provide Information

Private Discussion	Talking with parents, answering their questions, giving explanations, clarifying notions, and changing misconceptions.
Demonstration/ practice sessions	Providing demonstrations while parents observe and, then, giving an opportunity for parents to practice.
Positive reinforcement	Giving parents a smile and a word of encouragement, e.g., "You waited for Chad to try that by himself. He did it! Waiting a little but really can pay off."
Modeling	Arranging and encouraging a parent to "model" for another parent.
Bulletin boards	Designing simple, clever, visual, concise and, sometimes, even humorous bulletin boards to emphasize specific concepts.
Posted information	Posting short quotes, statistics, and "helpful hints" from the related literature periodically.
Formal presentations/ discussions	Scheduling formal presentations and discussions at routine parent meetings; presentations may be given by parents, school staff, psychologists, medical specialists, and therapists, followed by a discussion.
Informal presentations/ discussions	Inviting parents to school to have an informal observation or a lunch-time or snack-time show-and-discuss activity; parents and staff have an opportunity to briefly share information relative to program and/or individual objectives.
Handouts	Distributing handout materials to parents, such as copies of short articles, annotated bibliographies, quotes, suggestions, and home programs.
Recommendations/ announcements	Providing parents with recommendations and announcements in written or multimedia format (e.g., newsletter, facsimile, email, cassette/video tapes, CDs).

Source: Mapes, M.K., Mapes, J.C., & Lian, M-G.J. (1988). *Education of children with disabilities from birth to three.* Springfield, IL: Charles C. Thomas.

involved in activities such as (1) educational assessment; (2) development of long-term goals and short-term objectives; (3) support and continued implementation of programs at home; participation in specific problem-solving projects (e.g., behavioral projects, feeding, and toilet training); and (4) prevention of child abuse and neglect, or other parenting concerns (e.g., overprotection, or emotional problems).

Turnbull and Turnbull (1990) indicated that parents' role in educational programs for their children with special needs have shifted from the source of their children's problems and recipients of professional decisions to service developers, organization members, political advocates, and educational decision makers. In other words, parental and family involvement

Table 11.5 Parent Rights in Brief

Student Records:
1. Right to inspect and review records;
2. Right to obtain copies of records at no cost;
3. Right to be informed of all types and locations of records being collected, maintained or used by the agency;
4. Right to ask for an explanation of any item in the records;
5. Right to ask for an amendment of any record on the grounds it is found inaccurate, misleading or in violation of privacy rights;
6. Right to a hearing if the agency refuses to make the requested amendment.

Confidentiality of Information:
1. Right to restrict access to your child's records;
2. Right to be informed before information in your child's file is to be destroyed or disclosed.

Notice:
1. Right to notice before the agency initiates or changes the identification, evaluation or placement of your child;
2. Right to have that notice in writing, in your native language, or other principal mode of communication, at a level understandable to the general public;
3. Right to have the notice describe the proposed action, explain why it is proposed, describe the options considered and explain why those other options were rejected;
4. Right to be notified of each evaluation procedure, test, record or report the agency will use as a basis for any proposed action.

Consent:
1. Right to give consent before an evaluation is conducted and before initial placement is made in special education;
2. Right to revoke consent at any time.

Evaluation Procedures:
1. Right to have a case study evaluation of your child's educational needs completed within 60 school days of referral;
2. Right to have more than one criterion used in determining an appropriate educational program for your child;
3. Right to have the evaluation performed by a multidisciplinary team;
4. Right to obtain a copy of the multidisciplinary conference report;
5. Right to have your child assessed in all areas related to the suspected disability;
6. Right to have a reevaluation every three years or more frequently if conditions warrant or if you or your child's teacher requests it.

Least Restrictive Environment:
1. Right to have your child educated with nondisabled children to the maximum extent possible;
2. Right to have placement in the school your child would attend if nondisabled unless the individualized education plan requires some other arrangement;
3. Right of your child to participate with nondisabled children in nonacademic and extracurricular services and activities, such as meals, recess, counseling, clubs, athletics, and special interest groups.

Source: Illinois State Board of Education. (1998). *A parent's guide: The educational rights of students with disabilities.* Springfield, IL: ISBE.

Table 11.6   Legal and Financial Planning Workshop

Parents and family of a person with disabilities may find some legal and financial workshops to be beneficial. The ARC of Illinois provides a series of related workshops which address the unique needs that families have in planning for the financial and legal future of their relative with a developmental disability. Topics in these workshops include:

1. Negotiating the Social Security maze.
2. Preserving eligibility for government benefits through proper financial planning.
3. Special needs trusts.
4. Guardianship and less restrictive alternatives-the implications for consent.
5. Health care proxies.
6. selecting a knowledgeable attorney.

have changed from being passive to positive and active. Today in many countries, they are perceived as stakeholders of their children's education.

Davis, Kroth, James, and Van Curen (1991) provided the following principles for enhancement of parental and family involvement:

1. Families are not a homogeneous group; therefore, services and programs should be individualized based on family's needs and preferences and a variety of types and levels of activities should be provided.
2. Parents are the true experts of their children and have to be recognized as educators; professionals, including teachers, psychologists, pediatricians, and others, need to learn to be consultants.
3. All families and children have strengths.
4. Most parents do care and do want to help their children; however, sometimes they lack the skills. These skills are teachable.
5. Lack of involvement may reflect overriding primary family needs which take first priority, not lack of caring or concern.
6. A variety of legitimate family forms can promote health child and family development.
7. Acceptance of and respect for diverse cultural, ethnic, and racial heritages, lifestyles, and values is essential.
8. Family involvement is critical across the years of childhood and adolescence.
9. Family involvement is not a separate distinct component, but is integrated throughout the entire education service system.
10. Successful family involvement is a long-term process. Program development takes time, commitment, and extensive work. (p. 3)

The Heart of Illinois Low Incidence Association (HILIA), for example, conducted inservice workshops for the field practitioners to enhance *teaming with parents* through parent-friendly and need-based multidisciplinary conference (MDC) and individualized educational planning (IEP) meetings. Objectives of the workshop included:

1. to examine characteristics of effective, meaningful MDC/IEP meetings,
2. to hear directly from parents, their perceptions of MDC/IEP meetings; to identify aspects of the MDC/IEP process that are the most and least helpful to parents; and to discuss ways to elicit parent input and involvement throughout the process, and
3. to examine methods for improving climate, content, and organization of MDC/IEP meetings, with particular emphasis on parent involvement and need-based decision making.

Scharf and Lian (1991) gave detailed suggestions for parents when they are communicating with school or when attending parent-teacher conferences and individualized educational program (IEP) meetings:

Preconference Communication

1. Insure that the time of meeting is convenient.
2. Reschedule meeting if time suggested by the school is inconvenient.
3. Obtain any information which you believe will be helpful at the meeting, including your child's medical records.
4. Ask yourself the following questions:
   - What are realistic goals — what would you most like your child to learn?
   - Within these realistic goals, what would you most like your child to learn?
   - Are there concerns about your child's functioning at home that could be addressed by work at school?
   - What areas of your child's behavior do you believe need to be improved?
   - What are your child's strengths and weaknesses?
   - What methods have you found to be effective in rewarding your child.
   - To what extent does your child play with children in the neighborhood?

- What are your feelings about providing opportunities for your child to interact with nondisabled children?

Initial Conference Proceedings

1. If you are not introduced at the meeting to any persons you do not know, introduce yourself to all team members.
2. Make a note of the names and positions of everyone at the meeting.
3. Ask questions to clarify the particular role of other team members if this is not explained initially.
4. If you bring friends or advocates, introduce them and explain their role.
5. If you have a time limit for the meeting, let other team members know.
6. Ask the chairperson to state the purpose of the meeting and review the agenda, if this is not done.
7. If you have any questions about your legal rights, ask for more information.

Interpretation of Evaluation Results

1. Insure that the teacher, psychologist, speech/language pathologist, social worker, physical/occupational therapist, or other school professional states all tests that were administered and the specific results of each.
2. You may make a record for yourself or ask for a written copy of the test results and evaluations of your child. This may become an important part of your records on your child.
3. Insure that the classroom and educational program implications of the evaluation results are identified.
4. If any professional "jargon" is used which you do not understand, ask for definitions.
5. Ask how your child was classified in regard to a particular disabling condition (e.g., physical/health impairments, mental retardation, learning disabilities).
6. If you disagree with evaluation findings or classification, state your disagreement.
7. If your disagreement cannot be resolved within the meeting, ask for another meeting or an independent evaluation to be administered by an appropriate professional outside the school.

Development of the IEP Goals and Objectives

1. If the school's description of your child's performance is not as you perceive it, do give your description of his/her performance level.
2. State the skills and content areas which you believe are most important for your child's program.
3. If you have a question about the goals and objectives suggested by the school, ask for reasons.
4. Insure that all subjects requiring specially designed instruction are included in the IEP.
5. If your child receives instruction from two different teachers (e.g., regular and resource teacher) ask how the manner in which the responsibility for teaching the objectives will be shared.
6. If you are willing to assume responsibility for teaching or reviewing some of the objectives with the child, make this known to the committee.
7. Insure that the procedures and schedules for evaluation of goals and objectives are specified.

Placement Decision and Related Services

1. State the placement (regular classroom, resource program, special class) which you believe is most appropriate for the child.
2. Be sure all necessary related services you believe your child needs (e.g., speech therapy, physical/occupational therapy, transportation) are included. Remember that the school is not obligated to provide related services that are not written into the IEP.
3. If the school does not agree with you on placement and related services and you are convinced you are right, ask for the procedural guidelines for mediating a disagreement.
4. If you agree on a placement, and you are unfamiliar with the teacher, ask about the teacher's qualifications (training and experience).
5. Insure that your child has appropriate opportunities to interact with nondisabled children.

Conclusion of Meeting

1. If the chairperson does not initiate it, ask for a summary of the meeting to review major decisions and follow-up responsibility.

2. If follow-up responsibility has not been specified, ask who is going to be responsible for each task.
3. Describe what responsibilities (e.g., teaching objectives, increasing socialization opportunities during after-school hours) you will assume.
4. Ask for the approximate time for reviewing the IEP on at least an annual basis.
5. State in what ways and how frequently you would like to keep in touch with the teacher.
6. State your desire and intent to work closely with the school.
7. Express appreciation for the opportunity to share in decision-making and for their interest in your child.

Parental and family participation continues after the patent-teacher conference and IEP meeting. They are encouraged to monitor and support their children's educational program and follow-up with home activities. The Center for Research, Development, and Services of the Department of Educational Psychology at California State University-Northridge provided a working manual, the *Parent Behavior Progression* (PBP), for enhancing parent-infant interaction and early intervention for children at risk. The following are selected sample items (Bromwich, 1997):

Level i, #4   Parent spontaneously talks about things her infant does that please her.

Level ii, #6   Parent makes reference to infant's temperamental and behavioral characteristics (i.e., attentiveness, physical vigor, intensity of response, reaction to change, etc.).

Level ii, #8   Parent is sensitive to/talks about the amount of stimulation the infant can handle and profit from.

Level iii, #7   Sequences or chain of pleasurable interaction between parent and infant suggest mutuality in the relationship.

Level iv, #7   Parent takes into account the infant's state and current interests in providing experiences/materials for him.

Level iv, #13: Parent gives infant opportunity to communicate his needs/wants rather than always anticipating them.

Level iv, #18: Parent sets reasonable and developmentally appropriate limits, encouraging behavior which elicits positive feedback from others.

Level v, #10:   Parent experiments with ways of dealing more effectively with infant's developmentally inappropriate and unacceptable behavior.

Level vi, #8: Parent tries to respond in a balanced manner to the infant's needs as will as her own needs and those of the rest of the family.

Level vi, #9: Parent exercises her own reasonable judgment before following suggestions of "experts"(i.e., pediatricians, relatives, friends, books, etc.). (pp. 383–384)

SUMMARY

1. Parents and other family members play an important role in the life of a child with special needs. There is a strong rationale for parental and family involvement in the child's school programs.

2. Parents and families tended to be neglected in the history of special needs education. Nevertheless, they organized themselves to share information, exchange experience, provide support, lobby for legislation and legal actions, request funding, protect rights, and enhance/assure quality of education and related services.

3. Most of the schools of children with special needs in Hong Kong to some extent have involved parents and families in educational programs. PTA and parent resource centers were established. In addition, there have been active parent organizations since early 1980s, with dedicated missions to enhance disability awareness in the community, support families, and improve educational opportunities and outcomes for children with special needs.

4. School professionals need to be aware of parental/family responses when having a child with exceptionalities, as well as their specific needs, and provide appropriate assistance and support.

5. There are effective approaches for changing parents' and families' attitudes and enhancing productive home-school relationships.

6. Ways of providing parents and families with appropriate information include private discussion, demonstration, positive reinforcement, modeling, bulletin boards, posted information, formal/informal presentation and discussion, handouts, and recommendations/announcements.

7. Parents and families have protected rights to access their child's records, keep confidentiality of information, receive notice, give consent, and participate in the evaluation procedures.

8. Teachers and other school professionals need to arrange events and activities with assistance and encouragement in an attempt to enhance parental and family participation in special needs education and related services.

ACTIVITIES

1. Invite parents and other family members as guest speakers to share experiences of having and raising a child with special needs.
2. Assign students to visit schools in Hong Kong as well as to interview coordinating staff of the Education Department in order to collect information relating to opportunities and strategies for enhancing parental and family involvement. Schedule for students to present findings in class.
3. Form small groups to review related literature and list parental and family involvement in special needs education of various countries.
4. Conduct a survey of parents' and family's needs in their effort to provide or assure better quality of education and related services for their children with exceptionalities.
5. Engage role-playing activities for students to practice on active listening and positive, productive, outcome-based conversation.
6. Design and prepare parent/family handbooks for providing appropriate information and encouraging parental and family participation.

RESOURCES

Resources in Hong Kong

Babamama.com
Web address: http://www.babamama.com

仙人掌特殊教育網頁
Web address: http://cactus-sped.uhome.net/

Equal Opportunities Commission
Unit 2002, 20/F, Office Tower, Convention Plaza, 1 Harbour Road, Wanchai, Hong Kong
Tel.: 852-2511-8211   Fax: 852-2511-8142
Web address: http://www.ied.edu.hk/educode

Heep Hong Society 協康會
G1-11, Tung Yu House, Tai Hang Yung Estate, Kowloon
Tel.: 852-2776-3111   Fax: 852-2776-1837
E-mail: info@heephong.org
Web address: Http://www.heephong.org

Hong Kong Association for Specific Learning Disabilities
Web address: http://www.asld.org.hk

Hong Kong Education Department
Web address: http://www.ed.gov.hk/

The Hong Kong Society for the Deaf — Parent Resource Centre
Room 903, Duke of Windsor Social Service Building
15 Hennessy Road, Wanchai, Hong Kong
Tel.: 852-2854-2676 or 852-2854-2713
Web address: http://www.deaf.org.hk

香港唐氏綜合症協會
九龍東頭村振東樓東翼地下 Kowloon
Tel.: 852-2718-7774-8   Fax: 852-2718-0811
E-mail: asdkh@glink.net.hk
Web address: http://www.healthbasic.com/downsyndrome/index/index1.
  html

Hong Kong Family Welfare Society
E-mail: hoffice@hkfws.org.hk
Web address: http://www.hkfws.org.hk

The Parents' Association of Pre-school Handicapped Children
香港九龍鑽石山鳳德村紫鳳樓地下1-2A室 Hong Kong
Tel.: 852-2324-6099   Fax: 852-2352-4991
E-mail: info@parentsassn.org.hk
Web address: http://www.parentsassn.org.hk

Resource Center for Parents with Hearing Impaired Children
Podium Floor, Hong Shing Court, Healthy Village
No. 668 King's Road, North Point, Hong Kong

Society for the Welfare of the Autistic Persons (SWAP)
Room 210-214, Block 19, Shek Kip Mei Estate, Kowloon
Tel.: 852-2788-3326   Fax: 852-2778-1414
Web address: http://www.swap.org.hk

Special Education Society of Hong Kong
香港特殊教育學會
Tel.: 852-2320-3452
Web address: http://www.seshk.org.hk/

Resources in Taiwan

大手牽小手
Web address: http://residence.educities.edu.tw/suiheng/

Children's Epilepsy Association of Taiwan
中華民國兒童癲癇協會, 石牌路二段號, Taipei, Taiwan
Tel.: 886-02-2871-2121 Ext. 3661   Fax: 886-02-2871-3557
Web address: http://www.childepi.org.tw/about.htm

中華民國智障者家長總會
3F, No 285 Chien Kuo S.RD. Sec. 1 Taipei, Taiwan, R.O.C
Tel.: 886-02-2701-7271   Fax: 886-02-2754-7250
E-mail: papmh@papmh.org.tw
Web address: http://www.papmh.org.tw/partner/partner.htm

台北市學習障礙者家長協會
台北市和平東路三段12號10樓之一
Tel.: 886-02-2739-6942   Fax: 886-02-2739-6975

Syin-Lu Social Welfare Foundation
財團法人心路社會文教基金會
Web address: http://www.syinlu.org.tw/

International Resources

Human Services Research Institute, National Center for Family Support
850 Lancaster Drive SE Salem, OR 97301 U.S.A.
Tel.: 1-503-362-5682 Fax: 1-503-362-7729
http://www.familysupport-hsri.org/

The National Parent Network on Disabilities (NPND)
1130 - 17th Street, NW, Suite 400
Washington, DC 20036 U.S.A.
Tel.: 1-202-463-2299 Fax: 1-202-463-9405
Web address: http://www.npnd.org

South Dakota University Affiliated Program (SDUAP),
Dictionary: For Parents of Children with Disabilities
Web address: http://www.usd.edu/sduap/Dictionary/Dictionary.htm#A

REFERENCES

Bromwich, R. (1981). *Working with families and their infants at risk.* Austin, TX: Pro-ed.

Buscaglia, L. (1975). *The disabled and their parents.* Thorofare, NJ: Charles B. Slack.

Davis, D.T., Kroth, R., James, A., & Van Curen, S. (1991). *Family involvement guide* (2nd ed.). Plantation, FL: South Atlantic Regional Resource Center.

Featherstone, H. (1980). *A difference in the family: Life with a disabled child.* New York: Basic Book.

Garshelis, J.A., McConnell, S.R. (1993). Comparison of family needs assessed by mothers, individual professionals, and interdisciplinary teams. *Journal of Early Intervention, 17*(1), 36–49.

Gorham, K. (1975). A lost generation of parents. *Exceptional Children, 41,* 521–525.

Hallahan, D.P., & Kauffman, J.M. (1988). *Exceptional children: Introduction to special education* (4th ed.). Englewood Cliffs, NJ: Prentice Hall.

Hollingsworth, C.E., & Pasnau, R.O. (1977). Mourning following the birth of a handicapped child. In C.E. Hollingworth, & R.O. Pasnau (Eds), *The family in mourning: A guide for health professionals* (pp. 95–99). New York: Grune & Stratton.

Illinois State Board of Education (1998). *A parent's guide: The educational rights of students with disabilities.* Springfield, IL: ISBE.

Kingsley, E. (1989, November 5). Welcome to Holland. [In the Dear Abby Column] *The Pantagraph,* p. C5.

Levine, M.D. (1985). *Parent questionnaire for developmental, behavioral, and health assessment of the elementary school children.* Cambridge, MA: Educators Publishing Services.

Lian, M-G.J. (1984). Counseling parents of exceptional children. *Special Education Quarterly, 11,* 18-22.

Lian, M-G.J. (1999). *Getting to know individuals with physical disabilities and health impairments.* Normal, IL: University Communications, Illinois State University.

Lian, M-G.J. (2000). *Teaching children and adolescents with physical and multiple disabilities.* Normal, IL: Communication Services, Illinois State University.

Lian, M-G.J., & Aloia, G.F. (1994). Parental responses, roles, and responsibilities. In S.K. Alper, P.J. Schloss, & C.N. Schloss (Eds.). *Families of students with disabilities: Consultation and advocacy* (pp. 51–93.

Mapes, M.K., Mapes, J.C., & Lian, M-G.J. (1988). *Education of children with disabilities from birth to three.* Springfield, IL: Charles C. Thomas.

Massie, R., & Massie, S. (1975). *Journey.* New York: Knopf.

Menolascino, F.J. (1974). Understanding parents of the retarded: A crisis model for helping them cope more effectively. In F.J. Menolascino, & P.H. Pearson

(Eds), *Beyond the limits: Innovations in services for the severely and profoundly retarded* (pp. 172–209). Seattle, WA: Special Child Publications.

Murray, J.N. (1980). *Developing assessment programs for the multi-handicapped child.* Springfield, IL: Charles C. Thomas.

Peterson, N.L. (1987). Parenting the young handicapped and at-risk child. In N.L. Peterson (Ed), *Early intervention for handicapped and at-risk children: An introduction to early childhood special education.* Denver, CO: Love Publishing Co.

Powell, T.H., & Olge, B.A. (1985). *Brothers and sisters: A special part of exceptional families.* Baltimore, MD: Paul H. Brookes.

Scharf, M.K., & Lian, M-G.J. (1991, February 28). *Training parents communication skills.* Paper presented at the conference of Illinois Chapter of the Association for Persons with Severe Handicaps, Chicago.

Sexton, D., Burrell, B., & Thompson, B. (1992). Measurement integrity of the family needs survey. *Journal of Early Intervention, 16*(4), 343–352.

Turnbull, A.P. (1985). The dual role of parent and professional. In H.R. Turnbull, & A.P. Turnbull (Eds), *Parent speak out: Then and now* (pp. 137–141). Columbus, OH: Merrill.

Turnbull, A.P., & Turnbull, H.R. (1990). *Families, professionals, and exceptionality: A special partnership* (2nd ed.). Columbus, OH: Merrill.

Yeh, C.C., Morreau, L., & Lian, M-G.J. (1993). *Perceptions of Chinese parents toward mainstreaming their children with disabilities and service needs.* Unpublished manuscript, Illinois State University, Normal, Il.

12

Assistive Technology

ADVANCED THINKING

Answer the following questions as you read:

1. What is the rationale for the use of assistive technology in education and daily life of persons with special needs?
2. What is assistive technology?
3. What are generally included in assistive technology services?
4. How do we assist persons with special needs for them to successfully access various assistive technology devices?
5. How does assistive technology enhance communication, academic performance, and independent living?
6. What are general suggestions for selecting appropriate assistive technology devices?
7. What can be implemented in order to meet individualized needs for assistive technology among persons with special needs?
8. What are the potential advantages of organizing a technological assistance team (TAT)?

KEY TERMS AND PHRASES

adaptive switch
alternative communication
alternative keyboard
assessment
assistive technology
AT devices
AT lab
AT services

auditory output device
augmentative communication
case study
e-mail
environmental control
expanded keyboard
follow-up services
high tech

IEP
information technology
input access
instructional technology
internet
interview
joystick
keyboard
keyboard guard
keyboard moisture guard
low tech
observation
optical pointer
output access

pointer
screen reader
simulation program
speech dictated program
speech synthesizer
technological assistance team
touch window
training
TTY/TDD
visual receptive communication device
voice recognition device
word predict program
word processor
world wide web

INTRODUCTION

During the past two decades, a variety of assistive technology (AT) devices have been rapidly developed for children with special needs to successfully overcome barriers in their school and daily living environments. These devices help students with physical, mental, sensory, emotional/social, and other learning challenges achieve their individualized life goals. As Abbey (1983) indicated "Technology has advanced to where it can be used by many people, ... allowing them to become productive members of our society" (p. ii).

Lian and Stearns (1988) pinpointed that, for persons with special needs to be fully included in general school programs and community living, many assistive technology devices have made what used to be impossible possible. Assistive technology can make life of a person with special needs easier; it helps him/her perform specific tasks, becomes the door to opportunity, and assists a person in realizing his/her potential. To this, Wall and Sevener (1998) stated that "technology can be a great enabler and an equalizer of opportunity" (p. 4).

Matt is a high school student with a visual disability. When asked to describe how he felt about the assistive technology he used, he simply wrote, "Freedom. That's what assistive technology means to me" (Bersani, 2000, p. 11). He added that, having the right kind of assistive technology tools would greatly increase his will to participate in his own life.

Trollinger and Slavkin (1999) described that, "technology is changing the world in which we live and the schools in which we work" (p. 10). Data from Clasberry and Lian's (1998) survey among teachers and other school practitioners, for example, indicated that assistive technology is one of the effective strategies for enhancing inclusion programs for children with special needs. Through technological assistance, progress could be made toward inclusive school and community.

The Council for Exceptional Children (CEC) developed a set of standards for providing special needs education and related services. These standards emphasize knowledge and skills of using "appropriate adaptations and assistive technology ... to allow students with ... disabilities full participation and access to the core curriculum" (CEC, 1997, p. 182). Chambers (1997) asserted that all individualized educational program (IEP) team members should consider assistive technology when developing an educational plan for a student with special needs.

Realizing the importance of assistive technology in school education and rehabilitation for persons with special needs, governmental agencies and professional organizations in many countries and areas (e.g., Australia, Hong Kong, Singapore, Taiwan, U.K., U.S.) have devoted increasing efforts in an attempt to explore and develop advancement programs. The National Council of Social Services (NCSS) and the Association for the Deaf of Singapore, for example, worked together to establish the Disabled Assistive and Rehabilitation Technology (DART) Network (Chan). The National Science Council (NSC) in Taiwan created a website to list a great number of NSC-funded or self-funded assistive technology programs. Many local schools in Hong Kong have started assistive technology (AT) as well as information or instructional technology (IT) programs for students with special needs.

The beginning of the new century will continue the era of information network in special needs education and related services. Policy makers need up-to-date information regarding assistive technology to determine the direction of school education and social welfare, and provide timely leadership and administrative support, while field practitioners need to have knowledge of most recent models of assistive technology equipment and services so that they can provide more effective instructional and rehabilitation programs. The information networks need to have universal access, i.e., convenient and equal access for immediate, mass sharing. Providing alternative and augmentative communication devices for children with special needs in Guatemala, Duncan (2000) added that global promotion of assistive technology needs to be culturally sensitive and responsive. As she said, "We need a coherent set of strategies aimed at helping individuals in specific settings and offering assistance to community and governments … at the same time, we must respect different cultural understandings of disability, education, and human rights" (p. 8).

ASSISTIVE TECHNOLOGY DEFINED

According to the Technology-Related Assistance for Persons with Disabilities Act of 1988 in the United States, *assistive technology devices* "… are any item, piece of equipment or product system, whether acquired commercially off the shelf, modified, or customized, that is used to increase, maintain, or improve functional capabilities of individuals with disabilities" (20 USC 33). These devices may be utilized to enhance various areas of an individual's life. For example, AT devices for enhancing academic performance may facilitate learning and lead to accomplishment of school tasks such as reading, writing, math, doing homework, and taking exams. In addition, "the independent living and environmental control systems may enhance self-feeding, dressing, grooming, doing house chores (e.g., cooking, setting room temperature), and participating in leisure/recreational activities" (Lian, 1998, p. 1).

According to Wobschall and Lakin (1995), "assistive technology is just a subset of tools used by human beings, providing assistance in ways and places that are needed by relatively few people with significant impairments in 'normal' physical, sensory, or cognitive abilities" (p. 1). To this, Thompson, Wall, and Winchip (1998) explained:

> Just as a gardener uses a shovel to dig a hole because digging with one's hands is inefficient and ineffective, some people use technologies to perform tasks which they could not perform effectively or efficiently if they had to rely solely on the capacities of their own body. For example, some people who cannot produce voice use augmentative communication devices with voice synthesizers to expressively communicate. Another example would be a person who cannot visually distinguish characters on a computer monitor or a keyboard. When using a computer, this individual might use a screen magnifier to enlarge the information on the computer screen and an adapted keypad with keys that can be discriminated by the individual. (p. 7)

School professionals and parents of children with special needs need to be aware that assistive technology does not have to be always complex and expensive. Assistive technology systems may include *high-tech components* (e.g., more complex electronic technology) and *low-tech components* (e.g., less complex or no electronic technology) (Thompson & Beck, 1998). The decision to choose high-tech or low-tech devices should be based on whether they meet individualized needs in school and daily living environments. The "Ten-dollar Tech" sharing corner in the newsletter of Illinois Assistive Technology Project (IATP) is an example of encouraging field practitioners and consumers to first consider less costly but creative and practical assistive technology options.

ASSISTIVE TECHNOLOGY SERVICES

Mandated by the Individuals with Disabilities Education Act (IDEA) of the United States, schools for children with special needs should provide *assistive technology services,* which include the responsibility to directly assist the student with an exceptionality in the process of selecting, acquiring, or using an AT device (20 U.S.C., 1401). Common AT services are (Thompson, Wall, & Winchip, 1998):

1. the evaluation of the needs of a child with a disability, including a functional evaluation of the child in the child's customary environment;
2. purchasing, leasing, or otherwise providing for the acquisition of assistive technology devices by children with disabilities;
3. selecting, designing, fitting, customizing, adapting, applying, retaining, repairing, or replacing assistive technology devices;
4. coordinating, and using other therapies, interventions or services with assistive technology devices;
5. training or technical assistance for a child with disabilities or, where appropriate, the family of a child with disabilities; and
6. training or technical assistance for professionals. (p. 7)

ASSISTIVE TECHNOLOGY DEVICES

Assistive technology devices may be utilized for (1) accessing other AT devices, (2) enhancing communication, (3) enhancing academic performance, and (4) enhancing independent living. School professionals and parents of children with special needs may follow a set of convenient guidelines to select appropriate AT devices and related services.

For Accessing AT Devices

Input Access

According to Illinois Assistive Technology Project (1996), "*Input access* refers to the ability to build-in and add-on adaptations to make all components (hardware, operating system, applications) accessible to all individuals using the system" (p. 8). Traditional computer keyboards and the input systems of many technological devices (e.g., an augmentative communication device) tend to have small, non-flat keys. Persons with motoric disabilities may make erroneous or unintended multiple key strikes (Lian, 1984). They may also find a mouse with click buttons difficult to handle. In this case, persons with special needs may rely on specific adaptive devices in their attempt to access and operate the input systems of assistive technology. These devices include adaptive switches, joystick, keyboard guard/moisture guard, alternative or expanded keyboards, and voice recognition devices.

Schaeffler (1988) gave practical suggestions for children with cerebral palsy to access electronic and non-electronic devices:

1. Maintain *stabilization* in case children have uncontrolled movement of hands or only one hand control; stabilization can be accomplished by having the object clamped to a table of wheelchair, or simply utilizing masking tapes and Velcro.
2. Have *boundaries* in case an object's movement needs to be restricted within reach of the child and easy for him/her to retrieve.
3. Provide *grasping aids* and *manipulation aids* in case children lack fine motor dexterity.
4. Utilize *switches* for children who need adapted remote control to turn on/off power and operate electronic devices.

Adaptive switches may be utilized to provide opportunities for accessing computers and other assistive technology devices. Lian (2000) listed a variety of adaptive switches in a handbook for teachers of children with special needs, including thumb switch, touch switch, flat pad or pressure pad switch, latch switch, grasp switch, air cushion ("squeeze") switch, motion (mercury) switch (e.g., head switch), mouth tube ("puff") switch, ribbon or leaf ("floppy") switch, and wheelchair mounting switch. There are also adaptive switches with commercial names, such as Jelly Bean (colorful touch) switches, soft switch, Jumbo Plate (enlarged flat pad) switch, and P-switch (for minimal skin or muscle movement, e.g., raising eyebrow).

The following are additional switches and/or related devices:

1. From Adaptation, Inc., the *Taction Pads* (i.e., "tactile action pad") are clear, adhesive-backed, touch sensitive patches that can turn nearly any surface or object into a switch. Users of this device are instructed to peel the backing off and stick it to nearly any surface and object. The newly formed touch sensitive patches will only work with products of Adaptation, Inc.

2. The *LightSwitch* from Ability Research, Inc. is a light-activated switch which can be used to operate various assistive technology devices. When a focused light spot of up to three inches in diameter is directed at the LightSwitch, it provides switch closure.

3. The *voice-activated switch* can be operated by voice or sound. It has adjustable sound threshold level to which the switch will respond and length of time switch stays on.

In their experimental study, Tanaka and Lian (1995) not only reviewed optional adaptive switches, but also tried various body parts of a person with special needs for successfully accessing and operating specific switches. These body parts may include thumb or other fingers, palm or back of hand, elbow, shoulder, chin, mouth, eye, forehead, side or back of head, knee, inside or outside of thigh, ankle, and foot.

Joystick is a device used to be designed and installed for persons with physical disabilities to operate his/her wheelchair. It is also available for accessing various assistive technology devices. In addition, young children may benefit in using it to learn directionality and other relationships.

From Assistech, Inc., the plastic full-formatted *keyboard guard* has slide insert for custom templates to expose particular keys on keyboard to fit software requirements. Templates made of opaque plastic to slide over keyboard guard and hook around pin at end. The *keyboard moisture* guard from Don Johnston Incorporated is a thin, flexible device which protects against dust, moisture, and liquids.

A variety of pointers (or sticks) have been introduced for persons who have difficulties to manually type on a keyboard. Alternative parts of a human body may make it possible to utilize a head pointer, mouth or tongue pointer, chin pointer, or foot pointer to access assistive technology devices. Different textures of the tip of a pointer are available for specific purposes, e.g., activating adaptive switches, typing, drawing, turning pages, inserting/ retrieving computer diskettes or CDs, and operating the printer.

There have been a variety of *alternative keyboards* and *expanded keyboards*. These adaptive keyboards may provide enlarged keys, flat keys, and alternative keys (e.g., the color keys on the Muppet Learning Keys and the "Zap" key for ending or re-starting a software program). Many alternative and expanded keyboards also have available keyguards and/or moisture guards.

Optical pointer, usually attached to the side of a person's head (as an optical head pointer), may be utilized to activate keys of a specially designed keyboard as well as the computer screen or its replacement. The Light Talker (LT) from the Prentke Romich Company, for example, makes it possible for a nonvocal person without capable hand movement to "look at" the keyboard, activate selected keys, and send out synthesized speech messages.

Touch window is a touch screen that attaches easily to a computer monitor. It allows touch input, which is one of the most direct and natural ways for a child to interact with the computer; the child points and touches to make selections, move objects, and draw graphics.

Individuals who have difficulty in manually operating traditional and adaptive input systems may need to utilize a voice recognition device. This device includes a microphone and a "voice dictation" software program. The Dragon Naturally Speaking Essentials v.5 from the Dragon Systems, Inc. is one of the popular voice recognition programs. Users of this device operate a computer or other electronic system to work on school assignments, access world wide web, send e-mail messages to a friend, and update data-based files "hands-free" (by natural voices).

Persons with a visual disability may find it more convenient to use a Braille input system. The *Braille-'N-Speak 2000* from the Freedom Scientific, Blind/Low Vision Group is an electronic talking Braille note-taker and personal organizer which has a combination of speech access and a standard, Perkins style* Braille keyboard (*Perkins School for the Blind).

Output Access

Persons with specific disabling conditions, such as visual and/or hearing impairments may need adaptive output systems of assistive technology. *Output access* is "the ability of build-in and add-on adaptations to make all components (hardware, operating system, application) of a [technological] system accessible to an individual's use" (IATP, 1996, p. 9). Traditional computer systems provide visual outputs (through color monitor and printer) and auditory outputs (through speakers, e.g., beeping, voice, and music). Persons with sensory exceptionalities may not be able to perceive these outputs.

Adapting visual outputs may include the arrangements of:

1. having visual information enlarged on screen or a printout,
2. having visual information transformed into an alternative mode, such as speech output (through a screen reader system) and tactile output (through vibration or Braille displays).

The *JAWS for Windows* from the Freedom Scientific, Blind/Low Vision Group is a popular *screen reader*. Illinois Assistive Technology Project (1996) suggested that "screen readers may be used in conjunction with other enhancement devices, such as magnification systems, or they may replace all visual output" (p. 10).

The device of *Braille displays* may be used to convert visual information on computer screen (e.g., English or Chinese messages and graphics) into "touchable" Braille messages (DeMario, Leigh, & Dina, 1998).

Traditional telephone amplifiers and visual receptive communication devices, such as *text telephone* (TTY) and *telecommunication device for the deaf* (TDD), have been available for persons with hearing impairments to make or answer a phone call (Lartz, 1998). Today, additional options like facsimile, e-mail, and a chat room on the world wide web (W.W.W.) are available and convenient.

For Enhancing Communication

A variety of *alternative* and *augmentative communication devices* have been developed and made available for persons with nonvocal or nonverbal conditions. The following are a few examples:

1. The *SpeakEasy Communication Aid* of AbleNet can be used to store 12 messages for a total of four minutes and 20 seconds of recording time. The messages are accessible via keypad or external switches.
2. The *Cannon Tape Communicator*, available through Crestwood Company, stores up to 7,000 characters and prints out frequently-used phrases. This communication device provides speech and enlarged print and can be operated by adaptive switches for raw and column scan intersect.
3. The *DynaVox 2 and 2c Augmentative Communication Devices*, available through the Sentient Systems Technology, Inc., assist persons with physical disabilities in natural language formation. For users' convenience, the devices do not confine an individual

to the limitations of a fixed keyboard, so there is no need to memorize hundreds of complicated codes that get in the way of real communication. Instead, the devices use a dynamic "touch-screen" display that leads the user smoothly through the same natural message-formation process that produces normal speech.

4. The *Liberator* of Prentke Romich Company (PRC) is a device with high quality DECtalk gender and age-appropriate speech for persons with nonspeech conditions. It is user-friendly with convenient overlays, switch interface, keyguard and moisture guard, and various scanning set-ups. Liberator can also serve as an alternate keyboard to most computers and can operate an environmental control.

Readers are referred to Chapter 7 for more detailed description of AT devices for communication,

For Enhancing Academic Performance

Assistive technology may provide students with motivating, multisensory stimuli for students to (1) receive information and build important concepts, and (2) explore and repeatedly practice for becoming skilled in learning and outcome-based academic performance (Lian, 1984). Bakken (1998) indicated that students who have mild mental, learning, and emotional/behavior disabling conditions may face challenging situations in listening, reading, writing, and organizing information; these students can benefit in assistive technology through adapted "computers, taped books, spellers, tape recorders, readers, calculators and electronic books" (p. 1). Bakken further provided detailed description of in-classroom and home-based AT devices and approaches for children with mild disabilities to get and stay organized, to stay on-task, and to make their academic performance more manageable:

1. Highlighters for important information.
2. Index cards to help organize information.
3. Frames to highlight problems.
4. Color-coding for organizing similar information.
5. Graph paper for grouping.
6. Beepers/buzzers to help stay on-task.
7. Digital clocks, digital watches, talking watches to help stay on-task.

8. Headphones or earplugs to shut out distractions.
9. Tape recorders to record information that might be missed.
10. Mini pocket recorders allow the user to verbally store and retrieve telephone numbers, appointments, and individual notes (to-do lists).
11. Voice-activated day planners operate with voice-input technology.
12. Software programs, such as personal data managers and free-form databases. (p. 4)

Persons with specific learning difficulties may face the challenging tasks of perceiving and processing visual information. A student with dyslexia, for example, may read words on computer screen incorrectly. Bakken (1998) recommended the following assistive technologies for making visual tasks less strenuous:

1. Tape recorded lectures or presentations.
2. Software program options that enable the user to change background and text colors or to change font size.
3. Large print written materials.
4. Large print transparencies for prolonged viewing of computer screens that may reduce the eyestrain of the individual.
5. Magnification hardware (special monitor screen) or software (program applications) that enlarges and enhances the text and graphics displayed as well as enlarging text, the user can alter colors, fonts, and print size.
6. Enlarged cursor control panels that allow the users to choose from a number of big cursors, as well as the options of a "lefty" cursor for those people who are left-handed.
7. On-screen keyboards and keyboards that speak, that provide voice output.
8. Talking, large print browsers that allow users with visual processing problems to search the Internet.
9. Books on disc, once on the computer screen, that can be enlarged and read back to the user with voice output.
10. Material that is scanned, enlarged, and read back to user with voice output.
11. To capitalize on visual learning strengths, material presented through videotape (using a VCR) or videodisc (using a computer [or VCD player]).
12. Large computer monitors for easier viewing. (p. 6)

The following are additional assistive technology devices which may be used for enhancing academic performance in students with special needs:

1. The *Flexible Wheelchair/Table Mounting Kit* of Crestwood Company can clip items such as adaptive switches, books, augmentative communication devices, and other teaching and learning as well as vocational and recreational materials up to three pounds to wheelchair or table. Another device, the Crestwood *Tri Mounting Kit*, can be used for mounting membrane and button switches easily and securely to wheelchair or table. The switches are mounted to one of three plates in kit.

2. The *IntelliKeys* of IntelliTools, Inc. supports physical, visual, and cognitive access to computers or other microprocessors. This device provides enlarged keyboard with customized overlay and touch tablet. It can also be operated with the *Snap-In* keyguard or a keyguard for standard overlay, or by adaptive switches.

3. Developed by the Don Johnston, Inc., the *Discover Board* is for IBM system and *Discover Ke:nx* is for Macintosh computers. Both are for the purpose of replacing traditional keyboards, so that students with disabilities may have easier access to classroom computers, more convenient data-input process, and more successful performance on educational software programs. They may provide sounded feedback to confirm students' effort of operating substitute and expanded keyboards (Lian, 1999)

4. The *All-Turn-It spinner* of AbleNet Inc. may allow students to participate in regular class activities. This double spinner has (1) inner overlay and arrow which spin independently, and (2) dice overlay which allows students to participate in commercially-available games.

5. The *Co:Writer* of Don Johnston Inc. is an intelligent *word prediction* program that allows individuals with physical, cognitive, or learning disabilities to write with whole words when writing letter-by-letter is a challenging situation. It cuts down the number of keystrokes needed to type words.

For Enhancing Independent Living

Persons with specific disabling conditions today can utilize appropriate assistive technology devices in an attempt to achieve more successful independent living. Through these devices, individuals who used to face existing barriers in school, home, and community environments realize their potential and become "more independent, self-confident, productive, and integrated into the mainstream of community living" (Wall & Sevener, 1998, p. 6).

Assistive technology may increase a person's opportunity to accomplish daily living tasks of food preparation and eating, personal hygiene and grooming, dressing, other house chores, career development, personal finance, and leisure/recreation activities. The following are a few examples of utilizing available AT devices to achieve independent living goals:

1. The *Vee-Zee Reachers* of Maddak Inc. are reaching aids specially designed to provide an extra measure of support, comfort, and ease. They feature flexible arm supports made of soft metal sheathed in vinyl tubing, which may be attached for either right- of left-handed use and bent to any shape by the user or care provider.

2. The *ULTRA-4 Remote System*, available through Crestwood Company, can be used as an ultrasound transmitter to remotely control immediate environment. The color-coded ultrasonic signals of this device can be sent to receivers of same color. The system controls up to four electrical items such as TV, radio, tape recorder, and table lamp.

3. The *Basic Environmental Control Unit* of Crestwood Company can be operated by head movement, using adaptive switches. As a result, a radio, TV set, tape recorder, or light can be plugged into the receiver module and activated by ultrasonic signals.

Selecting Appropriate AT Devices

Wall and Sevener (1998) suggested the following considerations for selecting appropriate assistive technology devices for persons with special needs:

1. Easy to use.
2. Accuracy, speed, and efficiency.
3. Ability to complete work and life tasks.
4. Compatibility with other home, work, and/or school equipment.
5. Availability.
6. Durability.
7. Noise level.
8. Portability, if needed.

9. Impact or temperature on equipment.
10. Maintenance requirement.
11. Longevity or ability to upgrade.
12. Versatility/flexibility of device.
13. Cost.
14. Manufacturer support.
15. Business history.
16. Trial rental period.
17. Loaner equipment during servicing.
18. Technical support line access.
19. Maintenance packet.
20. Warranty. (p. 14)

Wall and Sevener (1998) further recommended Batavia's (1989) evaluation criteria for school professionals to follow when selecting appropriate assistive technology devices for a person with exceptionality:

1. Effectiveness.
2. Affordability.
3. Operability.
4. Dependability.
5. Portability.
6. Durability.
7. Compatibility.
8. Flexibility.
9. Ease of maintenance.
10. Securability.
11. Learnability.
12. Personal acceptability.
13. Physical comfort.
14. Supplier repairability.
15. Physical security.
16. Consumer repairability.
17. Ease of assembly. (in Wall & Sevener, 1998, p. 14)

MEETING INDIVIDUALIZED NEEDS

To fulfill individualized AT needs of students with exceptionalities, a team approach is recommended. Members of the *technological assistance team* (TAT) may include teachers, speech/language pathologists, physical and occupational therapists, and other school professionals. TAT meetings are held regularly (e.g., once a week) for the purpose of:

1. Sharing up-to-date information and resources,
2. Assessing specific students' needs for, and potential of, using assistive technology,
3. Recommending and implementing appropriate assistive technology services, and
4. Evaluating effectiveness of assistive technology services.

The school may support efforts of TAT by providing opportunities for staff development (e.g., sponsoring inservice workshops and attendance at external professional conferences) and securing funding for facilitating an *assistive technology lab* and its function, i.e., assessment, training, and follow-up services.

Assessment

There have been a number of AT assessment guides. Some are with a checklist or data collection forms. The following suggestions were given by a field practitioner for an informal adaptive switch assessment:

1. Observe the individual with disabilities in a comfortable or natural environment.
2. Watch the individual's natural movement.
3. Record all potential locations for placing a switch.
4. Connect the switch to a preferred item or an item which is likely to be preferred by a peer of the individual.
5. Place appropriate switch in a location where the individual's movement was previously observed and documented.
6. Verbal and/or physical prompt the use of the switch.
7. Count the number of activations.
8. Watch for fatigue.
9. Try all locations where movements were observed and documented.

Thompson et al. (1998) emphasized the use of observation and interview in fulfilling individualized needs for assistive technology. *Observation* should be conducted in the environment where a student needs assistive technology (e.g., classroom, playground, lunchroom, home, or job site). Information collected through observation may include:

1. The student's entry-level abilities, e.g., cognitive development,

perceptual-motor coordination, receptive/expressive language skills, social/emotional development, and motivation;

2. The environment (i.e., the setting) and the persons and situations (e.g., equipment and activities) involved in it; and

3. Patterns of the student's interactions with others and equipment as well as his/her responses to, and participation in, the activities.

Observation should be ongoing before and during implementation of assistive technology services for a student. If applicable, videotaping can be utilized to facilitate formal and informal observation.

In addition to observation, TAT members need to conduct *interviews* to confirm their observation and collect additional information. As Thompson et al. (1998) indicated, "It can be very helpful for a special educator to interview a student, parent, teacher or any other individual involved with the student's performance related to assistive technology" (p. 16).

Training

Generally, it is almost not possible for a student with special needs to pick up an assistive technology device and immediately use it. It usually takes some time for him/her to get familiarized with it and repeatedly practice the way to access and operate it. This is especially true when the student has a severe mental, physical, sensory, learning, and/or emotional/behavior disability.

A student may need to try out on a number of options in order to find one which most fits him/her. TAT members may provide the student with motivation, demonstration, and task analysis approaches for his/her continuous practice and drill until the efficiency of using a specific AT device is at application level in the classroom and daily living environment.

Follow-up Services

The completion of training should not be the conclusion of an assistive technology service. It is the beginning of the next stage of the TAT work — to follow-up with supporting activities. *Follow-up services* may include:

1. Trouble shooting in case the AT device or the user is having a problem, and

2. Periodic evaluation to check effectiveness and need for revision of the assistive technology plan.

Case Study

Tables 12.1, 12.2, and 12.3 provide examples of case study evaluation and the individualized AT plans developed and implemented by the technology assistance team.

Table 12.1   Case Study Evaluation Example I

Reymundo was 6 years old. Born with severe spastic cerebral palsy, he habitually lied in a supine position on the floor with his arms and hands flexed (with thumbs adducted) and with his legs adducted and hyperextended. All of his joints were stiff. He lacked head and trunk control. He was not feeding or dressing himself and he was not toilet trained. He usually seemed unaware of objects and people and did not seem to communicate in any way. He cried sporadically in a way that seemed to be related to hunger or discomfort. Responses to visual and auditory stimuli had not been noted. He had never been in a school or preacademic program before and had spent much of his life at home. Reymundo cried and hyperextended when handled. He did not attend to his name nor seemed interested in objects or people in his environment.

A comprehensive case study evaluation was conducted based on Reymundo's needs for improvement in the following areas and an assistive technology plan was developed and implemented:

1. Reymundo needed to have appropriate positioning in order to eliminate disturbing motor patterns and develop functional postural control and motor movement. A bolster was placed under his abdomen and was rolled back and forth gently to help him relaxed. A wedge was then used for prone positioning which reduced his hyperextension pattern in trunk, increased extension of upper and lower extremities, and encouraged use of his elbows for weight bearing. A corner chair was also utilized to increase body symmetry/alignment and head/trunk control.
2. The assistive technology plan included use of a TumbleForm Scooter which provided opportunities for prone positioning and increased mobility.
3. The SpeakEasy Communication Aid of AbleNet was introduced for Reymundo to indicate his basic needs. After a four-month period, he began to indicate his needs, such as hungry and thirsty, by reaching for the enlarged keys with pictures of foods and drinks.
4. Reymundo demonstrated significant progress in sensory (auditory and visual) stimulation and consistent response (S-R) activities using the adaptive switches connected to perceptual-motor and cause-effect computer software programs.
5. A feeder chair was utilized for Reymundo's upright but relaxed sitting position during feeding time. The feeder chair reduced hyperextension of his trunk and encouraged head in midline. The IEP team is currently preparing padding and support for once he is ready to work on the toilet trainer.

Source: Lian, M-G.J. (1998). Technologies for persons with physical disabilities. In J.R. Thompson, M.E. Wall, & S.M. Winchip (Eds), *Assistive technology: Competencies and skills for teachers*. Normal, IL: University Communications, Illinois State University.

Table 12.2   Case Study Evaluation Example II

Bea was a 10-year-old, Caucasian girl in school. She exhibited foot placing reactions, parachute, and mild extensor thrust reflexes. She rolled from back to stomach and then crawled and pulled to a standing position holding on to a table. She showed fairly good head and trunk control. She was schedule trained but might wet her pants if not taken to the toilet every 2 hours or less. She tried to feed herself with a spoon held in a pronated fist. She ate everything but did not exhibit tongue or jaw rotation. She could put on a jacket and hat but did not otherwise dress herself. She spoke 4-word sentences such as "I go school 'morrow'" (tomorrow). She was able to sort objects according to their colors, sizes, or shapes. Her academic skills were below her age level. She was very active and she liked to interrupt others during a classroom activity.

A comprehensive case study evaluation was conducted based on Bea's needs for improvement in the following areas and an assistive technology plan was developed and implemented:

1. Bea seemed to be ready for standing and beginning walking with appropriate support. A standing table was used to increase her balance and endurance. A walker was also utilized, with an adult's physical prompting, to further enhance her standing balance and practice of stepping forward.
2. The assistive technology plan included an adapted tricycle for Bea to continue working on reducing her extensor thrust pattern, increasing parachute and protective reactions, and enhancing mobility.
3. Bea was scheduled to attend 30-minute sessions of speech/language therapy three days a week. Her mean length of utterance (MLU) and use of complete sentences was significantly improved.
4. The Co: Writer program of Don Johnston Inc. was introduced to help Bea in spelling and increase her pace of typing on computer.
5. Bea was scheduled to work with an occupational therapist in more functional way of holding spoon and increase of tongue lateralization and jaw rotation when chewing. The OT's suggestions were implemented during lunch time by the teacher and teacher's assistant.

Source: Lian, M-G.J. (1998). Technologies for persons with physical disabilities. In J.R. Thompson, M.E. Wall, & S.M. Winchip (Eds), *Assistive technology: Compe-tencies and skills for teachers*. Normal, IL: University Communications, Illinois State University.

Table 12.3   Case Study Evaluation Example III

An African-American boy, Richard was 16 years old and had resided in a hospital school since his infancy. His legs were flaccid sitting in a wheelchair and he had severe scoliosis and heart/kidney disorder. He tended to be shy and a little withdrawal. He did not speak and he used a traditional communication board. His receptive language was well developed, but he was always showing underachievement in his academic work. He had fairly good arm and finger movement. He fed himself but needed others to get foods ready for him to eat (i.e., chopping the meat, pouring milk, etc.). He kept this same dependence when needing to dress and using toilet. Being aware of the trend of deinstitutionalization, his parents were thinking about taking him home and getting him more involved in the public school and other community activities.

A comprehensive case study evaluation was conducted based on Richard's needs for improvement in the following areas and an assistive technology plan was developed and implemented:

1. Richard needed to have an opportunity to be in standing position to help strengthen muscles in his legs, maintain the head of his thighbone in the hip socket, and enhance blood circulation. A supine stander was utilized to gradually increase weight bearing in his lower extremities. A sidelyer was also used to prevent further development of scoliosis.
2. The assistive technology plan included use of the Mobil Adaptive Stander of Flaghouse Inc. to continue his opportunity of maintaining in upright standing position and weight bearing in hip and legs, while he could freely move around to increase mobility.
3. The Liberator, purchased from Prentke Romich Company, greatly increased his expressive language in communication and his appropriate use of social request for help in preparing foods and dressing.
4. Richard's academic curriculum was modified to increase concepts and skills of community living and the competencies of hiring, training, and supervising a personal care assistant (PCA).
5. The ULTRA-4 Remote System, available through Crestwood Company, was used for Richard to remotely control immediate environment, including his TV, radio, tape recorder, and table lamp.

Source: Lian, M-G.J. (1998). Technologies for persons with physical disabilities. In J.R. Thompson, M.E. Wall, & S.M. Winchip (Eds), *Assistive technology: Competencies and skills for teachers*. Normal, IL: University Communications, Illinois State University.

Further Recommendations

Thompson et al. (1998) gave 10 dos and don'ts to guide school professionals in planning and providing assistive technology services:

1. Do insist that [individualized educational planning] teams truly consider the assistive technology needs of all students with disabilities and don't settle for uninformed or dismissive discussion at IEP meetings.
2. Do make sure that the performance and interests of the student are considered before a device is purchased and don't make any AT decision without a student's input.
3. Do become part of a network of professionals who share information and ideas about assistive technology. The importance and value of brainstorming and problem solving in identifying appropriate technological solutions cannot be overstated. Don't

hesitate to consult with others who may know less than you, or to seek consultation from those who may know more than you.

4. Do become familiar with all potential funding sources. Don't allow a child to go without a device because of the cost of the device.

5. Do insist on professional training that builds true competency in the area of assistive technology. Don't settle for training that is outdated, disjointed, or irrelevant.

6. Do learn how to expertly operate any and all AT devices that your students use so that you can troubleshoot problems and maintain devices in good condition. Don't depend on a student's family or on a "specialist" to fulfill this role.

7. Do plan and schedule opportunities for students to use newly acquired devices throughout the school day. Don't rely solely on natural "teachable moments" to provide students with opportunities to use technology.

8. Do try out a device to get a good idea how it may work for a student before a final purchasing decision is made. Don't let anyone talk a school or a child's parents into purchasing a device before you know how it works for that individual.

9. Do take good care of devices, especially expensive ones, and try to educate students, peers, and family members about the value and care AT equipment. Don't leave electronic devices in hot cars, unsecured on table ledges, or in any other place where they can be easily damaged or destroyed.

10. Do keep believing in the potentials of assistive technology, regardless of the temporary setbacks that are bound to occur. Don't lose your vision or smile! (pp. 18–19)

Summary

1. Many assistive technology devices have been developed in order to help persons with special needs overcome physical, mental, sensory, emotional/behavior, and learning barriers and achieve individualized life goals.

2. Governmental agencies and professional organizations in Hong Kong as well as other countries and areas have increased awareness and devoted increasing efforts to explore and develop assistive technology advancement programs.

3. Assistive technology devices are any item, piece of equipment or

product system that can be used to increase, maintain, or improve functional capabilities of individuals with special needs. There are high-tech (more complex electronic) devices and low-tech (less complex or not electronic) devices.

4. School assistive technology services may include the responsibility to directly assist students with special needs in the process of selecting, acquiring, or using an assistive technology device.

5. Assistive technology devices may be utilized for accessing other AT devices, enhancing communication, enhancing academic performance, and enhancing independent living.

6. Detailed guidelines are available for school professionals and parents to follow when selecting an appropriate assistive technology device.

7. It is recommended that a technological assistance team (TAT) be established to meet individualized assistive technology needs of students with special needs.

8. An assistive technology lab may serve as a convenient and efficient vehicle for (1) conducting case studies through assessment, training, and follow-up services, (2) planning individualized educational programs, and (3) implementing assistive technology projects.

ACTIVITIES

1. Assign small groups to review assistive technology programs in a country or areas, e.g., China, Hong Kong, Singapore, Taiwan, the United Kingdom, and the United States. Each group will present its findings to the class.

2. Invite assistive technology practitioners, e.g., AT or IT teachers, therapists, and rehabilitation technicians, to speak to the class and demonstrate available devices and programs.

3. Invite assistive technology consumers to share with class their personal experiences and how specific AT devices and services helped to overcome barriers and achieve individualized goals in school and daily living environments.

4. Schedule for the class to visit a few assistive technology labs in local schools or rehabilitation settings, followed with a discussion with the in-charge teacher or program coordinator.

5. Assign each student to evaluate a child or an adult with special needs, review his/her personal goals in education and/or independent living, determine needs for assistive technology devices and services, and

develop an AT plan with detailed objectives, selected devices, and approaches.

6. Design and prepare a user-friendly booklet to introduce the "what," "where," "when," and "how" of assistive technology to other school personnel and parents of children with special needs, i.e., "What is assistive technology?" "Where and when is it needed?" and "How is it provided?"

RESOURCES

Resources in Hong Kong

John F. Kennedy Centre, Information and Technology Education Project
15 Sandy Bay Road, Hong Kong
Tel.: 852-2817-0131   Fax: 852-2817-3730
Web address: http://www.jfk.edu.hk/

Caritas Lok Kan School, Computer Room
42 St. Francis, Wanchai, Hong Kong
Tel.: 852-2528-5991   Fax: 852-2528-4363
Web address: http://lk.hkcampus.net/

Hong Kong Blind Union
Tel.: 852-2711-2777
E-Mail: info@hq.hkbu.org.hk
Web address: http://www.hkbu.org.hk/chinese/resources/link/

The University of Hong Kong, Faculty of Education
Pokfulam Road, Hong Kong
Tel.: 852-2859-2784   Fax: 852-2858-5649

William and Anita Newman Library
Web address: http://newman.baruch.cuny.edu/about/v_tour/chinese_trad/
    tour_23.htm

Resources in Singapore

Tan Tok Seng Hospital, Department of Rehabilitation Medicine
Study: "Rehabilitation and Assistive Technology for the Disabled in
    Singapore"
Web address: http://cares.nsc.gov.tw/Paper/William_Chan.html

Resources in Taiwan

National Science Council, Specific Assistive Technology Information
台北市和平東路二段106號
Tel.: 886-02-2737-7992   Fax: 886-02-2737-7566
Web address: http://www.nsc.gov.tw/y2k/English_Version/Assistive_T/
  result.htm

National Taiwan Normal University, Special Education Center,
Special Education Technology Program
台北市和平東路一段162號
Web address: http://140.122.65.63/special/index.html

International Resources

Ability Research, Inc.
P.O. Box 1721, Minnetonka, Minnesota 55345 U.S.A.
Tel.: 1-612-939-0121   Fax: 1-612-890-8393
E-mail: ability@skypoint.com
Web address: http://www.skypoint.com/~ability

AbleNet Inc.
1081 Tenth Street S.E.
Minneapolis, Minnesota 55414-1312 U.S.A.
Tel.: 1-800-322-0956 or 1-612-379-0956 Fax: 1-612-379-9143
Web address: http://www.ablenetinc.com/

Adaptive Consulting Services, Inc.
403-A Hawk Street, Rockledge, Florida 32955 U.S.A.
Tel.: 1-800-515-9169
Web address: http://www.augmentative.com/acs-dv2c.htm

Assistive Technology, Inc.
1642 W. 64th Street, Hialeath, Florida 33012 U.S.A.
Tel.: 1-305-827-3686   Fax: 1-305-827-3687
Web address: http://assistivetech.com/

Closing The Gap, Inc.
P.O. Box 68, 526 Main Street, Henderson, Minnesota 56044, U.S.A.
Tel.: 1-507-248-3294   Fax: 1-507-248-3810
Email: info@closingthegap.com
Web address: www.closingthegap.com

Crestwood Company
6625 N. Sidney Place, Milwaukee, Wisconsin 53209-3259 U.S.A.
Tel.:1-414-352-5678   Fax: 1-414-352-5679
Web address: http://www.communicationaids.com

Council for Exceptional Children, Division of Technology and Media
Web address: http://www.cec.sped.org/dv-menu.htm

Deaf World Web
Web address: http://dww.deafworldweb.org/

Don Johnston Incorporated
1000 N. Rand Road Bldg 115, Wauconda, IL 60084-0639 U.S.A.
Tel.: 1-800-999-4660   Fax: 1-847-526-4177
Web address: http://www.donjohnston.com/

Don Johnston Special Needs Ltd.
18 Clarendon Ct., Calver Road, Winwick Quay Warrington, England WA2
   8QP
Tel.: 44-01-925-241642   Fax: 44-01-925-241745
E-Mail: jmunro@djsn.u-net.com

Dragon Systems, Inc.
320 Nevada Street, Newton, Massachusetts 02460 U.S.A.
Tel.: 1-617-965-5200   Fax: 1-617-630-9707
Web address: http://www.dragonsys.com/

DynaVox Systems Inc.
2100 Wharton Street Suite 400, Pittsburgh, PA 15203 U.S.A.
Tel.: 1-800-344-1778
Web address: http://www.sentient-sys.com

Freedom Scientific, Blind/Low Vision Group
11800 31st Court North, St. Petersburg, Florida, 33716-1805 U.S.A.
Tel.: 1-800-444-4443
Web address: http://www.blazie.com/

Illinois Assistive Technology Project (IATP)
1 West Old State Capitol Plaza, Suite 100
Springfield, Illinois 62701 U.S.A.
Tel.: 1-217-522-7985 TTY: 1-217-522-9966 Fax: 1-217-522-8067
Web address: http://www.iltech.org/

IntelliTools, Inc.
55 Leveroni Court, Suite 9, Novato, Virginia 94949 U.S.A.

Tel.: 1-800-899-6687 Fax: 1-415-382-5963
Web address: http://www.intellitools.com/

J. A. Preston Corporation
60 Page Road, Clifton, New Jersey 07012 U.S.A.
Tel.: 1-800-631-7277

Maddak Inc.
Pequannock, New Jersey 07440 U.S.A.
Tel.: 1-201-628-7600
Web address: http://www.maddak.com/

Mayer-Johnson
P.O. Box 1579, Solana Beach, California 92075-1579 U.S.A.
Tel.: 1-800-841-8923 Fax: 1-609-921-0483
Web Address: http://www.mayer-johnson.com/

National Assistive Technology Research Institute (NATRI)
Department of Special Education and Rehabilitation Counseling
University of Kentucky
Lexington, KY 40506 U.S.A.
Web address: http://natri.uky.edu

National Information Center for Children and Youth with Disabilities
P.O. Box 1492 , Washington, DC 20013 U.S.A.
Tel.: 1-800-695-0285
E-Mail: nichcy@aed.org
Web address: http://www.nichcy.org

The National Rehabilitation Information Center (NRIC)
1010 Wayne Avenue, Suite 800, Silver Spring, Maryland 20910 U.S.A.
Tel.: 1-301-562-2400 TTY: 1-301-495-5626 (TTY) Fax: 1-301-562-2401
Web address: http://www.naric.com/index.html

Prentke Romach Company
1022 Heyl Road, Wooster, Ohio 44691 U.S.A.
Tel.: 1-800-262-1984
Web address: http://www.prentrom.com/index.html

Sentient Systems Technology, Inc.
2100 Wharton Street, Pittsburgh, PA 15203 U.S.A.
Tel.: 1-800-344-1778 Fax: 1-412-381-5241
Web address: http://www.sentient-sys.com

State University of New York , University at Buffalo,
Center for Assistive Technology and Rehabilitation
515 Kimball Tower, Buffalo, NY 14214 U.S.A.
Tel.: 1-716-829-3141 Fax: 1-716-829-3217

Technical Aids & Systems for the Handicapped, Inc. (TASH)
Unit 1 - 91 Station Street, Ajax, Ontario, Canada L1S 3H2
Tel.: 1-800-463-5685 or1-800-841-8923 Fax: 1-905-686-6895

Words+, Inc.
40015 Sierra Highway, Building B-145
Palmdale, California 93550 U.S.A.
Tel.: 1-800-869-8521 Fax: 1-805-266-8969
Web address: http://www.words-plus.com/

REFERENCES

20 USC 33. *Technological-related Assistance for Persons with Disabilities Act of 1988.*
20 USC 1401. *Individuals with Disabilities Education Act of 1990.*
Abbey, J.B. (1983). *I'm handicapped! How can I use computers?* Clifton, NJ: J.A. Preston Corporation.
Bakken, J.P. (1998). Technologies to complete academic tasks. In J.R. Thompson, M.E. Wall, & S.M. Winchip (Eds), *Assistive technology: Competencies and skills for teachers.* Normal, IL: University Communications, Illinois State University.
Batavia, A.I. (1989). *Consumer criteria for evaluating assistive devices: Implication for technology transfer.* Proceedings from the RESNA 12th Annual Conference, New Orleans, La.
Bersani, H. (2000). Me and my assistive technology: High school students write about their assistive technology. *TASH Newsletter, 26*(10), 11–14.
Chambers, A.C. (1997). Has technology been considered? *A guide for IEP teams.* Reston, VA: Council of Administrators of Special Education and Technology and Media Division of Council for Exceptional Children.
Chan, W. Rehabilitation and assistive technology for the disabled in Singapore. [online] http://cares.nsc.gov.tw/Paper/William_Chan.html.
Clasberry, G., & Lian, M-G.J. (1998). *Strategies for an inclusive school: A handbook for teachers & program coordinators.* Project ID# H023B60037, CFDA 84.023B, funded by U.S. Department of Education, Washington, DC.
Council for Exceptional Children. (1997). *NCATE-approved curriculum guidelines: Basic and advanced programs in special education.* Reston, VA: CEC.
DeMario, N.C., Leigh, K., & Dina, G. (1998). Technologies for persons with visual

impairments. In J.R. Thompson, M.E. Wall, & S.M. Winchip (Eds), *Assistive technology: Competencies and skills for teachers*. Normal, IL: University Communications, Illinois State University.

Duncan, J.M. (2000). Providing AAC systems for children in a Guatemalan orphanage: How do we help in culturally responsive ways? *TASH Newsletter, 26*(10), 8–10.

Glennen, S., & DeCoste, D.C. (1997). *The handbook of augmentative and alternative communication*. San Diego: Singular Publishing Co.

Illinois Assistive Technology Project (1996). *Computer technology access for students with disabilities*. Springfield, IL: IATP.

Lartz, M., & Prendergast, S. (1998). Technologies for people who are deaf and hard of hearing. In J.R. Thompson, M.E. Wall, & S.M. Winchip (Eds), *Assistive technology: Competencies and skills for teachers*. Normal, IL: University Communications, Illinois State University.

Levin, J., & Scherfenberg, L. (1990). *Selection and use of simple technology in home, school, work, and community settings*. Minneapolis, MN: AbleNet, Inc.

Lian, M-G.J. (1984). Increasing physically disabled individuals' opportunities to access computer. *Special Education Quarterly, 14*, 34–38

Lian, M-G.J. (1997). *Special adaptations for students with physical disabilities*. Normal, IL: University Communications, Illinois State University.

Lian, M-G.J. (1998). Technologies for persons with physical disabilities. In J.R. Thompson, M.E. Wall, & S.M. Winchip (Eds), *Assistive technology: Competencies and skills for teachers*. Normal, IL: University Communications, Illinois State University.

Lian, M-G.J. (1999). Technology and humanities: Assistive technologies with physical disabilities. *Sino-U.S.-Canada Science and Technology*, 1–2

Lian, M-G.J. (2000). *Teaching students with physical disabilities and health impairments*. Normal, IL: University Communications, Illinois State University.

Lian, M-G.J., & Stearns, K. (1988). *Success through technology*. [Video tape] Normal, IL: Media Services, Illinois State University.

Lloyd, L.L., Fuller, D.R., & Arvidson, H.H. (1997). *Augmentative and alternative Communication: A handbook of principles and practices*. Boston: Allyn and Bacon.

Orelove, F.P., & Sobsey, D. (1991). *Educating children with multiple disabilities: A transdisciplinary approach* (2nd ed.). Baltimore, MD: Paul H. Brookes.

Schaeffler, C. (1988). Making toys accessible for children with cerebral palsy. *Teaching Exceptional Children, 20*(3), 26–28.

Schwarz, S.P. (1998, January/February). Creating an accessible home with projects under $100. *Enable Magazine*, 52–53.

Tanaka, N., & Lian, M-G. J. (1995, Spring). The operation of a computer adaptive switch by a child with cerebral palsy using two body sites. *Physical Disabilities: Education and Related Services, 13*(2), 31–42.

Thompson, J.R., & Beck, A. (1998). Technologies for communication. In J.R. Thompson, M.E. Wall, & S.M. Winchip (Eds), *Assistive technology: Competencies and skills for teachers*. Normal, IL: University Communications, Illinois State University.

Thompson, J.R., Wall, M.E., & Winchip, S.M. (1998). Ready, set, go! The promises and challenges of assistive technology. In J.R. Thompson, M.E. Wall, & S.M. Winchip (Eds), *Assistive technology: Competencies and skills for teachers*. Normal, IL: University Communications, Illinois State University.

Trollinger, G., & Slavkin, R. (1999). Purposeful e-mail as stage 3 technology: IEP goals online. *Teaching Exceptional Children, 32*(1), 10–15.

Wall, M.E., & Sevener, G.A. (1998). Technologies for school, work, and community living. In J.R. Thompson, M.E. Wall, & S.M. Winchip (Eds), *Assistive technology: Competencies and skills for teachers*. Normal, IL: University Communications, Illinois State University.

Wobschall, R., & Lakin, C. (1995). Feature issue on assistive technologies, *IMPACT, 8*(3), 1.

Woltosz, W.S. (1994, February 14). *Augmentative and alternative communication: The next generation*. Paper presented at North Carolina Augmentative Communication Association Conference, Winston-Salem, Nc.

Glossary

Absence seizure. A seizure in which there is a short lapse in consciousness.

Acquired immunodeficiency syndrome. A normally fatal medical syndrome caused by infection with human immunodeficiency virus.

Acuity. Sharpness of response to visual, auditory, or tactile stimuli.

Adaptive skills. The ability of an individual to function in an environment.

Advisory service. One of special education services provided by the educational system for children with special educational needs. It is relevant to professional advice on how to meet students' special needs and how to promote teaching skills of special education teachers, etc.

Adventitious blindness. Blindness acquired after the age of two.

Age of onset. The age at which a disability occurs.

Aggression. Hostile and attacking behavior, which can include verbal communication, directed toward self, others, or the physical environment.

Americans with Disabilities Act (ADA). Disability anti-discrimination legislation passed in 1990 in the United States.

Anencephaly. A condition in which the brain fails to completely develop or is absent.

Anxiety. A state of painful uneasiness, emotional tension, or emotional confusion.

Aphasia. Loss or impairment of language ability due to brain injury.

Articulation problems. Abnormal production of speech sounds.

Asphyxia. Deprivation of oxygen, often through near drowning or smoke inhalation.

Assistive technology. Devices that help students with disabilities in their daily lives; they include hearing aids, wheelchairs, computers that offer augmentative communication, and a wide array of equipment that helps compensate for an individual's disabilities.

Association. In thinking, the ability to see relationships among different concepts or knowledge bases.

At risk. A predisposition or high possibility of mental retardation and other learning problems based on the child's environment, life circumstances, or physical characteristics.

Attention deficit disorder (ADD). A condition that describes students who display hyperactive behaviors, have difficulty attending to the task at hand, and tend to be impulsive.

Attention deficits. A characteristic often associated with learning disabilities in which students do not pay attention to the task or the correct features of a task to learn how to perform it well.

Attentive listening. Focusing on one form or source of communication.

Audiogram. A graph drawn from the results of hearing tests using an audiometer; it charts individuals' thresholds of hearing at various frequencies against sound intensities, in decibels.

Audiological service. One of special education services provided by the educational system for children. It involves such services as audiological diagnosis, production and issue of ear moulds and advisory and training support for pre-school hearing impaired children, etc.

Audiologist. Professional trained to diagnose hearing losses and auditory problems.

Augmentative communication systems. Alternative methods of communication that employ non-speech alternatives, such as communication boards, communication books, sign language, and computerized voices.

Autism. A severe disorder of thinking, communication, interpersonal relationships and behavior.

Behavior management. Systematic use of behavioral technologies such as behavior modification to control or direct responses.

Behavior modification. Systematic use of the principles of learning, including rewards and punishment, to increase desired behaviors and decrease undesired behaviors.

Behavioral disorders. A condition of disruptive or inappropriate behaviors that interferes with a student's learning, relationships with others, or personal satisfaction to such a degree that intervention is required.

Blindness. Not having a functional use of sight.

Braille. A system of reading and writing that uses dot codes that are embossed on paper, developed by Louis Braille in 1929.

Bulimia. Chronically causing oneself to vomit, limiting weight gain.

Cataract. Clouding of the eye lens, which becomes opaque, resulting in visual problems.

Categorical system. A system of classification using specific categories such as learning disabilities or mental retardation.

Center schools. Separate schools (some residential), typically dedicated to serving students with a particular disability.

Central vision. The main field of vision in the eye, usually greater than 20 degrees.

Cerebral palsy. A disorder of movement and posture caused by a defect in the developing brain.

Classification. Classification is categorical, organizing special needs into the categories.

Cleft palate. An opening in the roof of the mouth, causing too much air to pass through the nasal cavity when the individual is speaking.

Cognitive behavior modification. Instructional strategies that teach internal-control methods (such as self-talk) in structured ways to help students learn how to learn.

Collaboration. An effort engaged by two or more persons, e.g., general education teacher, special education, therapist, and parent, who interact with and support each other in an effort to achieve a mutual goal.

Communication. The transfer of knowledge, ideas, opinions, and feelings.

Communication board. A flat device on which words, pictures, or other symbols are used to expand the verbal interactions of people with limited vocal abilities.

Community-based instruction. A strategy of teaching functional skills in the environments they occur in; for example, shopping skills should be taught in the local market rather than a classroom "store".

Computer-assisted instruction. Self-contained instructional software programs that students use to supplement or replace traditional teacher-directed instructional methods.

Conceptualize. Generate questions and formulate abstract ideas.

Conduct disorder. A type of behavioral disorder in which persistent negative, hostile, and antisocial behavior impairs functioning in daily life.

Conductive hearing loss. Hearing loss caused by an impairment of the outer or middle ear that prevents transfer of sound to the inner ear.

Congenital. Present at birth.

Congenital rubella. German measles contracted by the expectant mother; causes a variety of problems including mental retardation, visual and hearing impairments, and other neurological problems.

Continuum of services. A graduated range of educational services; one level of service leads directly to the next one.

Cooperative learning. Groups of more than two students collaborating as they learn the same material.

Creativity. A form of intelligence characterized by advanced divergent thought, the production of many original ideas, and the ability to develop flexible and detailed responses and ideas.

Curriculum based assessment. A method of evaluating children's performance by objectives of a student's curriculum as the criterion against which progress is evaluated.

Deaf. Unable to usefully perceive sounds in the environment with or without the use of a hearing aid; unable to use hearing as the primary way to gain information.

Decibel (dB). Unit of measure for intensity of sound.

Delayed speech. An individual has deficit in speaking proficiency in that speech is performed like someone younger.

Delinquency. Illegal behavior, which may or may not be the result of a behavioral disorder, which is committed by juveniles.

Depression. A state of despair and sad mood.

Diabetes mellitus. Familial constitutional disease characterized by inadequate utilization of insulin; results in disordered metabolism of fats, proteins, and carbohydrates.

Disability. Results from a loss of physical functioning or difficulties in learning and social adjustment that significantly interfere with normal growth and development. Americans with Disabilities Act defines it as "a physical or mental impairment that substantially limits the person in some major life activity."

Disorder. Disturbance in normal functioning (mental, physical, or psychological).

Direct instruction. Specifically focusing instruction on the desired, targeted behavior.

Down syndrome. A chromosomal disorder (Trisomy 21) that cause physical and cognitive disabilities.

Dyslexia. Severe impairment of the ability to learn to read.

Examination service. One of special education services provided by the educational system for children with special educational needs. These services include assessment of special needs of handicapped candidates for public examinations and recommendation for special arrangements for such candidates.

Exceptionality. A child with exceptionality may have difficulties or special talents in seeing, hearing, speaking, thinking, moving, or socializing.

Fetal alcohol syndrome (FAS). Congenital mental impairments, behavioral difficulties, and potential physical disabilities caused by mother's consumption of alcohol during pregnancy.

Full inclusion. An educational philosophy and approach by which all students, regardless of their disabilities and differences in learning capacities, receive all instruction in the general education classroom setting where support services are delivered as well.

Glaucoma. Disorder in the eye characterized by high pressure inside the eyeball.

Handicap. Limitation imposed upon an individual by the environment and the person's capacity to cope with that limitation.

Hard of hearing. Individuals with a deficient but somewhat functional sense of hearing.

Health disabilities/impairments. Disabling conditions characterized by limited vitality, stamina, or alertness due to chronic or acute health conditions such as AIDS, diabetes, epilepsy, asthma, lead poisoning, leukemia, rheumatic fever, hemophilia, tuberculosis, or a heart condition.

Hoover cane. Long, white cane used in the system of mobility and orientation to help individuals with visual impairments to move about independently and was developed by Richard Hoover in 1944.

Human immunodeficiency virus (HIV). A virus that reduces the immune system functioning in affected individuals and is linked to AIDS.

Hyperactivity. Excessive behavior in inappropriate circumstances.

Individualized education plan (IEP). An educational program developed and implemented to take into account the student's present level of performance; annual goals; short-term instructional objectives; related services; timeline for special education services; and an annual evaluation.

Inclusion. The practice of assuring that all students with disabilities participate with other students in all aspects of school.

Integration. Placing students with disabilities in general education classrooms alongside their nondisabled peers.

Labeling. Labeling identifies individuals or groups according to a category assigned to them.

Learning disabilities. A disability wherein a person possesses average intelligence but is substantially behind in academic achievement.

Least restrictive environment. Students with disabilities are educated to the maximum extent appropriate with their nondisabled peers.

Meninges. Membranes that cover the spinal cord and brain.

Meningitis. Inflammation of the membranes covering the brain and spinal cord.

Mental retardation. Individuals with this disability are characterized by significant sub-average intellectual functioning, existing concurrently with related limitations in two or more adaptive skills. The disability manifests itself prior to age 18.

Muscular dystrophy. A group of inherited, chronic disorders characterized by gradual wasting and weakening of the voluntary skeletal muscles.

Neurological impairments. Damages to the central nervous system, (CNS), i.e., brain and spinal cord.

Orthopedic impairments. Damages to muscles, bones, and/or joints.

Other service. One of special education services provided by the educational system for children with special educational needs. It includes examination service and training service (c.f., examination service and training service).

Phenylketonuria (PKU). A metabolic disability in processing one of the essential amino acids (phenylalanine), which leads to toxicity, mental retardation, and physical disabilities; PKU can be controlled by diet.

Psychological service. One of special education services provided by the educational system for children with special educational needs. This service includes psychological assessment for children with suspected learning/behavioral problem, consultation and support to guidance service in schools and counseling for parents and their children with behavioral and emotional problem, etc.

Related service. Special education services provided by the educational system for children with special educational needs. Its main purpose is to facilitate early diagnosis and treatment of impaired children so as to avoid becoming serious or permanent. These services include screening, referral and placement services, audiological service, speech therapy service, psychological service, resource teaching service, advisory service, school-based remedial support program, and other service (examination service and training service).

Resource teaching service. One of special education services provided by the educational system for children with special educational needs. This service involves remedial support to children with learning difficulties and physical handicaps and adjustment programs for children with behavior/adjustment problems.

School-based program. See school-based remedial support program.

School-based remedial support program. One of special education services provided by the educational system for children with special educational needs. It is relevant to professional advice to schools with a high intake of bottom 10% junior secondary students on the implementation of the SBRSP as well as professional support and training to teachers developed for the SBRSP.

Seizure (epilepsy). Behaviors that occur to respond to abnormal discharge of the electrical impulses of the brain.

Sensorineural hearing loss. Results from an abnormal sense organ (inner ear) and a damaged auditory nerve.

Sexual abuse. Form of mistreatment mainly from caretakers or parents involving behaviors such incest, assault, or sexual exploitation.

Special needs education. Special needs education serves for children who cannot derive full benefits from the curriculum provided for children of their age cohort and/or who cannot be catered for adequately in the ordinary educational setting.

Speech therapy service. One of special education services provided by the educational system for children with special educational needs. It is related to assessment of children with speech/language impairments or communication disorders and professional support to and supervision of speech therapy personnel in special school, etc.

Spina bifida. Developmental defect of the spinal column.

Training service. One of special education services provided by the educational system for children with special educational needs. This service is associated with orientation and professional courses/workshop on special education for teachers, etc.

Visual acuity. Sharpness of vision.

Author Index

Subject Index

本社其他相關題材的書籍

Leadership and Management in Education:
Developing Essential Skills and Competencies
David Thenuwara Gamage and Nicholas Sun-keung Pang (2002)

《家庭學校與社區協作：從理念研究到實踐》
何瑞珠著 (2002)

《課程、教學與學校改革：新世紀的教育發展》
李子健編著 (2002)

《有效的中文科教學法》
周漢光著 (2000)

《尋找課程與教學的知識基礎：
香港中小學中文科課程與教學研究》
黃顯華編著 (2000, 2002)

《課堂管理技巧》
David Fontana 著 (2000)

Future School Administration: Western and Asian Perspectives
Edited by Clive Dimmock and Alan Walker (2000)

《閱讀與寫作教學》
周漢光編 (1998)

Helping Students with Learning Difficulties
Edited by David W. Chan (1998)

《課程：範式、取向和設計》(第二版)
李子建、黃顯華著 (1996, 2002)